Safeguarding Babies and Young Children

Safeguarding Babies and Young Children

A Guide for Early Years Professionals

John Powell and Elaine Uppal

Open University Press

Open University Press
McGraw-Hill Education
McGraw-Hill House
Shoppenhangers Road
Maidenhead
Berkshire
England
SL6 2QL

email: enquiries@openup.co.uk
world wide web: www.openup.co.uk

and Two Penn Plaza, New York, NY 10121-2289, USA

First published 2012

A catalogue record of this book is available from the British Library

ISBN-13: 9780335234080 (pb) 9780335234073 (hb)
ISBN-10: 0335234089 (pb) 0335234070 (hb)
e-ISBN: 9780335240296

Library of Congress Cataloging-in-Publication Data
CIP data has been applied for

Typeset by Aptara Inc., India
Printed in the UK by Bell and Bain Ltd, Glasgow.

Fictitious names of companies, products, people, characters and/or data that may be used herein (in case studies or in examples) are not intended to represent any real individual, company, product or event.

The McGraw·Hill Companies

Contents

Acknowledgements   vii

Introduction   1

PART 1
Principles for practice: overview of issues and
considerations for early years professionals in
safeguarding babies and young children

1   Issues in safeguarding babies and young children from abuse   9

2   The rights of children   33

3   The baby and young child as the focus for safeguarding   48

4   Acting ethically: developing ethical practices in safeguarding
    contexts   65

5   The development of community involvement   84

PART 2
Practical considerations: exploring the actions and roles of
early years professionals in safeguarding babies and
young children

6   Raising concerns and identifying abuse   101

7   Providing support for 'at risk' babies and young children   116

8   Assessment and referral: passing on concerns   125

9   Teamwork and safeguarding   138

10 Working with the parents and carers of an abused baby or
    young child   152

**11 What might happen after the case has been referred: mapping
    the potential impact of intervention**   161

**12 Conclusions: reflections on considerations for developing future
    practice and detailed requirements of effective intervention**   176

References   190
Index   199

Acknowledgements

We would like to thank our editor, Fiona Richman, for her valuable support and advice as well as her patience. We are greatly indebted to the practitioners from all professions, as well as the students who will enter those professions, dealing with safeguarding and child protection issues on a daily basis.

John Powell

I would like to acknowledge my grateful thanks to friends and family for their support and patience and to my wife Rita for providing endless cups of tea at key moments and for helping with checking the text. I would like to thank colleagues for their unswerving belief in the book and for offering ideas and insights to consider. I would like to thank my friend Dr Derek Clifford for his invaluable advice and support in writing Chapter 4 on Acting ethically: developing ethical practices in safeguarding contexts. I would like to register particular thanks to Professor Lesley Abbott (retired), who was so supportive at the start of the writing for the book, and Professor Nigel Hall (retired) for his encouragement and advice in organizing and structuring the book. I would like to thank my daughter Catherine for her helpful criticisms and observations about how to connect the book to its audience.

Elaine Uppal

I would like to offer my thanks for support and encouragement from colleagues, friends and family, particularly Sam for solid support and technical advice, Tom, Eloise, Wynn and Honor. I would also like to thank Bolton Local Safeguarding Children's Board (LSCB) for its support of my doctoral research and use of its Child Action Model. Finally I would like to thank John for offering me the opportunity to collaborate on this project.

Introduction

Since we began writing this book, there have been a number of changes that have impacted upon safeguarding and child protection practice. The emphasis has now been returned by the current UK coalition government to child protection, while still acknowledging the relevance of features of prevention in safeguarding. What has never changed is the compelling need to develop a working understanding of the safeguarding system, which is still highly complex. We emphasize the importance of preventative interventions as a positive means of impacting on the lives of children and their families through such processes as the Common Assessment Framework (CAF), as well as maintaining the need within the system for responses to be made to urgent concerns that are more closely related to child protection processes as and when appropriate.

The government has set in motion a review of social work practice in child protection, which is led by Eileen Munro, Professor of social policy at the London School of Economics. The focus of the review appears to be concerned with emphasizing practitioners' professional skills in their ability to bring about change for children and at the same time reducing the need for bureaucracy and unnecessary red tape.

> She argues that the system has become preoccupied by individuals 'doing things right' rather than 'doing the right thing'. And she concludes this attitude has meant that learning from professional experience has been limited.
>
> (BBC News 2011b)

This book focuses on the relationship that an early years professional has with the family through parents and carers as a means of reprioritizing practice in safeguarding and child protection and emphasizing the importance of focusing on the skills needed to work successfully with families.

How to use this book

This book offers you the opportunity of being guided through current policies and procedures and rehearsing practice by applying your thinking to practical case studies. This will enable you to rehearse your potential responses to different types of safeguarding concerns that can arise.

In Part 1, the chapters are organized to provide you with a set of principles for practice. You will be introduced to a range of significant ideas, concepts and factual information to support your development as a principled and reflective practitioner. In Part 2, we link the ideas of Part 1 to practical examples for you to prepare your possible intervention in real-life situations.

We offer no strong guidelines about where to start reading the book; however, Part 1 introduces a number of different ways of shaping your practice that you can then apply to the scenarios in Part 2. If for example you are attempting to develop a better understanding of children's rights, you might want to refer to Chapter 2. It is also feasible to examine any of the individual scenarios in Part 2 and apply some of the tools and methods suggested there in further detail to chapters in Part 1.

The case studies in the book reflect real-life situations where links to practice can be made. In Chapter 1 there are examples from recent history where the dilemmas for the practitioners included whether attention should be given quite as fully as it was to the concerns of the carers covers or parents. Ethical values are important and referred to throughout the book.

In Chapter 2 we begin to explore the way in which the rights of children are an important consideration in safeguarding. Children's rights remain a central and overarching principle for any early years professional working in a social context with babies and young children. The concept of safer cultures introduced in Chapter 3 can be seen as a way for you to construct a framework based upon taking a proactive approach through your values and attitudes in relation to young children generally, and as a point of resonance for your personal beliefs and interactions. The focus of your beliefs and interactions should not only remain focused upon the context of the child's home and life experience but also include your workplace and the wider community. This is explored further in Chapter 5.

The idea then is to support the development of a core set of beliefs and practices for you to consciously reflect on how you relate within safeguarding situations towards parents, carers and children.

Principles and practice

We offer you guidance where theories, ideas and concepts form a set of principles that are applied in Part 2 to practical case studies that reflect real-life situations. If you are working closely with young children, their families and carers on a day-to-day basis, this provides a useful support to you in safeguarding babies and young children. When dealing with what can be very sensitive issues around safeguarding and child protection, you may feel uncertain about what your responsibilities are, what appropriate action should be taken, how other agencies can be involved, as well as the consequences when they proceed to take action or fail to. This book explores the role of early years professionals both in relation to child protection and the wider responsibility of safeguarding, as enshrined in the Children Acts of 1989 and 2004, and supports the development of more effective, holistic and integrated practices.

The aim of the book is to provide a highly practical discussion about safeguarding babies and young children. Part 1 is primarily focused on discussing the core concerns of safeguarding and child protection at the heart of each individual chapter. We believe the messages from these chapters are highly significant in providing a total and coherent set of professional resources that, together with the chance to anticipate situations in advance of experiencing them in real time, should be beneficial to all practitioners in this area of work.

Following a brief overview of essential concerns and issues and their relevance for practice, Part 1 presents a problem resolution approach to safeguarding babies and young children through a process that invites you to rehearse your possible approaches through a number of case studies. You are also supported in considering the issues that may arise from the actions that you believe to be most appropriate in supporting a child who may be suffering abuse. Part 2 draws together the potential messages for practice and again invites you to consider how you might apply them to your own practice. This book is relevant for all early years professionals and students concerned with safeguarding and child protection; it is also applicable to anyone working with babies and young children from a variety of contexts, including pre-school provision and health, education and social care settings.

Part 1, 'Principles for practice', provides an overview of issues and their relevance for practice.

Chapter 1, 'Issues in safeguarding babies and young children from abuse', explores the issues for practice when dealing with child protection, referring to previous significant cases and their influence on policy and the legislative framework, developing a constructive critique of the issues that were raised and how these have relevance today. Chapter 1 discusses definitions of abuse and the dilemmas that are likely to be present when attempting to recognize and identify whether a form of ill-treatment is likely to have taken place.

Chapter 2, 'The rights of children', considers the development of children as beings with rights, drawing on legislation and policy which inform this perspective. The chapter emphasizes the importance of viewing children as having rights and responding to them appropriately during times of crisis such as in child protection.

Chapter 3, 'The baby and young child as the focus for safeguarding', considers the importance of maintaining the baby and young child as the central focus of concern particularly in relation to child protection. The chapter discusses recent history and cites examples where this focus became unstable or blurred and how this led to difficulties for children in need. The chapter also discusses the legal requirements expected from practitioners in situations where concerns are being felt for children who may be being abused. The chapter explores the concept of safer cultures as an effective way of working with parents and carers.

Chapter 4, 'Acting ethically: developing ethical practices in safeguarding contexts', considers the importance of developing and maintaining a series of ethical principles at the centre of professional practice to inform appropriate action on behalf of babies and young children. The chapter also offers the opportunity for reflection in relation to power dynamics and argues that an anti-discriminatory ethical practice is essential in this area of work. Anti-discriminatory practice helps develop the discussion surrounding reflexivity and the part that we play as social practitioners in influencing the outcomes of interventions.

Chapter 5, 'The development of community involvement', explores the important development of community involvement which has been rediscovered recently through policies such as Sure Start and Every Child Matters. A wider historical context is explored in which communities are discussed as either being helpful or unhelpful in supporting vulnerable babies and young children in relation to safeguarding concerns.

Part 2, 'Practical considerations', discusses the actions and roles of early years professionals in safeguarding babies and young children. Part 2 presents a problem prevention and resolution approach to safeguarding babies and young children through a process that invites you to rehearse possible approaches using scenarios and case studies. These build in terms of level of need, complexity and the amount and nature of intervention required as the chapters progress. You are encouraged to consider the issues arising from actions you believe may be the most appropriate in supporting a child who may be at risk of or suffering abuse. The child's perspective will be of paramount consideration throughout, focusing on the child's journey in the process of safeguarding and child protection practice.

Each chapter in Part 2 presents a case study and a set of tools for you to apply in order that you may develop strategies that you will find valuable in real-life everyday practice. In addition to the scenarios presented, a template is provided to support coherent strategies first for use with the scenario in the book but which we expect can be employed in situations in your own practice or studies. This supports a more personal set of reflections concerning developing appropriate practices for safeguarding babies and young children who may be suffering from some form of abuse. Chapter 12 draws together the central messages for practice and advice for future development in safeguarding babies and young children, inviting you to consider how you might apply them to your own practice.

Part 2 is chiefly organized around applying the messages for practice from Part 1 through the use of case studies. However, in difficult and intransigent cases it is worth while to introduce a number of strategies which are not always appropriate in earlier stages of intervention, but we recognize that you will be the best judge of that. More complex issues will be explored in order to introduce potential means of overcoming any difficulties or barriers to effective action that you may encounter within your practice. Part 2 is arranged so that the case studies that are used appear as progressively more problematic and complex.

Chapter 6, 'Raising concerns and identifying abuse', introduces the practical concerns surrounding the early moments when the practitioner begins to suspect or believe that a baby or young child may be being abused. Considerations and dilemmas surrounding the recognition of abuse are explored within the safeguarding framework and linked to a case study. The focus for the discussion provided by the case study will invite you to examine and explore possible actions or inactions and their likely consequences. A general formula for personal reflection is based around feelings and emotions, anxieties and the social, physical, intellectual impact that abuse may have on a baby or young child.

Chapter 7, 'Providing support for "at risk" babies and young children', discusses the real and effective ways that practitioners are able to support children who may be being abused at the point before which any referral to an outside agency has been made. Later in the chapter (using a different case study than the one in Chapter 6), ways of supporting babies and young children in abuse situations are considered after these initial referrals have been made. This will deal with the feelings that parents and carers may have in relation to the practitioner who made the referral. The chapter also considers how babies and young children may be emotionally sustained following abuse, discussing important practices that may be applied.

Chapter 8, 'Assessment and referral: passing on concerns', examines the procedural requirements relating to assessment and referral. The involvement of a multiprofessional and multidisciplinary workforce and its purpose in supporting this particular stage of information gathering is fully considered. A case study exploring the likely dynamics of a multiprofessional group involved in assessment identifies key strategies for developing a coherent approach to understanding the nature of safeguarding concerns relating to an abuse case and then explores likely and appropriate responses to it.

Chapter 9, 'Teamwork and safeguarding', explores current legislation which emphasizes the importance of coherent teamwork practice particularly in relation to safeguarding babies and young children. The chapter considers the nature of teams and the ways in which by working together effective safeguards may be afforded to vulnerable or abused babies and young children. A case study examines the aims and objectives as well as the roles and functions of teamworking in relation to a specific case.

Chapter 10, 'Working with the parents and carers of an abused baby or young child', discusses the likely nature of working through a safeguarding investigation with the parents or carers of an abused child. A case study illustrates the complexity of emotion and anxiety that may surround professional intervention. The intention of the chapter is to develop potential strategies for dealing with difficult dilemmas while remaining focused on the needs of babies and young children.

Chapter 11, 'What might happen after the case has been referred', uses a case study to reflect on the potential for the future of a baby or young child and their family following a child abuse investigation under Section 47 of the Children Act 1989. The case study highlights potential difficulties for both children and families who have been the focus of concern to become rehabilitated back into their local communities. The chapter considers positive strategies that may lead to successful outcomes for the future safeguarding of babies and young children while making clear the importance of remaining vigilant.

In Chapter 12, 'Conclusions: reflections on considerations for developing future practice', key messages arising from Parts 1 and 2 are explored. This supports a more personal set of reflections concerning developing appropriate practices for safeguarding babies and young children who may be suffering from abuse. Key practical, ethical and anti-discriminatory positions are highlighted for readers and practitioners to consider in their daily practice. Detailed points and requirements when managing a safeguarding case are set against a background of all the case studies. This includes making explicit the need for verbatim and contemporaneous recording, confidentiality and its complex meanings particularly in multidisciplinary teamwork contexts as well as many other important messages arising from the analysis of the case studies. This chapter draws together the central messages for practice and the advice for future developments in safeguarding babies and young children.

Part 1

Principles for practice

Overview of issues and considerations for early years professionals in safeguarding babies and young children

1 Issues in safeguarding babies and young children from abuse

---

Chapter Overview

This chapter discusses the issues associated with the safeguarding of babies and young children, not only recognizing the complexity that this area of work and study represents, but also highlighting future opportunities for overcoming them. The chapter explores the issues for practice that are present when dealing with child protection, referring to previous significant cases and their influence on policy and the legislative framework, developing a constructive critique of the issues that were raised and how these have relevance today. The chapter discusses definitions of abuse and the dilemmas that are likely to be present when attempting to recognize and identify whether a form of ill-treatment is likely to have taken place.

Historical overview

The following rather brief selective history introduces just a few of the many influential cases that have, over the years, revealed a range of issues arising from protecting young children. By revisiting cases, a number of tensions and constraints will be revealed. These may usefully guide and support you in understanding the current safeguarding context.

The growing involvement of the state in the lives of families

There have been major incursions into the daily life of the family unit by the state from the late nineteenth century when the earliest child protection legislation was introduced. The increase in state interest in family life can be linked to an improvement in national wealth and a growing sense of morality and justice. Myers (2004) gives an American perspective, pointing out that:

The colonists drew on principles of English law, under which parents could use 'reasonable' corporal punishment. Corporal punishment of children was well accepted and rooted in the Bible. The government seldom interfered with the parental prerogative to discipline children.

(Myers 2004: 31)

Cunningham (1995) refers to parent–child relationships in the seventeenth and eighteenth centuries in England being experienced differently depending on social class. Children from the upper classes often had fairly distant relationships with their parents, who sent them to boarding school around the age of 10. Cunningham (1995) indicates generally that:

in the schools and in the home, corporal punishment, often very brutal, was the norm, the late sixteenth and early seventeenth centuries being 'the great flogging age'. Children were taught to behave with great formality in the presence of their parents and to defer to them at all times.

(Cunningham 1995: 11–12)

There is a clear suggestion that hitting children was an acceptable practice prior to the nineteenth century (it is still legally acceptable for parents to physically chastise children in the UK as long as it is done within *reasonable limits*) and that policies relating to safeguarding and child protection are relatively new phenomena. There was a general lack of interest from the state into what went on in the privacy of the home and in that respect children were not considered of much interest as long as they behaved themselves for their parents. Cunningham (1995: 107) goes on to argue that 'once the child had acquired some economic usefulness parental attitudes noticeably changed', making the connection of the need of the family to call upon the skills of its children where their efforts in the workplace could create income for the family. Clearly this argument chiefly applies to children who are both physically and mentally able. A different experience could be expected for children with disabilities, depending on the nature and severity of them.

Corby (2006) charted historical abuse of children ranging from Roman infanticide as a form of birth control that was not criminalized until AD318, common abandonment of children in the Middle Ages, to Victorian baby farming and child labour. During the industrial revolution, 'to patrol industry on behalf of the young was England's Christian duty. To patrol the home was a sacrilege' (Behlmer 1982: 9). There was apparently much less concern generally for children as the subject of an agenda of child protection before the late nineteenth century and consequently less interest for western governments to legislate in this area. However, from the nineteenth century onwards, in particular the latter part of it, there was a growing awareness of children's issues with the emerging development of a safeguarding platform in legislation and social policy. For instance, the 1880s saw the inception of the National Society for the Prevention of Cruelty to Children (NSPCC), with the first legislation to protect children evident in the Prevention of Cruelty to Children Act 1889, ironically later than the animal cruelty Acts. Further Acts in 1894 and 1904 set the principles for present-day legislation, with more specific legislation also evident in the Infant Life Protection Act 1897, Children Act 1908 and Punishment of Incest Act 1908. The Children and Young Persons Act 1932 broadened the powers of juvenile courts and introduced supervision orders for children at risk. A year later, the Children and Young Persons Act 1933 consolidated all existing child protection legislation into one Act.

Between the First and Second World Wars, a change in focus was evident, perhaps due to improved parenting and welfare, resulting in perceivably less child abuse. Concern about high numbers of children in care led to an increasing focus on parenting, particularly the mother as evidenced in Bowlby's (1951) maternal deprivation hypothesis. The political connotations of men returning from the Second World War and women being encouraged to return to home-making should not however be neglected. A simultaneous focus on delinquency rather than abuse and recognition that prevention may be better than cure particularly in terms of financial cost was evident in the Children Act 1948.

There is little documentation regarding joint working between agencies until the 1950s, when growing awareness of child maltreatment was addressed by a joint circular from the Home Office and the Ministries of Health and Education (1951) to gain cooperation between statutory and voluntary agencies and to discuss significant cases of neglect and all cases of ill-treatment. Coordinating committees were established to facilitate this process. Arguably this is not dissimilar to the current set-up of Local Safeguarding Boards and could raise the question why improvements in joint working practices remain an issue of debate and concern, as highlighted in the Laming inquiry into the death of Victoria Climbié (Laming 2003).

The Ingleby (1960) report highlighted the importance of detecting families at risk with investigation and diagnosis of the particular problem and treatment in the form of the provision of facilities and services to meet the families' needs and to reduce the stresses and dangers that they face. This is perhaps characteristic of the perceived parent focus of services and laissez-faire attitudes of professionals at this time. Similarly the Children and Young Persons Act 1963 highlighted increasing emphasis on supporting families in the home. The Seebohm (1968) report saw the formation of new social services departments to meet the social needs of individuals, families and communities.

At the same time the 1960s was a time of medical innovation leading to better diagnosis due to technology such as radiology. Kempe's work on the battered child syndrome highlighted the need for a multidisciplinary approach (Kempe et al. 1962). Non-accidental injury was becoming a concern of the medical profession, leading to the formation of the Tunbridge Wells Group, with other disciplines encouraged to join the debate. Potential difficulties and tensions began to emerge, particularly in terms of coordinating activities (Stevenson 1963). At this time awareness of child abuse was increasing, with emphasis on previously unrecognized aspects such as the psychological needs of children and the issue of neglect. This was evident in the Children and Young Persons Act 1969, which focuses on neglect as a cause of delinquency.

Significant cases that inform current practice

The cases that follow illustrate the growing concerns developing within contemporary western societies in relation to safeguarding babies and young children. They are selective and represent only a small proportion of the total number of cases that have come to public attention over the years. It is important to mention that these cases are often concerned with mistakes made by practitioners that have led to a continuation of child ill-treatment and sometimes resulting in death. However, there are occasionally cases where the outcome is positive for the child, as in the first case for discussion.

Mary Ellen Wilson 1864–1956

An important case arising in the nineteenth century in the United States was that of Mary Ellen Wilson. Mary Ellen was cared for by Mary and Francis Connolly, where according to Myers (2004):

> Mary Ellen spent eight long years . . . filled with neglect and cruelty . . . [she] was not allowed to play outside with other children . . . she was beaten routinely . . . she had only one item of clothing . . . she slept on a piece of carpet on the floor beneath the window.
>
> (Myers 2004: 129)

Mary Ellen came to the attention of a local missionary, Etta Angell Wheeler, who was eventually able to successfully intervene through the courts and free her from her abusing carers (Myers 2004: 130). Of central interest to the experience of Mary Ellen is the way in which Wheeler acted as a 'concerned citizen' and through the interest of the press, which covered the court case, there was a general raising of public awareness in child protection, leading later to the introduction of the New York Society for the Prevention of Cruelty to Children (NYSPCC), the immediate model and forerunner of the Liverpool Society for the Prevention of Cruelty to Children and later the NSPCC in the UK. The introduction of child protection societies in the late nineteenth century was underpinned by new child protection legislation, first in the United States and then a few years later in the UK.

In child protection contexts the importance of the concerned individual pursuing the concerns of a child lies at the heart of current practices. Wheeler's persistent intervention on behalf of Mary Ellen represents an early model for practice for social care, education and health professionals working with families and their children. It is important to remember that Mary Ellen survived her ordeal, due in no small measure to Wheeler, unlike several later cases which also became well known.

There are a number of practices which Wheeler brought to bear. First, she was observant, identifying in Mary Ellen clear indications of what appeared to be and later turned out to be child abuse. However, she could not get the police to act because they needed clear evidence to do so. This prompted her to seek an alternative route to safeguarding (this terminology was not in place in the nineteenth century and is a recent phenomenon) by putting her case before an influential figure associated with animal welfare, who in his capacity as a magistrate was able to advise about the appropriate steps that needed to be taken to protect Mary Ellen.

Mary Ellen emerges as both 'vulnerable' and as 'property' that belonged to the family, an understanding recognized as having some relevance in contemporary society (see Reder et al. 1993). This interpretation recognizes issues of power that may operate between adults and children in abusive or damaging relationships (Powell 2005a). However, it would be far too simplistic to view Mary Ellen as being completely powerless. Through the courts she was able to articulate the facts of her experience and, by doing so, was able to influence the judge in determining who should care for her. Thus Mary Ellen, by showing that she had the ability to represent herself within a formal context, leads us to see her with the potential of being a strong child with something to say about her own destiny. The involvement of the child as central to expressing their views on issues concerning their own safeguarding will be dealt with later in Chapter 4, but it is important to point out that this is a complex matter, with a great deal at stake for the child's future. As practitioners concerned to better understand issues of safeguarding maintaining the inclusion of the child and her or his voice is an important aspect of practice but one which should be seen as a significant strand within a wider assessment process. Powell (2005a) compares the cases of Mary Ellen Wilson in 1873 America with more recent cases such as that of Maria Colwell and Victoria Climbié in terms of the handling of the proceedings and particularly the centrality of the child's voice. The link between public concern, inquiry findings, legislation and their subsequent impact on professional practice is highlighted (Reder et al. 1993; Powell 2005a).

The appropriate practices for safeguarding that would relate to contemporary society can be shown to be concerned with:

- recognizing ill-treatment and acting accordingly
- making an appropriate referral
- including the child's voice, wherever possible.

Additional factors supporting successful intervention include acknowledging concerns and acting upon them when triggered, being zealous even when others (possibly more senior than you) are attempting to minimize these concerns, and promoting an emotional commitment to the well-being of the child. In Mary Ellen's case her saviour Wheeler also appears to have had effective communication skills which she was able to bring to bear with a range of external agencies, including the police and the courts. Interestingly there are few documents and examples of good practice in more current cases, perhaps reflecting an overemphasis on poor outcomes in the media.

Maria Colwell 26 March 1965 – 6 January 1973 and other cases

We now explore concerns arising from later inquiries into the deaths of children such as Maria Colwell (see Department of Health and Social Security (DHSS) 1974) and Victoria Climbié (see Laming 2003) (it is important to remember that Mary Ellen survived her early ill-treatment and went on to live into her nineties). When Maria Colwell was asked about where she would prefer to live, she stated that she wished to remain in the care of her aunt and uncle rather than go to live with her mother and her new stepfather. Unlike Mary Ellen, Maria's wishes were not felt to be in her 'best interests'. This view was influenced by the belief prevalent at that time that most children's emotional and social needs were generally better met if they were living with their birth parents. Consequently Maria was returned to live with her mother and siblings as well as the children of William Keppel, who was now her stepfather, and at whose hands she later died. It appears that more weight in this instance was given to the effects of contemporary child development rather than to foregrounding the child's voice as a key stakeholder or to the inclusion of other professional perspectives before a decision was made about returning Maria to the family home.

This began to change in the 1970s in response to Maria's death and the ensuing inquiry (DHSS 1974) highlighting communication failures between agencies and calling for more monitoring and inter-agency work. Increasing identification of professional responsibility led to more detection, investigation and monitoring. Training was recommended for clerical and administrative staff. Social services training needs included recognition and response, record keeping and supervision. Health professionals became more involved in safeguarding in the form of Area Review Committees, the forerunners of Area Child Protection Committees (ACPC) and procedures were formulated including child abuse registers, dominated by physical abuse and non-accidental injury. Multi-agency child protection conferences and the child protection register were established.

The subsequent Children Act 1975 highlighted the needs of children as distinct from rights of parents, setting up future emphasis on the child being central in proceedings. Additionally children were not to live in same house as a Schedule 1 offender (offences of violence and indecency towards children as set out in the Children Act 1933) in response to the Susan Auckland case (see DHSS 1975). Susan was killed by her father, who had previously been convicted of manslaughter of another of his children. Further medical research around this time by Meadows (1977) also led to initial recognition of Munchausen's by proxy, now referred to as fabricated or induced illness.

Some clarification regarding types of abuse was provided by a DHSS (1980) Circular highlighting four categories of abuse or risk of abuse: physical injury; physical neglect; failure to thrive incorporated with emotional abuse; and living in the same house as someone convicted under Schedule 1 of the Children and Young Persons Act 1933. Sexual abuse was not considered a category for registration unless connected to physical injury. Although it was a prominent issue in the United States, it was only just beginning to emerge or be recognized as a social problem in the UK.

The 1980s can be marked as a time of guidelines and more guidelines, perhaps in response to the numerous cases seen in the Department of Health (DH 1991) study of inquiry reports, which considered cases from 1980 to 1989 such as Jasmine Beckford (London Borough of Brent 1985), Kimberley Carlile (London Borough of Greenwich 1987) and Tyra Henry (London Borough of Lambeth 1987), emphasizing the importance of coordination. The large number of cases is alarming, but it is difficult to know if this merely reflects the increasing emphasis on improving practice and working together better. Arguably society was simultaneously becoming more aware of child abuse, perhaps due to increasing media attention. Previously the rule of optimism had been prevalent (Dingwall et al. 1983) with both practitioners and the public being guilty of making the best interpretation of allegations of abuse, reframing signs and symptoms to be normal due to the natural love assumed of parents – 'if it is assumed that all parents love their children as a fact of nature, then it becomes very difficult to read evidence in a way which is inconsistent with this assumption' (Dingwall et al. 1983).

This led to a dichotomy between a firm stance on child abuse and working with families, and counter-concerns regarding over-intrusive and heavy-handed practice. This was evident in the Cleveland affair of 1987 (Butler-Sloss 1988), where a phenomenal 121 children tested positively for sexual abuse, perhaps as a result of an increase in recognition combined with overzealous response and inappropriate handling of the situation. Indeed the anal reflex dilatation test used by medical staff was arguably a form of abuse in itself. Despite the official drive towards inter-agency work, social services were increasingly taking the lead.

Child protection practice was placing further emphasis on the child rather than the parents, as evidenced in the Cleveland inquiry (Butler-Sloss, 1988), which argued that professionals failed to recognize parents' rights. Yet practitioners had previously been criticized in public inquiries into deaths (Jasmine Beckford, London Borough of Brent 1985; Kimberley Carlile, London Borough of Greenwich 1987; Tyra Henry, London Borough of Lambeth 1987) for accepting too readily what adults say. This apparent confusion and divergent practices serve only to emphasize the importance of multi-agency working. Increasingly the need not only to communicate, but also to cooperate was recognized, with particular reference to information sharing and record keeping. *Working Together* (DHSS 1988) highlighted the need for training for all staff in contact with children, with distinction being made for those requiring specialized training. This brings to mind the current practice of varying levels of training dependent on level of contact and working with children. Yet the commonality of concerns and understanding of the concept of abuse, local procedures, recognition and response and the development of good working relationships is essential for all agencies and staff.

The 1980s ended on a good note in terms of the Children Act 1989, which emphasized the importance of putting the child first while cooperating and sharing parental responsibilities. The local authority would hold corporate responsibility for services to children, recognizing that a range of services is required for children in need. The principle of paramouncy of the welfare of the child was created in law. Additionally, it was established that delay and drift is not in the child's best interest and should be avoided. It suggests that the child and young person's wishes must be taken seriously, promoting principles of working together and working in partnership.

Despite the Children Act 1989 it could be argued that confusion persisted into the 1990s, perhaps evident in the 1991 Orkney case of ritualistic abuse (Clyde 1992). Although this was not the only investigation into ritualistic abuse (Rochdale and Nottingham also had cases), it was certainly the most prominent in the media at the time. During the course of interviewing the children from one family who were suspected of having been sexually abused by their father and siblings, allegations of ritualistic sexual abuse of nine children from four other families were also made, implicating their parents and a local minister. These children were subsequently removed from their homes in Orkney in a joint police and social care manoeuvre, flown to mainland Scotland and placed in foster care. They were subjected to much interviewing and denied any contact with their parents. Six weeks later a decision was reached at the Sheriff's Court that the legal proceedings that had taken place were incompetent and the return of the children to their parents was ordered. The inquiry did not consider whether or not the abuse had taken place but the reasonableness of the actions of the child protection professionals in the light of the evidence they had available to them. The inquiry also considered the treatment of the children and their parents. The findings were similar to Cleveland (Butler-Sloss 1988), especially regarding the style and quality of the interviewing of children, the manner of removal (dawn raids) and the ban on contact.

The subsequent Clyde report (1992) concentrated on the response rather than the actual abuse, criticizing the approach of professionals which appeared heavy handed, perhaps in reaction to some high profile cases in the 1980s; an increase in recognition and response, and overzealous interpretation of the Children Act 1989. Interestingly *Working Together under the Children Act 1989* (DH and Home Office 1991) sets training agendas in terms of joint training for those involved in working with children and specialized training for those with major child protection roles; police and social care interview techniques were also raised as an area requiring further training.

The publication of *Child Protection: Messages from Research* (DH 1995) emphasized that child protection services had become over-concerned with detecting and investigating physical and sexual abuse cases (i.e. more overt forms of abuse in the public eye). In fact these forms of abuse constituted a minority of referrals, but were subsequently dominating professionals thinking to the detriment of neglect cases. This research summary also confirmed the findings from the Cleveland (Butler-Sloss 1988) and Orkney (Clyde 1992) reports, particularly with respect to parental perspectives and showed that many findings were viewed as intrusive, stigmatic and unhelpful. This emphasized the need to consider quality of life provided by parents for children as well as the actual abuse incidents – with a family approach preferable to the assertive or even aggressive child protective approach. Again the decade ended on a positive note with the publication of *Working Together to Safeguard Children* (DH 1999) spelling out the purpose of training with enormous implications for the organization and delivery of training.

Victoria Climbié 2 November 1991 – 25 February 2000

In spite of the development and refinement of structures to enhance inter-agency collaboration and clear guidance from government policy, poor inter-agency collaboration is still cited as a key factor in child death inquiries. Despite the increasing profile of inter-agency working and training, further tragedy came with the Victoria Climbié case. The decade started with the *Framework for the Assessment of Children in Need and Their Families* (DH 2000) providing clear guidance for multidisciplinary assessment. Past experiences were highlighted in a review of serious case reviews (Sinclair and Bullock 2002), identifying training deficits and the need for regular and relevant training. Indeed Victoria's death and the subsequent inquiry (Laming 2003) served only to highlight deficits and reinforce training needs. It also highlighted the prospect of cultural relativism (Dingwall et al. 1983) in that some of Victoria's behaviours were wrongly attributed to her ethnicity rather than indicators of abuse.

Victoria Climbié was killed by her great-aunt Marie-Thérèse Kouao and her great-aunt's boyfriend Carl John Manning in 2000. On 12 January 2001, Kouao and Manning were convicted of her murder. An inquiry was set up under the chairmanship of Lord Laming later in 2001 to investigate. In all 108 recommendations were made by the inquiry, significantly impacting upon professional practices. The following recommendation is of particular significance for most practitioners working with babies and young children:

> **Recommendation 12** Front-line staff in each of the agencies which regularly come into contact with families with children must ensure that in each new contact, basic information about the child is recorded. This must include the child's name, address, age, the name of the child's primary carer, the child's GP, and the name of the child's school if the child is of school age. Gaps in this information should be passed on to the relevant authority in accordance with local arrangements.
>
> (Laming 2003: 373, Paragraph 17.97)

This recommendation relates to most staff who see families and children regularly. The concern of this recommendation is to gather appropriate and relevant information about a child. Earlier in the report Laming (2003) identifies the qualities required of frontline social care, education and health practitioners as follows:

> I recognize that those who take on the work of protecting children at risk of deliberate harm face a tough and challenging task. Staff doing this work need a combination of professional skills and personal qualities, not least of which are persistence and courage.
>
> (Laming 2003: 3)

Many of the qualities which Laming refers to were present in the case of Mary Ellen Wilson in the person of Etta Wheeler, whose persistence made such a difference. Similar attempts in the case of Victoria Climbié to hear the child's voice were frustrated because her first language was French, which acted as a barrier to her communicating her concerns whenever she came into contact with practitioners (Powell 2005a). It is possible that the very involvement of a diverse group of practitioners, without clear lines of communication or coordination, obscured a clear insight into Victoria's situation. In other words, the fact that professionals failed to coordinate or communicate their efforts in a clear and consistent manner was detrimental to effective intervention.

A key message arising from the tragic deaths of Maria Colwell in 1973 and Victoria Climbié in 2000 appears to be the inability of practitioners to share concerns in a coherent manner and this clearly contributed to their deaths. Reder et al. (1993: 72) suggest that in Maria's case 'the mother and Social Worker [also] functioned together as a closed thinking system'; they had shared expectations that Maria would return to the birth mother's care. This pact privileged values and thinking, which were not apparently open to the views of other practitioners. This practice, which Laming would have been critical of, occurred perhaps because in 1973 there was no formal structure in place within the context of child protection where such an exchange could easily or formally take place.

Working with children and families

Arguably Victoria's death was pivotal in the policy development that followed, particularly *Every Child Matters* (Department for Education and Skills (DfES) 2003b) to develop measures to improve services through professional accountability and service reform. *Every Child Matters: Change for Children* (DfES 2004a) focuses on a shared programme of national change to provide services around the needs of children and young people in order to integrate services and achieve better outcomes such as being healthy, being safe, enjoying and achieving, making a positive contribution and achieving economic well-being.

The Children Act 2004 emphasized reform within children's services with local arrangements to safeguard and promote the welfare of children and national initiatives such as the Information Sharing Index, containing basic information about all children and families to track children who are born or enter the United Kingdom. *Working Together to Safeguard Children: A Guide to Inter-agency Working to Safeguard and Promote Welfare of Children* (DH 2006) contained statutory and non-statutory guidance, providing a national framework for policies, procedures and practice. It promotes safeguarding training which must be consistent with common core principles, while individual agencies are responsible for ensuring that staff are competent and confident to carry out safeguarding responsibilities.

It is important to note that each agency has its own guidance, while legislation is relevant to all agencies. One such example is the Education Act 2002, which emphasizes the duty to make arrangements to safeguard and promote the welfare of children; ensure training and pastoral support; and identify designated staff to coordinate and manage child safeguarding practice. It promotes policies and procedures to safeguard children and working in partnership with other agencies. *Safeguarding Children in Education* (DfES 2005) sets out the duty of local education authorities, schools and further education to have arrangements to safeguard children.

The *National Service Framework for Children, Young People and Maternity Services* (DH 2004) is a ten-year programme aiming to develop long-term and sustainable improvements in children's health. Standards include promoting health and well-being; identifying needs and intervening early; supporting parenting; child, young person and family-centred services; growing up into adulthood; and safeguarding and promoting the welfare of children. All services and staff in the children's workforce must be competent and trained to promote children's welfare and safeguard them from harm. While this plan targets health, it suggests that many factors can impact on outcomes.

The legal framework

Working with children and families is supported by a legal framework which informs policy and practice. The guidance offered by the legal framework includes when and what actions may be considered to protect a child from ill-treatment. *Working Together to Safeguard Children (DCSF 2010)* states:

> Although all organizations that work with children and families share a commitment to safeguard and promote their welfare, many agencies have specific roles and responsibilities to do so that are underpinned by a statutory duty or duties.
> (Department for Children, Schools and Families (DCSF) 2010)

Key principles include parental responsibility, duties of care and the welfare of the child. The Children Act 1989 and all subsequent legislation emphasizes that the primary responsibility for looking after children rests with parents and the role of the local authority and other agencies is to help families fulfil this responsibility, even if the parent's responsibility has been restricted by a Court Order.

Thus the Act aims to find a proper balance between the need to promote the welfare of the child, and the need to respect the rights of parents. This is seen particularly in the various legal safeguards which families have, reflected in the provisions of the Human Rights Act 1998. Under Section 17 of the Children Act 1989, the local authority has specific duties to safeguard and promote the welfare of children 'in need' and to promote the upbringing of such children by their parents, so far as this is consistent with their welfare duty to the child, by providing an appropriate range and level of services.

Under Section 17(10) of the Act, a child is in 'need' if:

a. He/she is unlikely to achieve or maintain, or have the opportunity of achieving or maintaining, a reasonable standard of health or development without the provision for him/her of services by a local authority;

b. His/her health or development is likely to be significantly impaired, or further impaired, without the provision for him/her of such services; or

c. He/she is a Disabled Child.

A welfare checklist (set out in Section 1(3) of the Children Act 1989) has to be considered by a court before making any orders under the Act other than emergency orders. The matters on the checklist include:

i. The ascertainable wishes and feelings of the child (considered in light of his or her age and understanding)

ii. The child's physical, emotional and educational needs

iii. The likely effect on the child of any change in circumstances

iv. The child's age, sex, background and any characteristics which the Court considers relevant

v. Any harm which the child has suffered or is at risk of suffering

vi. How capable each of the child's parents (and any other person in relation to whom the Court considers the question to be relevant) is of meeting the child's needs

vii. The range of powers available to the Court in the proceedings in question.

A local authority is under a duty to investigate in the following circumstances:

a. When a Court in family proceedings directs that a local authority investigate a child's circumstances (under Section 37(1) of the Children Act 1989).

b. Where the local authority is informed that a child who lives, or is found, in its area is the subject of an Emergency Protection Order (granted to a person other than the local authority) or is in Police Protection or has contravened a ban imposed by a curfew notice made under the Crime and Disorder Act 1998 (Section 47(1)(a) of the Children Act 1989).

c. Where a local authority is informed, or has cause to suspect, that a child living in their area has suffered Significant Harm or is likely to suffer such harm (Section 47(1)(b) of the Children Act 1989).

Investigations, assessments and types of orders are considered in more detail in Part 2 of the book. You may also find it useful to refer to Chapter 2 regarding children's rights.

Signs on the child

The discussion has so far has explored the historical context of safeguarding, suggesting that concerns for children's well-being have been around for a considerable period of time. The emphasis within the discussion has highlighted the failings surrounding certain practices at the same time exploring some of the more effective ways of intervening on behalf on babies and young children. One of the major issues experienced by most practitioners is how to recognize abuse or ill-treatment, when it is extremely unlikely that a baby or a young child will be able to explain what has happened to them. It is also highly likely that in the majority of cases, ill-treatment will occur in the privacy of the home and out of the view of professionals, which means that practitioners will have to use their judgement in determining whether a child appears to be showing signs of abuse or not. In addition, because babies and young children are normally unable to fully participate in verbal interaction, they can only give limited clues as to what may have happened to them.

Peter Connelly (also known as Baby P or Baby Peter, 1 March 2006 – 3 August 2007)

Although it is not always possible for babies and very young children who may not yet have the language to articulate their concerns adequately, their body language may nonetheless suggest a degree of unhappiness. This is perhaps reflected in the more recent case of Peter Connelly, who died in 2007, aged 17 months, despite having been examined by a paediatrician 48 hours earlier (Haringey LSCB 2008). He had also been on Haringey Council's child protection register (now termed as being under a child protection plan) for the eight months preceding his death following suspected non-accidental injuries. Without the benefit of hindsight it is easier to attribute potential signs of abuse – such as an overly fractious child, bumps and bruises – to behavioural aspects and accidental injuries. Yet this was essentially a child under supervision following several injuries and concerns, including an unexplained bump on the head, 'easy bruising' being reported by the mother (despite being only six months old at the time), and falling down the stairs resulting in bruising to his left breast and cranium. Although Peter had been removed into care for a period of time, this was to a friend of the mother and he was subsequently returned to the care of this manipulative woman, who effectively disguised potential signs of abuse not only with misinformation about who was living in the house but also physically by covering facial injuries with smeared chocolate. The effect of this case has been significant in terms of the increase in the number of Section 31 Care Order applications by 113 per cent, named the 'Baby Peter effect' by the Children and Families Court Advisory and Support Service (CAFCASS 2009). This suggests that practitioners are taking more notice of potential signs of abuse and the need to take care to remain vigilant without being alarmist. While such a large rise in Section 31 applications might be seen as resulting from practitioners resorting to a more 'tick box mentality' to ensure that they appeared to be appropriately vigilant in protecting children, it could also be an example of overreaction to potential risks. However, only the benefit of hindsight can truly answer this in each case. There will be further discussion of balancing risks and benefits later in the book, particularly in Chapters 6 and 7.

The ability and the willingness to enquire about a child who appears to be displaying an injury or mark or any other suggestion that causes concern or suspicion is an extremely important practice that should be carried out by any early years professional at the point of contact. This requirement should be irrespective of the context that the early years professional works in and applies equally to those practitioners in childminding, Sure Start children's centres, crèches, nurseries, schools or working in the community as a health practitioner or social worker.

It is acceptable to enquire how a mark was caused but the initial question to a child should be one reflecting a 'light touch' approach, such as 'Oh dear, how did you get that bruise?' and should never be a leading question, for example by asking the above question but adding 'Did Daddy do it?' Similarly with parents or carers it is acceptable to ask how an injury came about so that a note can be made for perhaps a record of an accident if the child is at nursery or crèche – or in fact to rule out the possibility that an injury took place outside the care of the parents or carers. Any suspicion regarding potential sexual abuse should be shared with fellow professionals in the first instance and kept confidential. There are clearly some aspects of child protection and safeguarding that can be addressed in a more direct manner so that it is perfectly legitimate to enquire how an injury came about. Indeed in the majority of cases where some concern is felt for a child's well-being, practitioners may already be monitoring and ready to follow up with appropriate questions. In the case of sexual abuse the signs of ill-treatment are unlikely to be as apparent, but information may come to you that may make you suspicious that a child is being sexually abused. However, it is clearly a very sensitive area and you need to proceed cautiously in order to avoid alerting the perpetrator and placing the child at further risk. A more acceptable practice that we would recommend would be to convene a strategy meeting with appropriate practitioners from both inside and outside your agency, including the police and social care practitioners, and then agree on a plan of action. Of course this means that the risk to the child remains unaddressed inasmuch as an intervention does not immediately follow. However it is important that when an investigation does begin that it does so on a sound basis that sometimes may not be related to sexual abuse but to some other form of ill-treatment.

Defining safeguarding: getting to grips with the guidance and the legal infrastructure

It is important to begin the discussion around identification and recognition with a note of caution. Despite the apparent helpfulness of the above definitions they must be applied to particular situations and this is where it can be problematic. Of course, there may be occasions, though these will tend to be less frequent when a baby or young child who is displaying very clear indications that she or he may have been abused should result in rapid action by discussing the situation urgently with a line manager. If you are on a student placement and notice a sign on a child that raises your concern, you should similarly refer this matter immediately to your direct line manager. Your line manager has a responsibility of care to both the identified child and to you as having referred the matter and should follow this up by contacting your tutor at the university or college to ensure that they are kept in the picture. You should also contact your tutor so that the implications of making the referral can be discussed along with any other support that might be deemed appropriate.

Part of the developing policies and guidance arising from the Every Child Matters documentation is *Working Together to Safeguard Children: A Guide to Inter-agency Working to Safeguard and Promote the Welfare of Children* (originally published by DH 2006; updated by DCSF 2010). This document through its very title tells readers what it will be concerned with. Safeguarding can really be achieved only when the child is perceived as central to practitioner interest and concern. Children will need to have aspects of their lives safeguarded, it suggests, in order to ensure that they are able to participate more fully in life. This can be achieved through the promotion of children's welfare, through a range of practitioners coming to work together to ensure that these aims are realized.

This raises the question of what safeguarding might mean, and the document helpfully offers a working definition of safeguarding and promoting the welfare of children as follows:

> The process of protecting children from abuse and neglect, preventing impairment of their health and development, and ensuring they are growing up in circumstances consistent with the provision of safe and effective care that enables children to have optimum life chances and enter adulthood successfully.
>
> (DCSF 2010: 27)

This definition highlights the particular elements from which safeguarding is constructed and therefore is emphasizing the importance of prevention and the promotion of children's welfare as a global concept and therefore the responsibility all citizens. This is significantly different from the situation prevailing in childcare, before the implementation of *Every Child Matters* (DfES 2003b) and shows the state symbolically through the work of practitioners coming in contact with babies and young children as an attempt to micro-manage families and carers with children.

The *Working Together to Safeguard Children* guidance (DCSF 2010) goes on to clarify the above by setting out further elements that help to clarify what is meant by 'safeguarding', 'child protection' and 'children in need' which are all terms that are referred to throughout the guidance. Safeguarding and promoting the welfare of children is defined for the purposes of this guidance as:

- protecting children from maltreatment
- preventing impairment of children's health or development
- ensuring that children are growing up in circumstances consistent with the provision of safe and effective care
- undertaking that role, so as to enable those children to have optimum life chances and to enter adulthood successfully.

(DCSF 2010: 34)

The general headings above suggest a wide-ranging set of concerns to facilitate support that will lead to maximizing the child's life experience. In relation to child abuse the Department for Education and Skills (DfES 2006b) guidance under Section 4.1 of *What To Do If You're Worried a Child is Being Abused* reintroduces the concept of *significant harm* (also referred to in the Children Act 1989), which is described as 'the threshold that justifies compulsory intervention in family life in the best interests of children' (DfES 2003b: 8). Local authorities have a duty to make enquiries, 'where it has a reasonable cause to suspect that a child is suffering, or likely to suffer, significant harm' (Section 47 of the Children Act 1989).

Categories of child abuse

A range of definitions of child abuse are set out in government advice such as Department of Health (2003: 3). These include inflicting harm or failing to prevent harm within a family, institutional or community setting, by those familiar to them or a stranger. Specific types of abuse are now traditionally categorized as:

- physical abuse
- emotional abuse
- sexual abuse
- neglect.

However, the attention and emphasis given to each has shifted culturally over time.

Indeed the assessment of situations as abusive or not may also rely on a practitioner's insights and preconceptions that include personal as well as professional values, attitudes and experiences in decision-making. There is an important point being made here since this will generally mean that each practitioner will tend to approach a specific concern with different sets of beliefs and attitudes making it likely that there will always be a range of differing perceptions as to what counts as abuse or ill-treatment (Powell 2005a). At least this position taken by each practitioner in relation to whether a child appears to be vulnerable or ill-treated has to start with a practitioner raising concerns and sharing them with colleagues. It was evident in the Laming (2003) report that this area of communication was lacking, non-existent or contradictory. An important lesson arising from Laming (2003) was the vital importance of clear, understandable communication within and across agency and professional boundaries as a core requirement of effective intervention.

As we have seen, different forms of ill-treatment are defined as physical abuse, emotional abuse, sexual abuse and neglect. The categories of abuse as defined in the guidance *Working Together to Safeguard Children* (DCSF 2010: 4.2) are described below.

Physical abuse

Physical abuse may involve hitting, shaking, throwing, poisoning, burning or scalding, drowning, suffocating or otherwise causing physical harm to a child. Physical harm may also be caused when a parent or carer fabricates the symptoms of illness, or deliberately induces symptoms of illness, or deliberately induces illness in a child.

Emotional abuse

Emotional abuse is the persistent emotional ill-treatment of a child such as to cause severe and persistent adverse effects on the child's emotional development. It may involve conveying to the child that they are worthless or unloved, inadequate, or valued only in so far as they meet the needs of another person. It may feature age or developmentally inappropriate expectations being imposed on children. It may involve seeing or hearing the ill-treatment of another; serious bullying causing a child to feel frightened or in danger; or the exploitation or corruption of a child. Some level of emotional abuse is involved in all types of ill-treatment of a child, though it may occur alone.

Sexual abuse

Sexual abuse involves forcing or enticing a child or young person to take part in sexual activities, including prostitution, whether or not the child is aware of what is happening. The activities may involve physical contact, including penetrative (e.g. rape or buggery) or non-penetrative acts. It may include non-contact activities, such as involving children in looking at, or in the production of, pornographic material or watching sexual activities, or encouraging children to behave in sexually inappropriate ways.

Neglect

Neglect is the persistent failure to meet a child's basic physical and/or psychological needs, likely to result in serious impairment of the child's health or development. Neglect may occur during pregnancy as a result of maternal substance abuse. Once a child is born, neglect may involve a parent or carer failing to provide adequate food and clothing, shelter including exclusion from home or abandonment, failing to protect a child from physical and emotional harm or danger, failure to ensure access to appropriate medical care or treatment, or the failure to ensure access to appropriate medical care or treatment. It may also include neglect of, or unresponsiveness to, a child's basic emotional needs.

Further guidance in identifying abuse

While these definitions may be useful as a guide, it is important to bear in mind advice given in the *Working Together to Safeguard Children* document which under Section 1.28 makes the important point 'there is no absolute criteria on which to rely when judging what constitutes significant harm' (DCSF 2010: 36). However, this guidance highlights that under Section 31(9) of the Children Act 1989 as amended by the Adoption and Children Act 2002: 'harm' is defined as 'ill-treatment or the impairment of health or development, including, for example, impairment suffered from seeing or hearing the ill-treatment of another'; 'development' as 'physical, intellectual, emotional, social or behavioural development'; 'health' as 'physical or mental health'; and 'ill-treatment' as 'including sexual abuse and forms of ill-treatment which are not physical' (DCSF 2010: 36). Further advice in understanding and identifying significant harm suggests considering:

- the nature of harm, in terms of maltreatment or failure to provide adequate care
- the impact on the child's health and development
- the child's development within the context of their family and wider environment
- any special needs, such as medical condition, communication impairment or disability, that may affect the child development and care within the family
- the capacity of parents to meet adequately the child's needs
- the wider and an environmental family context.

(DCSF 2010: 37)

Significant harm suggests a tipping point towards intervention, but safeguarding provides the opportunity for practitioners to become involved in supporting children prior to significant harm being part of the concern. Early years professionals are excellently placed to consider the children's development against the five outcomes listed in *Every Child Matters: Change for Children* (DfESa 2004: 9) and which are as follows:

1. *Being Healthy:* enjoying good physical and mental health and living a healthy lifestyle.
2. *Staying Safe:* being protected from harm and neglect and growing up able to look after themselves.
3. *Enjoying and Achieving:* getting the most out of life and developing broad skills for adulthood.
4. *Making a Positive Contribution:* to the community and to society and not engaging in anti-social or offending behaviour.
5. *Economic Well-Being:* overcoming socio-economic disadvantages to achieve their full potential in life.

The above outcomes are endorsed by law in the form of the Children Act 2004 as key factors towards ensuring children's well-being and as a benchmark for acceptable parental practices.

Child protection is still to be found as a significant part of safeguarding and promoting welfare and according to *Working Together to Safeguard Children*: 'this refers to activity that is undertaken to protect specific children who are suffering, or at risk of suffering, significant harm' (DH 2006: 35). In other words child protection begins at the point where prevention is believed to be inadequate in dealing with issues of significant harm and a more concentrated and statutory engagement is likely to be initiated. This is not to say that child protection as a response to serious concerns is always part of a continuum of intervention; it can also be used as an immediate way of supporting and protecting a child in need.

This general concern relating to safeguarding is linked with children in need who are referred to in *Working Together to Safeguard Children* (DCSF 2010) as:

> Children who are defined as being 'in need' which under Section 17 of the Children Act 1989 are those whose vulnerability is such that they are unlikely to reach or maintain a satisfactory level of health or development, or their health and development will be significantly impaired, without the provision of services (Section 17 (10) of the Children Act 1989) plus those who are disabled.
>
> (DCSF 2010: 35)

The advice from *Working Together to Safeguard Children* (DCSF 2010) suggests that the critical factors to be taken into account in deciding whether a child is in need under the Children Act 1989 are:

- What will happen to a child's health or development without services being provided, and
- The likely effect the services will have on the child's standard of health and development.

> (DCSF 2010: 35)

The ways that safeguarding is defined and located, alongside child protection and children in need, clearly connects it to the Children Act 1989 as well as to more recent legislation. There is therefore a clear relationship which is emphasized in the government's legislative framework of the safeguarding agenda being concerned with both prevention and protection as a balanced set of professional concerns to ensure children's well-being and development. This suggests that practitioners' decision-making concerning whether a child may have been ill-treated may not solely rest on an injury that is perceived as suspicious but a number of factors which taken together indicate its likelihood. This having been said there are also situations that occur where a child suffers an injury that requires the professional intervention immediately.

Prevention and protection

The concern for measures to be put in place that could lead to the prevention of babies and young children being ill-treated has been around for some time and as Parton (2006: 78) suggests, 'the 1989 Act had extended . . . responsibilities to providing family support for "children in need".' There was a concern at the time of the Children Act 1989 being enacted that still remains that prevention could lead to the reduction of child abuse if family difficulties could be identified and resolved. This view of prevention suggests intervention as a set of strategies focused on working with families before problems that could lead to child abuse could take form. In the case of babies and young children, this could result in early concerns relating to safeguarding leading to a multi-agency approach to working with the family in an attempt to support the family in resolving difficulties.

The term 'protection' refers specifically to maltreatment and the professional responsibilities that support intervention. It arises when immediate concerns for a child's well-being are identified. It is important that when such concerns are identified that there is the opportunity to share this with another responsible member of staff to ensure that appropriate action can be initiated. There are therefore twin aspects to safeguarding as referred to above, one concerned with the wider support available to families, carers and their children. While this book will be referring to both prevention and protection, it is chiefly concerned with protection and supporting readers in making informed choices when presented with safeguarding concerns.

Personal feelings

It is important to begin any intervention by examining your own feelings as a key factor in bringing to light the nature of a safeguarding concern. Each individual has their own core of values and beliefs concerning childcare and children's welfare, and it is this set of personal factors, which will immediately come into play and inform the individual about what their concern is related to.

Practice reflection points

Considering your own values and beliefs
- Considering the previous discussion relating to safeguarding and child protection, how would you inform your values and feelings as to what represented a safeguarding situation? Consider the kinds of parental practices which you might disapprove of as well as what might signal concern about a child.

- What do you believe has helped to form your personal beliefs about parenting and child rearing? How helpful does having a sense of parenting standards influence your decision about whether a situation is one that should be considered in safeguarding terms or not?

- Is it always useful and productive to have a strong point of view from which it might be considered by a parent that you were judging them from?

Of course it is very difficult to be able to anticipate how you might feel in a particular situation concerning safeguarding. However, you probably have a general idea of what your tendencies are likely to be when you have concerns for a baby or young child. By imagining individual responses, a more productive set of practices may be considered because the last thing you would want to do would be to alienate the parent or carer and leave the baby or young child at risk of avoiding contact.

When to intervene (early moments): from concern to actions

The question of knowing how or when to intervene can be extremely difficult, dependent upon the nature of the relationship that the practitioner may have with the parent or carer and the anticipation of the likely reaction to any possible interpretation of interference.

The ability to share and discuss professional concerns with a colleague or directly with a parent or carer relating to a baby or a young child would probably count as an initial intervention. Before doing so it may be better to reflect on how this possibly sensitive and even delicate matter might be articulated by you as an early years professional. Once a form of words has been decided upon, and you feel comfortable that you will be able to make your point and not alienate anyone, it might then be possible to discuss the concern. Of course, for some parents and carers it will be difficult for them to not feel that they are being judged as not coping or even worse as poor parents. Therefore, direct communications should remain open and honest, while remaining sensitive towards the other person's feelings. This may be easier to do when there is already an established positive relationship. For instance, it might be possible to say, 'I've noticed a small bruise on the baby's hand and wondered how it got there.' What follows should receive your full attention as it may lead to the need for a discussion with a colleague. Even when an explanation appears plausible, it should be recorded so that later it can be reflected upon with any other incidents that may have happened as part of a history of possible ill-treatment.

Developing trust in relationships is a key area for working together in partnership with parents, so that factors which may cause stress and may lead to possible overreaction with a baby or young child can be discussed. Alternative strategies may be considered including possible referral to a range of different support groups. Of course, each case of concern varies enormously, but there will be a detailed discussion taking place throughout the book which we hope will cover most of these concerns.

The discussion must necessarily consider some of the difficulties of communicating across professional boundaries and of course how some of those difficulties may be overcome.

Practice reflection points

The multidisciplinary team

- Identify those colleagues both within your workplace and beyond, with whom you can share your thoughts with relating to a child where you have concerns about any aspect of safeguarding.

- In responding to the above, consider the accessibility of the practitioners that you have identified and whether that is something that can be improved.

- Did you manage to identify a range of practitioners, or did they tend to be mainly from within your workplace?

- How can you improve contact with external agencies, first in the more general way, and second specifically in relation to a safeguarding concern about a child?

Working closely across professional boundaries with parents and carers: communication

One of the key findings of the Laming inquiry and his subsequent report (Laming 2003) was that there was a significant lack in the ability of care practitioners to liaise and intervene effectively. Central to all of these concerns was a breakdown in communication, as Laming reminded agencies in the inquiry: 'Effective action designed to safeguard the well-being of children and families depends upon sharing relevant information on an inter-agency basis' (Laming 2003: 1, 45).

Key messages

Several important messages in this introductory chapter relate to issues in safeguarding babies and young children. We began by examining some safeguarding cases, because of the way in which they still have a good deal of relevance to offer modern safeguarding practice. A discussion of the types of signs and symptoms that may be displayed by and on children led to an examination of recent policy and guidelines. We explored some of the definitions of surround safeguarding with its emphasis on both prevention and protection. There was then a brief examination concerning the earliest moments, where concerns are just beginning to emerge and the need perhaps of shaping up what and how to voice concerns with parents and carers. Listed below are some of the main issues that arise around safeguarding:

- You need to have the child central to any concerns. This may sound rather obvious, but it is a factor that can be easily overlooked. See for example the cases of Maria Colwell and Peter Connelly.
- You should recognize the shift that has taken place about safeguarding and child protection in current social policy and legislation and understand that all early years professionals are expected to respond proactively in relation to children's well-being and see that as being an opportunity for positive and supportive preventative intervention. However when it is considered that the child is suffering from significant harm, it is important for you to treat this as a priority and for appropriate discussions to take place with other practitioners as a matter of urgency.
- You need to be able to articulate sensitively, but honestly, any concerns felt about a particular child to the parents or carer and colleagues. The issues here are concerned with personal feelings, values and beliefs; it is difficult to discuss childcare where there are considered shortcomings in the parents or carers, and for them not to feel offended for at least being considered a poor parent and not want to have further contact. This could be extremely problematic, particularly for the baby or young child concerned.
- You should be able to explore and assert your position with colleagues, both within the familiar workplace and also with those from outside agencies who may have a different set of values and perspectives.
- You need to be aware of current guidance and policy and to some extent the underpinning legislation that informs it. This is particularly important in the case of a situation such as where a professional action is being contemplated such as recording or visiting the home of a parent or carer. You should have a sense of security that the action that is about to be performed is appropriate, professional and linked to legal understandings.

- Most of all, it is essential for you to understand yourself as a vital resource for both babies and young children and their parents and carers. Failure to do so may result in the safeguarding agenda not been taken seriously which might result in the continuation of a safeguarding situation that otherwise might have been supported or resolved earlier.
- You should be persistent and focus on the needs of the child in each case, including his or her perspectives and experiences, giving the opportunity for the child to tell their side of the story. In our view your relationship with the parents or carers, while important, should always wherever possible allow the child to give voice to matters that clearly are important to them and their future well-being.
- Finally reflection is essential, because it will help you to review your actions or perhaps your lack of them as being part of a considered professional examination, leading to continuous learning opportunities and improvements.

2 The rights of children

Chapter Overview

This chapter considers the development of children as beings with rights, drawing on legislation and policy which inform this perspective. The chapter emphasizes the need for children's rights as a central tenet for the book. It is important to view children as having rights and to respond to them appropriately during times of crisis such as in child protection.

There has been a marked change from the relative absence of government involvement to a situation in contemporary society, signified by surveillance and anxiety for children's well-being. In this change in societal perspectives, the child has moved from the margins to the centre of concern and interest, to what is considered to be a more holistic way of thinking about children's needs and experiences. *Every Child Matters* (DfES 2003b) identified the five outcomes, which suggests a means by which children's well-being may be understood:

- Be healthy
- Stay safe
- Enjoy and achieve
- Make a positive contribution
- Achieve economic well-being.

As the Every Child Matters website pointed out:

> The project is all about making sure children and young people can have a good life, whoever they are, and no matter what problems they may face.
> The aim is to make everyone aware of the things children and young people need to help them to be happy, successful, healthy and safe. The Government wants people to work better together to look after the needs of children.
>
> (DfES 2003b)

Every Child Matters (DfES 2003b) located children at the very centre of the policy agenda, therefore supporting the position of children with rights able to articulate their experience and concern about a range of different areas, which directly or indirectly affect them. They were encouraged to share concerns with a range of early years professionals who can then interpret them in relation to the five outcomes. Many of the concerns relating to children being able to articulate and share concerns or worries about the ways that they are treated are enshrined within the Children Act 2004, which for the first time identified the need for a Children's Commissioner to act as the adult champion of children's concerns.

The Children's Commissioner's role, outlined by the Children Act 2004, has the functions and responsibilities shown in the text box.

The role of the Children's Commissioner

(1) The Children's Commissioner has the function of promoting awareness of the views and interests of children in England.
(2) The Children's Commissioner may in particular under this section:-
   (a) encourage persons exercising functions or engaged in activities affecting children to take account of their views and interests;
   (b) advise the Secretary of State on the views and interests of children;
   (c) consider or research the operation of complaints procedures so far as relating to children;
   (d) consider or research any other matter relating to the interests of children;
   (e) publish a report on any matter considered or researched by him under this section.
(3) The Children's Commissioner is to be concerned in particular under this section with the views and interests of children so far as relating to the following aspects of their well-being:

   (a) physical and mental health and emotional well-being;
   (b) protection from harm and neglect;
   (c) education, training and recreation;
   (d) the contribution made by them to society;
   (e) social and economic well-being.

The Children's Commissioner is therefore an extremely significant person, whose role is to ensure that children remain at the centre of all childcare agencies' perspective whether they are from statutory, voluntary, private or independent sectors; and across all professional disciplines, particularly those who have regular contact with children such as Sure Start practitioners, teachers, healthcare practitioners, foster carers and childminders. The Children's Commissioner role was developed as a national watchdog and champion for children in order to monitor, protect and promote rights as advocated in the United Nations Convention on the Rights of the Child (UNCRC 1989).

On 1 March 2005, Professor Al Aynsley-Green was appointed as the first Children's Commissioner for England. He was also the National Clinical Director for Children within the Department of Health and still practising as a paediatric professor at Great Ormond Street Hospital. While the UK government aimed to demonstrate a commitment to children's rights and views with this appointment, it was ultimately criticized as tokenistic, as unlike Scotland, Wales and Northern

Ireland, the English Commissioner's role was effectively limited to raising awareness and reflecting the interests of children and not promoting and protecting their *rights* in a statutory framework. The 2010 Dunford review of the role recommended a statutory, independent and stand-alone body exclusively promoting and protecting the rights of children or a model with the Children's Commissioner heading up a distinct division or section, with statutory powers, dedicated staff and ring-fenced resources aimed at promoting and protecting children's rights (Children's Rights Alliance 2010; Dunford 2010). Other key representatives for children include the Minister for Children and the Education Secretary.

Practice reflection points

Key representatives for children

- Who is the current Minister for Children?

- Who is the current Education Secretary?

- Who is the current Children's Commissioner?

- Find out who directs children's services in your local area.

- How can these national and local figures make a difference to children's lives?

- How can they help you in your early years role?

The Children Act 2004 also emphasizes the importance of interprofessional cooperation as a means of improving inter-agency communication and coordination in supporting the well-being of babies and young children. In addition, the Act asserts that integrated children's services have a mandatory duty to work together cooperatively and that each of them should have regard to the need to safeguard and promote the welfare of children.

Applying children's rights to the safeguarding context

The discussion so far illustrates the location of the child as central to all safeguarding, and therefore central to babies and young children achieving their potential. Consideration also needs to be given to the difficulties that might be encountered in putting children's rights at the centre of professional practice. The question needs to be asked about what children's rights might mean and how the application of a rights-led approach could be important to safeguarding practices. The United Nations Convention on the Rights of the Child (UNCRC 1989) underpins the Children Acts 1989 and 2004 and the Every Child Matters agenda in the UK by providing a set of consistent principles, while informing relevant childcare legislation in other countries which are signatories to the convention. Although ratified by the UK, it would need to be incorporated into English law through legislation for children to bring any proceedings before national courts; none the less it is accepted by most governments worldwide, if yet not fully ratified by all.

Children's rights generally have been receiving increasing attention, with campaigning becoming more prominent since the International Year of the Child in 1979. Dimond (2003) advocated the incorporation of the United Nations Convention of the Rights of the Child into UK law, just as the European Convention on Human Rights (ECHR) was incorporated in the Human Rights Act 1998. However, the Human Rights Act 1998 was drawn up with adults in mind. Arguably children are entitled to the same rights as all persons; however, this can be perceived as conflicting with the needs of adults on occasions.

According specific rights to children could give them greater protection, so that they could legally challenge any infringement of their rights. This charter of children's rights (UNCRC 1989) comprises a consensus of agreed norms, concerning prevention, participation, protection and provision. However it is criticized for being aspirational rather than a legal entitlement, dependent on political will and resources. Crucially the best interests of the child shall be a *primary* consideration, not the *paramount* consideration. The difference is that a paramount consideration is above all others whereas a primary consideration is principal but not necessarily exclusive of other concerns. The Adoption and Children Act 2002 highlights the issue of paramouncy, as under the Adoption Act 1976 the child's welfare was first but not paramount. The Children Act 1989 was the first piece of legislation to give paramouncy to children's needs, a more child-centred approach.

Specific rights relate to issues such as the right to life, development and identity; separation from parents; to express views; civil rights; parental responsibilities; child protection; recipience of social welfare; and protection against social exploitation. The current policy context emphasizes that child protection cannot be separated from measures to improve child welfare; indeed the welfare principle is a feature of legislation.

General rights of children

On a general level a child should have the right to life and development (Article 6 of the UNCRC) and the right to an identity (Article 7). A child 'shall be registered immediately after birth and shall have the right from birth to a name, the right to acquire a nationality, and, as far as possible, the right to know and be cared for by his or her parents' with implications for the biological origins in adoption or donation of sperm or eggs. Preservation of identity (Article 8) concerns 'respect the right of the child to preserve his or her identity, including nationality, name and family relations as recognized by law without unlawful interference', this has issues for adoption, contact and parental responsibility. Additionally separation from parent(s) (Article 9) should be avoided unless such separation is necessary for the best interest of the child.

Child protection

Articles 19–24 relate specifically to child protection with reference to 'appropriate legislative, administrative, social and educational measures to protect the child from all forms of physical or mental violence, injury or abuse, neglect or negligent treatment, maltreatment or exploitation, including sexual abuse' (UNCRC 1989: Article 19). This includes protection against social exploitation (Article 32–35) relating to employment, sexual abuse, drugs, punishment, abduction and trafficking. Article 34 highlights the state's responsibility to undertake to protect the child from all forms of sexual exploitation and sexual abuse.

A child temporarily or permanently deprived of his or her family environment, or in whose own best interests cannot be allowed to remain in that environment, shall be entitled to special protection and assistance provided by the state. When considering solutions in a case where the child needs to be

> temporarily or permanently deprived of his or her family environment, or in whose own best interests cannot be allowed to remain in that environment...due regard shall be paid to the desirability of continuity in a child's upbringing and to the child's ethnic, religious, cultural and linguistic background.
>
> (UNCRC 1989: Article 20)

This cultural aspect is recognized in the Children Act 1989, meaning that children need to be placed in culturally sensitive care.

UNCRC four central tenets

- *Prevention* in terms of healthcare, harm, abduction, discrimination
- *Participation* in decisions that affect them
- *Protection* from abuse, conflict and exploitation
- *Provision* of basic needs, education, security

UNCRC specific rights

- The right to life and development
- The right to an identity
- Separation from parents
- To express views
- Civil rights
- Parental responsibilities
- Child protection
- Recipients of social welfare
- Protection against social exploitation

The Convention highlights the importance of nurturing babies and young children so that they reach their full potential, and at the same time recognizing that children have the right to live a life free from neglect, exploitation and abuse. The Convention recognizes the importance of parents and carers as having the most important role in bringing up children; however, the best interest of the child will be their basic concern (UNCRC 1989: Article 18:1). While families are undoubtedly the primary support mechanism for most children, the UNCRC highlights that the state (i.e. governments and communities) should take responsibility not only for providing direct care for some children, but also for supporting and sustaining families or carers to ensure positive outcomes for children. This means that the state should 'render appropriate assistance to parents and legal guardians in the performance of their child-rearing responsibilities and shall ensure the development of institutions, facilities and services for the care of children' (UNCRC 1989: Article 18:2). This state responsibility for welfare and service provision is also enshrined in the Children Act 2004. Several other articles relate to state provision such as: access to healthcare, including preventive medicine (Article 24); recipience of social welfare (Articles 26–31); and an adequate standard of living for the child's physical, mental, spiritual, moral and social development (Article 27).

Countries who are signatories to the UNCRC are obliged to facilitate children's rights and promote their welfare: this can be facilitated through policy, legislation and service provision. The important message for early years professionals is that they should have a clear working understanding of the rights of children as the basis from which they can build their practice and understand better any justification for intervention into family life, where there are babies and young children. The UNCRC also requires agencies that are working for the benefit and well-being of babies and young children in relation to safeguarding concerns should work together effectively in order to coordinate the most effective practice possible. The central message, running through the identification of rights in the UNCRC, is that everyone has a part to play in promoting awareness of children's rights as a means of ensuring that children remain at the centre of societal concerns and by so doing confirms the societal responsibility towards all babies and young children. There are several other Articles in the UNCRC that can be related to safeguarding as follows.

The voice of the child

Article 12 of the UNCRC refers to children's rights to express their own opinions and to have them taken into account in any matter affecting them, although this is according to their age and maturity. Children's rights to freedom of expression are defined in Article 13, which also says that they have a right to receive and disseminate information; again this would need to be age and maturity appropriate. Even if a child is not old enough to give their opinion, their perspective needs to be considered. This is a feature of legal proceedings with the appointment of a Guardian Ad Litem or what is commonly termed now a Children's Guardian. However, the child's needs being central can and should be facilitated in all contact with services and professionals. The above Articles provide a framework that confirms the inclusion of babies and young children at the heart of the safeguarding process as beings with rights and supported by parents, carers and external agencies whose work is subject to inspection as part of a process of receiving government approved and continuing support.

The practitioner can consider a model that is built upon the part that Articles from the UNCRC play in informing and influencing practice through its connection with the framework of childcare legislation in the UK. The model would show the child as central to all attention in relation to safeguarding and therefore the immediate care and concern for the child should wherever possible be provided by the child's parents and carers who represent the first line for providing all services and against whom the five outcomes are integrated as part of their daily practices. Supporting parents and carers involves a further range of diverse agencies which can be mainly located within the community such as childminders, Sure Start practitioners, health visitors and midwives, social workers and family support workers. National legislative and policy agendas such as Every Child Matters are in place to underpin and inform professional practices in safeguarding. Informing national governments are universal policies such as the UN Convention on the Rights of the Child, which is an agreed document for implementation between the signatories from all the nations who signed up to it.

Human Rights Act 1998

The Human Rights Act was implemented on 2 October 2000 and incorporated the European Convention on Human Rights; importantly proceedings can now take place in English courts. The Act was drawn up with adults in mind not children, therefore the applicability and relevance to children could be questioned; none the less children have the same rights as all persons.

Human Rights Act 1998 – Fundamental Rights

- The right to life
- Freedom from torture, inhuman and degrading treatment
- Freedom from forced labour or slavery
- The right to liberty and to a fair trial
- Freedom from facing retrospective crimes or penalties
- The right to privacy
- Freedom of conscience
- Freedom of expression
- Freedom of assembly
- The right to marriage and family
- Freedom from discrimination

How is policy translated into practice?

One of the key difficulties is interpreting the above Articles and legal requirements into a set of practices that allow early years professionals to develop effective engagement with babies and young children that encourages them to participate meaningfully and as fully as possible. Alderson (2000b) argues that the rights that are articulated through the UN Convention should be used to support the participation of the very youngest children in society. However, it is recognized by Alderson that some rights are not yet fully realizable and are therefore more aspirational because they are dependent upon the 'maximum extent of each nation's available resources' and are 'not *absolute* but *conditional*, affected by the evolving capacities of the child, the responsibilities, rights and duties of parents, the primary responsibility of the parents and the national law' (Alderson 2000b: 23, referring to the UNCRC 1989). Children under the UNCRC have clear rights that must be respected, and which are shared, inasmuch as all children as well as other human beings should be treated with dignity and respect. Of course there are legal protections built in to ensure the children's best interests at the forefront of practitioner and parental concerns. For example, the Children Act 1989 has as its first principle that the welfare of the child should be paramount and the Children Act 2004 emphasizes the need for services to work together

> with a view to improving the well-being of children in the authority's area so far as relating to:
>
> (a) physical and mental health and emotional well-being;
> (b) protection from harm and neglect;
> (c) education, training and recreation;
> (d) the contribution made by them to society;
> (e) social and economic well-being.
>
> (Children Act 2004: 2:10:2)

There are clearly a number of practices concerned with practitioners being clear to view babies and young children as having rights, and it is their responsibilities as practitioners to attempt to include children's voices in any interaction regarding their well-being. However, this raises the question of how can babies and young children convey a sense of engagement that informs any meaning they might be able to make of their situation to early years professionals, and how can practitioners understand what babies and young children might mean through their means of communication? This was discussed in Chapter 1 and relates to all the cases highlighted there.

It is important for all practitioners to remember that children are all different in terms of their development but equally are likely to experience different cultural and rearing practices. *The Birth to Three Matters Framework* (DfES 2003a) and the *Early Years Foundation Stage* (DfES 2007) both emphasize that children develop at different stages and rates, and that early years professionals 'as well as leading activities and encouraging child lead activities, [you] should support and extend all children's development and learning by being an active listener and joining in and intervening when appropriate' (DfES 2007: 12). Parents, carers and other practitioners are actively engaging through the practices similar to those described above, in carrying out the concerns identified by Alderson (2000b) to ensure children's rights are recognized by engaging with children by inviting her or his participation and communication as a central element of recognizing their individuality and personal needs as learners.

> Even before their first words they find out a lot about language by hearing people talking, and are especially interested when it involves themselves and their daily lives. Sensitive caregiving, which responds to children's growing understanding and emotional needs, helps to build secure attachments to special people such as parents, family members or carers.
> (DfES 2007: Child development overview, birth to 11 months)

Buckley (2003: 9) identifies several factors that support human communication. These include a fundamental need to have the motivation to engage, a conducive situation for communication, and that there is a recognizable relationship between the participants, which means that they have a degree of clarity about each other's roles (parents–child, childminder–child). There needs to be some appreciation of both parties taking turns and for an appreciation of not only verbal utterances, but also non-verbal communication and facial expression. For the sensitive adult communicator it will be important to extend the child's communication, which of course implies a degree of taking the lead from the child as part of a carefully scaffolded interaction.

Children as rights-holders

There are several situations which can undermine effective child-centred communication and which would therefore breach the child's right to participate. For example babies and young children who experience dysfunctional family life are likely to receive less attention from parents and carers, or alternatively may be on the receiving end of negative behaviour, including that which ignores them. Freeman (1983) suggests that children should be considered as rights-holders with a right to fundamental types of rights and suggests the following categories by which children's rights can be considered:

- *Rights to welfare:* this refers to children's access to universal rights such as education as well as certain rights to protection from harm.
- *Rights to protection:* this refers to children's rights to protection from any form of ill-treatment or abuse and suggests that children should have a minimum standard of care.

- *The right to be treated like adults:* Freeman argues that children are discriminated against on the basis of their age; but that they should be treated like adults in relation to social justice. However, he does concede that there are age-related differences which need to be taken into consideration, which should be continuously kept under review, and that children's ability to understand and make decisions can be made only on a step-by-step basis.
- *Rights against parents:* Freeman points to parents as being the child's representative, and that their decisions should be adhered to, as long as they are connected to more objective evaluations that can identify what is in the best interests of the child. Wherever parents are unable to perform this role then a representative from an external organization should be identified to represent the child instead of the parent.

The above rights that Freeman (1987) uses are helpful in seeing how rights are identified and applied through the UNCRC in a slightly different way. Freeman (1987) is quite clearly recognizing the importance of children to be seen as themselves, separate from others with their own ways of expressing themselves and behaving with others. This way of understanding can be applied to babies as well as young children, and while babies may have lots of points in common with each other they are also individuals who are able to express themselves in their own personal ways.

The role of adults in acting for children

Freeman (1987) points out there is sometimes a need for an adult to act on the child's behalf, particularly if the child is very young or lacks enough understanding to make appropriate decisions. The right for children to be able to express their views is found in Article 12(1) of the UNCRC, which states that the child capable of forming his or her own views has the right to express those views freely in all matters affecting them, adding the following: 'the views of the child being given full weight in accordance with the age and maturity of the child' (Powell 2001: 18). However, as Powell (2001: 8) points out: 'it does not always follow that the court is obliged to give effect to the child's preference'. The leading English case on children's views and wishes and feelings was decided in the case of Gillick v West Norfolk and Wisbech Area Health Authority (1986) AC 112 (now commonly referred to as the Fraser guidelines). The House of Lords recognized that a child under the age of 16 years could give valid consent to medical treatment without parental consent or knowledge provided that he or she (in that case she) was of sufficient age and understanding. This decision went against the wishes of the child's mother, who argued that a consultation between a child and a general practitioner (GP) should be shared with the child's parents.

So while a child apparently has a right relating to participation and decision-making, this is dependent upon the child's ability to understand the situation and to make an informed decision about it, which is something determined either by the court or by an officer of the court such as a probation officer, social worker, or Children's Guardian. Powell (2001: 19) points out that Lord Scarman in the Gillick case was specifically considering the issues relating to the confidential nature of the relationship between the patient and doctor in regard to the provision of contraception in this case for a child and whether it is in the child's best interest always to inform parents. Later, in his judgment he stated that 'until the child achieves the capacity to consent, the parental rights to make a decision continues save only in exceptional circumstances'. It is of course what constitutes an exceptional circumstance that can be disputed. But Lord Scarman identified: 'emergency, parental neglect, abandonment of the child, or inability to find the parents as examples of exceptional situations justifying the doctor proceeding to treat the child without parental knowledge and consent' (Powell 2001: 19). A child's right to be consulted about decisions that will affect them chiefly comes into play in exceptional circumstances. Parents usually maintain daily responsibilities towards their child's health and safety for most of the time.

Returning to the UN Convention on the Rights of the Child, it is important to consider some of the other rights that children have that should perhaps be considered alongside those rights that have already been discussed that referred to protection and prevention, and participation in decision-making. Powell (2001) argues that there are two stages of children's rights:

> In the first stage the child has a right to life, health, education, and to reasonable economic expectations. In the second stage, the child's rights extend to the facility and opportunity to thrive rather than simply to survive, to have a happy childhood and social rights equivalent to those enjoyed by adults. In the transition between the two stages the child's welfare moves from being an equal consideration, alongside other factors, to being a paramount consideration for courts and practitioners.
>
> (Powell 2001: vii)

Powell (2001) outlines here a useful legal model that begins with the child's basic rights to life and then acknowledges the importance of recognizing that children have the rights to thrive, and to experience a happy childhood.

The early years professional: reflection and reflexivity

Often before a situation can be identified as one which raises concerns for safeguarding and child protection, perhaps where early years professionals may have concerns for a baby or young child in relation to child-rearing practices, a number of initiatives that come under the safeguarding scheme can be implemented. One example is Sure Start children's centres, where there are a number of groups a parent or carer can attend with their baby or young child that may support parents and carers and give the opportunity to talk through any particular anxieties in their relationship with their children. The opportunity to join in groups can alleviate anxiety and confirm positive parenting practices which should give confidence to parents and carers to engage positively with their babies and young children. In the community, early childhood practitioners may identify families that need the support of colleagues such as family resource workers or outreach workers to support the parent or carer in developing their relationship with their baby or young child and with other families in the community.

However, it is clear that any such initiative is much more likely to succeed where the parent or carer agrees and is willing to participate in discussions about any concerns and that these concerns are listened to carefully by the early years professional dealing with them at the time. Often childhoods will fluctuate between appearing to be happy or not, and it is only really when a child appears to be in need, vulnerable or actually being abused, that it may be appropriate for a practitioner to be interventionist. Having said that, there will be moments when a child's performance or behaviour appears less positive to the extent that it is noticed by members of the staff group in the nursery, Sure Start children's centre or school. These moments may be linked to family circumstances, and in these types of situations practitioner contact should come about through the professional institution often directly communicating with the parent or carer.

The need for reflection

However, in virtually all situations it is advisable that all practitioners from whichever discipline they belong to reflect upon the situation that presents itself to them; it is important that they avoid a reactive response but communicate with sensitivity and empathy. A sensitive and reflective approach may be much more helpful in establishing a more 'inclusive' working relationship between the early years professional and the parent or carer is likely to help the relationship with the child to develop more emphatically, with greater possibility of cooperation.

> Working reflectively with the whole self entails harnessing artistic talents alongside other talents. If practice itself is an art, then reflection upon it is also an artistic process.
>
> (Bolton 2005)

An approach to reflective practice suggested by Bolton (2005) highlights the early years professional actively engaged in a process of thoughtful communication, both with themselves through a kind of internal voice and with colleagues and of course with the parents and carers. Communication is one of the key concerns highlighted in cases where there have been failures in safeguarding children (Reder et al. 1993). Reder et al. (1993) explain how different inquiry reports into the deaths of children have consistently raised concerns about communication; the difficulty, and lack of coordination between different professional services, the lack of shared assessment information, the inability of some services to share their information with practitioners from other disciplines, and inaccuracies in recording telephone messages. It is therefore extremely important for practitioners to develop and enhance their communication skills. There are moments within a safeguarding situation where the application of sensitive and articulate forms of communication are more likely to be successful and appreciated by another person. For example, it may well be that a child wishes to talk about something that is very difficult and even distressing. When communicating in this context, the practitioner needs to be empathetic, unshockable and always supportive.

Skills required by early years professionals in safeguarding and child protection

When discussing a safeguarding situation arising from a child's disclosure with a colleague, skills such as accurate recall are necessary in articulating the nature of the interaction and the content of the exchange. There will be other moments along the way when communication skills need to be adjusted and modified, dependent upon the context. Talking to parents about the concerns that the practitioner may have about a child can often be extremely upsetting to the parents and their reaction might be emotional, and even aggressive and hostile. Professional practice ought to incorporate moments of reflection in advance of the situation being experienced so that it can be better anticipated, and therefore responded to more appropriately.

Reflection is therefore a key communication and thinking skill, which can lead to a clearer understanding, a more engaged involvement with a variety of the other people and an ability to remain in control throughout the proceedings.

So far this chapter has considered reflection as a key element of communication. Reflexivity will now be discussed due to its connection to engaging with children's rights, while recognizing that children may not always be included or invited to participate as fully as they might within decisions that can affect them so much. It follows therefore that one of the essential reflections that any practitioner should have, if they are to work in the child's best interests, is to consider whether they are adequately reflecting on the rights of the child and whether these rights are being properly and appropriately respected by all the stakeholders who share safeguarding concerns.

The need to be reflexive

It is important to attempt to define what being reflexive might be and why it is important for early years practitioners to become not simply reflective but also reflexive in their practice.

Reflexivity is concerned with each of us individually concentrating attention upon ourselves in action. This should include 'thoughts, feelings, values, identity and their effect upon others, situations and professional and social structures' (Bolton 2005: 10). She goes on to point out that:

> the reflexive thinker has to stand back from belief and value systems, habitual ways of thinking and relating to others, structures of understanding themselves and their relationship to the world, and their assumptions about the way that the world impinges upon them.
>
> (Bolton 2005: 10)

Giddens (1991: 78) points to reflexivity as self-actualization, which he then goes on to explain as a balance between opportunity and risk.

As far as a reflexive approach is concerned, there is a continuous struggle to understand complex aspects of oneself and how they interact with the context and the other actors present in which practitioners find themselves involved. Reflexive practitioners attempt to understand why they, as practitioners, behave as they do, particularly when they have a strong view or no view at all about a situation concerning safeguarding a baby or young child; and the impact their positioning within an interaction may have on the child, his or her parents and carers, themselves as a practitioner, and other colleagues.

We are all a product of life experiences that have left us with individual bias and prejudice, and it is important that we acknowledge our usually felt but unspoken values, attitudes and beliefs, but which, despite not being said, will still be influencing the communication in an interaction. Our own sense of who we are, and the position we feel we occupy within social structures helps construct our identities but which can adversely affect, despite our best endeavours, our abilities to understand or even listen to the concerns of parents, carers, children and other practitioners from external institutional or disciplinary settings. To be effective as a practitioner in a safeguarding context requires both reflection and reflexivity as core practices and without them practitioners may become immune to the power differentials operating between different groups, which may lead to children's rights not being fully acknowledged.

Further children's rights for consideration

While this chapter has, appropriately, considered the rights of children that directly affect babies and young children in relation to safeguarding and child protection, there are other considerations relating to children's rights. Article 8 of the UN Convention on the Rights of the Child concerns the child's right to preserve their self-identity without interference. In relation to this specific article it is important for early years professionals to acknowledge the social divisions which construct a baby or young child. From a very early age children express their own sense of identity and expectations are also applied to them by parents, carers and other significant people in their lives. As Payne (2000) argues:

> We automatically perceive other human beings as being male or female, black or white, older or younger, richer or poorer, sick or well, or friend or

foe. In forming a perception of them, we placed in pigeonholes, adapting our behaviour and attitudes of them in terms of the slots into which we have placed them.

(Payne 2000: 1)

This set of perceptions that Payne (2000) refers to is noticed and interacted with a range of different individuals, including early years professionals. Within the social relationships lies the potential for discrimination, oppression and misrepresentation. Practitioners' own social identities and values may impact on the families and carers with whom they are working. Equally there can be differences, expressed as discrimination, operating between different practitioners, some of whom may think that they are rather more important than others and thereby create a barrier to effective inter-professional communications, which can lead to risk situations developing or even tragedy.

Key messages

The chapter has emphasized the key importance of children's rights, as the central principle guiding professional practice in the area of safeguarding.

- Children's rights can be maintained only if you are a vigilant practitioner who is prepared to continuously preface children's rights within any discussion on safeguarding.
- As a high priority you should recognize the importance of babies and young children being consulted, included and (where feasible) supported to participate in communicating about their thoughts and feelings.
- Children clearly have the right to a happy and contented childhood, free from abuse or ill-treatment.
- You should be aware of communication as an essential skill, and it is important that you maintain a more inclusive participatory relationship with babies and young children, parents and carers and other practitioners.
- You need to be clear about the ways in which you might behave in a discriminatory and even oppressive manner if you are not prepared to be reflective or reflexive in your practice.
- Babies and young children have identities, which you should acknowledge and respect.
- You should reflect on the diverse ways in which you interact with different aspects of social divisions.

3   The baby and young child as the focus for safeguarding

Chapter Overview

This chapter considers the importance of maintaining the baby and young child as the central focus of concern, particularly in relation to child protection. The chapter discusses recent history and cites examples where this focus became unstable or blurred and how this led to difficulties for children in need. The chapter describes the legal requirements expected from practitioners in situations where concerns are being felt for children who may be being abused. The chapter also discusses the responsibilities arising from safeguarding and the expectation it places on early years professionals. The chapter presents the concept of a 'safer culture' as a feasible working objective for practitioners.

Following the death of Baby Peter Connelly, Lord Laming (2009) reminded us that:

> Children are our future. We depend on them growing up to become fulfilled citizens well able to contribute successfully to family life and to the wider society. It is of fundamental importance that the life and future development of each child is given equal importance. Every child needs to be nurtured and protected from harm.
>
> (Laming 2009: 9)

Laming then discussed the needs of children and particularly focused on child protection issues in his progress report of 2009. While messages urging vigilance are clearly focal in safeguarding, it is also important for a balance to be maintained in the course of practitioner intervention and to appreciate the child as a holistic being reflected in *Every Child Matters* (DfES 2004a) through the five outcomes as the central element of the safeguarding agenda.

The Every Child Matters agenda is an attempt through the provision of a coherent framework to articulate a number of goals, as a set of standards that constitute 'well-being' for children and families. The five outcomes therefore offer a method for identifying a strong focus for safeguarding a child linked to professional concern.

The policy and legislative framework for safeguarding children is part of a continuing attempt by successive governments to facilitate more effective child protection, which has ultimately led to the current child and family support systems in place today. This system is more universal in terms of its goals which are to improve the lives of all children not just those likely to suffer from some form of ill-treatment (see Parton 2006). This suggests in effect a more integrated focus not only on prevention but also on early recognition of ill-treatment so that intervention can be triggered quickly and appropriately as a means of heading off problems before they become entrenched. With such a strong set of systems in place, it may be argued that they are acting as an early warning system for any kind of concern related to child rearing in parenting where it strays from orthodox or recognized methods. This in turn could lead to some relatively superficial concerns being over-interpreted as some form of ill-treatment raising the concerns of practitioners. Such a strong focus of concern directed towards communities and families and their treatment of babies and young children has led Furedi (2009) to argue that policies such as Every Child Matters have led to parents becoming far more paranoid about their parenting skills. At the same time this undermines children's ability to be resilient. In discussing risk Furedi points out that:

> It is easy to overlook the fact that the concept of children at risk is a relatively recent invention. This way of imagining childhood involves a redefinition both of the risk and of childhood. Until recently, risks were not interpreted by definition as bad things. We used to talk about good, worthwhile risks as well as bad, foolish ones. Risks were seen as a challenging aspect of children's lives. Today, we are so afraid of risk that we have invented the concept of children at risk. A child that is at risk requires constant vigilance and adult supervision.
>
> (Furedi 2009: 41)

Furedi's warning reinforces the message that practitioners apparently acting in the best interests of young children can in effect be working towards a counter-productive set of outcomes in families. This may leave a feeling of unease for practitioners involved in safeguarding babies and young children, particularly those children who are considered as being 'at risk': according to Furedi (2009) the very act of identifying a child as being at risk by a practitioner may heighten parents' and/or carers' feelings as 'poor parents'. This can become disempowering for parents' carers and children by assuming a hierarchy in which practitioners are assumed to know best. This in turn may lead to the development of a relationship built on the dependence of parents and carers on practitioners as 'those knowing how to make things safe'. On the other hand parents and carers might stay away from contact altogether from children's centres or nurseries to avoid their parenting being scrutinized. The alternative scenario is also a concern where practitioners may underestimate the perceived risks to a child, leading to them not responding rapidly and appropriately as safeguarding requires. It seems clear when it comes to safeguarding children, the field is potentially fraught with difficulties and also opportunities.

The safeguarding agenda therefore represents a difficult challenge for any practitioner working with families with babies and young children. There is a need to develop a discussion about the appropriate context and time when it seems right and proper to intervene and other occasions when it may not. As *Every Child Matters* (DfES 2004a) points out:

> From past inquiries into the deaths of Maria Colwell and Jasmine Beckford to recent cases such as Lauren Wright and Ainlee Walker, there are striking similarities which show some of the problems are of long standing. The common threads which led in each case to a failure to intervene early enough were poor coordination; a failure to share information; the absence of anyone with a strong sense of accountability; and frontline workers trying to cope with staff vacancies, poor management and a lack of effective training. The most tragic manifestation of these problems is when we fail to protect children at risk of harm or neglect. But the problem of children falling through the cracks between different services goes much further. Too often children experience difficulties at home or at school, but receive too little help too late, once problems have reached crisis point.
>
> (DfES 2004a: 5)

Early intervention, improved communication and coordination may all be helpful in supporting young children but one of the real challenges is to sustain an ongoing partnership with the parents and carers through the time of intervening to support babies and young children in what may be a real crisis in the family.

Practice reflection points

Developing a focus to safeguard children

List the opportunities and difficulties of developing a focus to safeguard children:

- Relating to children

- Relating to parents and carers

- Relating to other practitioners

The practice reflection exercise should illustrate the point that while there clearly are many difficulties in trying to develop a focus to ensure that children will be safe, there should also be an emerging set of values that emphasize the opportunities for change in any situation where concern may be felt for a child's well-being. This introduces the concept of 'safer cultures', an active assessment and relationship building tool which attempts to develop an understanding that can shed light on the influences that may impact on children, resulting in them suffering from ill-treatment. Safer cultures as an assessment method also identifies moments when families appear to be responsive and caring even if this goes against the perceived norm and that can offer the basis for future practice.

Professional expectations: worst case scenario

All practitioners in the caring services share a joint anxiety; indeed they have access to a nightmare that unites them, that a child who they have a responsibility for will end up either seriously injured, or even worse killed. It is important to reflect on how this sense of anxiety impacts on each practitioner's daily practice. Is it for instance making practitioners overly cautious and nervous about their dealings with dangerous families where children have already been identified as at risk of being ill-treated? There seems to be some anecdotal evidence that social workers, health practitioners, educators and indeed all practitioners involved in the caring services are becoming more careful about being seen to be taking appropriate and well-recorded steps to keep children safe. While this is clearly a laudable aim, which should result in some reduction in serious injuries to children, there are repercussions in the way that children are likely to be viewed as vulnerable and constantly at risk of something untoward happening to them. Will this result in anxiety around children being developed and grow to such an extent that they cannot be let out of the sight of their parents for fear of coming to grief? Will adults with any kind of interest in children be immediately suspected as potentially likely to abuse? Will this further mean that children may grow up with a sense of nervousness about relationships with others, both for themselves and for their own children when they have them? Is there a danger that we are expecting far too much from practitioners, who, after all, do not live in the same houses, or usually even in the same communities as the children over whom they are watching. This is reflected in media coverage, resulting in a likelihood that practitioners will become more guarded and careful in terms of leaving a paper trail, to ensure, that if the very worst happens and a child that they are responsible for in some way comes to harm, they will feel that there was nothing further they could do. More importantly, perhaps, they will be vindicated by those who come to judge them. Munro (2011) suggests that there has been an over-emphasis on the processes of child protection to the detriment of the focus on the child's journey or needs. In other words, the practice of those working within the field of early years has been directed towards a more bureaucratic system of recording rather than directing their gaze towards the specific needs of children and their families. The need for clearer and more detailed assessment and recording processes was set out in the Laming (2003) report. While this could be easily appreciated given the remit of the inquiry, they have tended to produce additional burdens on practitioners, which has undoubtedly impacted on the amount of time available for direct work with children and families.

Everyday practices

There is now something fundamental and vital that needs to be remembered and fully practised and which underpins the impact that procedures and guidelines and legal statute can have and that is to do with everyday practices. Some of these important basic ideas of practice will now be re-emphasized, which even for the most experienced practitioner are essential to continue to take into consideration.

Keeping focused

All practitioners should maintain a strong and clear focus on the baby or young child that they are concerned with. Indeed it has been argued that since the Laming (2003) report was implemented, there has been a slippage from the focus arising from direct work to the development of a greater emphasis upon process, recording and an increased bureaucratization of all services involved in safeguarding. However while all policy is important in emphasizing the need to protect, it is ultimately reliant on the practitioner to make sense of it and apply it. This however is complicated because early years professionals approaching their work through the professional codes and discourses that relate to their particular discipline are expected to work closely together, which can lead to roles overlapping, so that retaining a clear sense of professional identity and the boundary that surrounds it can be difficult. This requires them to have a good working knowledge of the roles that different professionals in the early years play and at the same time have a working understanding of each professional narrative relating to the child that each practitioner is responsible for.

The professional task also requires the development of partnerships with carers so that a meaningful relationship can result to the benefit of the baby or young child. Practitioner and carer relations can result in the attention which was intended for the child slipping to ensure that a useful and effective relationship and communications system is in operation. Multiprofessional, inter-agency communication is central to modern safeguarding and may result in procedures such as assessment of risk becoming a continual cyclical practice possibly resulting in inaction at times when action is necessary. In the official advisory booklet *What To Do If You're Worried a Child is Being Abused* (DfES 2006b), a number of processes are highlighted which are aimed at anyone including the general public who may come 'into contact with children and families in their everyday work... have a duty to safeguard and promote the welfare of children' (DfES 2006b: 3). What then follows is an explanation of what may happen next and what this might mean to the person if they contact and refer their concerns to the social services. There is little helpful advice in what may be done in practical terms if someone is to attempt to meet the immediate needs of the child by directly communicating with the carer if the situation seems to warrant it. Consider the practice reflection questions, which have been posed to a range of practitioners and students in early childhood studies and primary education.

Practice reflection point

Should you intervene?

Imagine that you are waiting in the checkout queue in a supermarket. In front of you are two fraught carers who you assume to be the parents of a toddling child and a baby, who is being held by the female carer. Suddenly the male seems to snap and begins to shout loudly at the toddler. His language is threatening and aggressive but instead of crying the toddler smiles, perhaps because of nerves. This enrages the adult, who takes hold of the child and begins to beat him quite harshly.

- What would you do?

- Is this a safeguarding or a protection concern at this stage?

- Is intervention a feasible option? Justify your thinking for either choice, if you think intervention is or isn't an option.

Reflecting on the practice reflection task

The responses that are given to the task can be varied but tend to reflect the difficulty of maintaining a composed view of what to do that will support the child most effectively. The problem suggests that an intervention might have a number of foreseeable outcomes such as the following:

- The parent might react by attacking you either verbally and/or physically. This at least might deflect attention from hitting the child, which ultimately could lead to official intervention by the police.
- The parent might ignore whatever you said.
- The parent might respond to your request, depending on the way that you communicated to them. Perhaps the most helpful way might include a sensitive even deflective strategy to gain the attention of the carer, while not placing the child or yourself at further risk from a backlash. This could include inquiries such as 'Can I help?' or 'They can be so difficult at that age, can't they'. This approach attempts to befriend but as a strategy would need to be reconsidered quite quickly if it had little effect on the parent–child interaction. If this initial attempt at deflection failed, you might say 'This has got to stop now or I will phone the police'. Try to ensure that you are not in striking distance when you say this but also appear serious in your intent.

Of course the term 'beat...quite harshly' is deliberately included in this brief scenario to conjure an image suggesting an event that is beyond what is reasonable to expect in public as it suggests a rather excessive reaction. The term 'beating' can be linked to a collection of extremely descriptive language including 'thrashing, whipping, thumping and pounding', which are all very easy to imagine psychologically but unlikely to be encountered in public in 'civilized society'. A key message from this example is that it is difficult to take action on behalf of a child without alienating the parent or carer, but nonetheless this might occasionally be the only action that can be taken to bring about a rapid change, albeit potentially short lived in a situation such as above. Finally if all situations are potentially learning opportunities – everyone involved should learn from it. The first lesson is that it is unacceptable to hurt children. The second lesson might be that it shouldn't happen in public places without members of the public potentially getting involved. This might lead to the conclusion that you shouldn't allow yourself to be seen doing anything to harm a child in the public domain, which is possibly why the majority of child abuse takes place in the privacy of the home (see Chapter 1).

Key reasons to intervene

- The child in the scenario is not being respected in terms of his or her rights.
- The child may end up seriously hurt if this treatment continues and is therefore at risk.
- You have a moral and legal responsibility as a member of the public to protect the vulnerable members of society such as children from harm. The child and the parents are members of your community and as such should expect your support – even if they do not actively seek it (see Section 58 of the Children Act 2004, which draws attention to the defence of reasonable chastisement).

Some of the issues

Over a long period practitioners and scholars concerned with safeguarding babies and young children have developed tools to inform understanding and so make the process of safeguarding more likely to be effective. This can be an area that presents most people with a high degree of complexity and difficulty, particularly if they are not used to safeguarding procedures. In addition they may feel uncertain how to respond to parents and carers, who can often be emotional, angry and even aggressive if they feel that an accusation is being made against them. Practitioners may also experience stress that can be associated with confronting a parent or carer over what may appear to be a suspicious injury since identification of abuse can be unclear and mistakes can be made. When this happens, the relationship between the practitioner and the parent or carer can be jeopardized, and it may take some time for trust to be re-established. In those situations where physical abuse is suspected because a mark has been left on the child's body, it is usual for a paediatrician or other medical practitioner to examine the baby or young child, so that a medical diagnosis can be made. It is then an assessment issue for early years professionals and in particular social workers to try to understand what may have happened to have caused the injury to the child.

However, this area is still potentially likely to be difficult to understand, because young children may develop injuries in unusual parts of their bodies that defy recognition even by experienced practitioners. It is even more problematic for paediatricians to diagnose with certainty cases of sexual abuse, where there has not been sexual penetration or other clear signs of inappropriate sexual activity (see Butler-Sloss 1988).

Can child abuse be recognized easily?

Child abuse is an area that contains several key issues relating to the identification and diagnosis of concerns and the process of clear communication between different practitioners within the culture of current practices of referral, as the previous discussion suggests.

For example in the case of Victoria Climbié (Laming 2003), when she was referred to the Central Middlesex Hospital the internal procedures deferred to the principle that Victoria would be examined by an appropriate practitioner with the specialist medical knowledge to do so. However, initially, she was seen by 'a senior house officer in the accident and emergency department' (Laming 2003: section 9.8, 239).

> a history [was taken] from Ms Cameron [the child minder] which, together with the results of a basic examination of Victoria, concerned him enough to refer the matter to a paediatric registrar. In his view there was a 'strong possibility' that this was a case of non-accidental injury.
>
> (Laming 2003: section 3.35, 29)

The internal hospital policy was now followed to the letter, with the paediatric registrar making a further and more detailed examination of Victoria and confirming the strong suspicion that this was a case of non-accidental injury. A further referral was then made to the 'on call consultant for child abuse' but when another medical examination took place, the revised diagnosis was that scabies was the major cause of the scratches and marks to Victoria's body.

The medical opinion in the Central Middlesex Hospital concerning Victoria Climbié takes a dramatic turn away from a child abuse or even child protection agenda, because of the final examination by a senior doctor. As Laming (2003) points out, there is clearly a difference of opinion between three medical practitioners within the same medical establishment but a discussion to share perceptions failed to materialize. This is reported by Laming (2003) as a difficulty caused by shifts and other working practices that are usual within the environment of a busy hospital. However Laming was very concerned that the opportunity to explore and either endorse or rule out the various observations that have been made by other practitioners was overlooked.

A further and important point to make is that even after the scabies diagnosis was made, a referral was not then made to the dermatological department because of lack of appropriate referral information. This in turn had the impact of changing the nature of communications between the hospital and the social services department by describing Victoria as a child in need because of housing issues, since she and her great-aunt were homeless at that time. There was an accumulation of information strongly suggesting child abuse, collated by two medical practitioners, but the third and more senior medical practitioner appears to overrule these earlier perceptions with an alternative perspective that carries the most weight. It is clear then that status and the attendant power that resides within an internal practitioner hierarchy are influential in this case.

Victoria Climbié was just 8 years old in February 2000 when she was killed. Her situation reflected the many missed opportunities for intervention and support which indicates the inability sometimes for practitioners and the institutions from which they work to fulfil their duty of care to vulnerable children within the community. This duty must take into account the importance of the perceptions of all practitioners and the clearest possible systems of communication to aid any professional intervention. The Victoria Climbié case emphasizes the ways that some key practitioners did not work together for most of the time and that therefore a tragedy resulted. However, in the majority of safeguarding cases the practitioners involved are experienced, well trained and usually influential in having a huge say in what ultimately happens, but also they are often extremely overworked, and may be lacking in resources. The chief commodity necessary to provide appropriate caring services, in addition to training and education, is that of time. It seems that in contemporary contexts, many agencies are likely to be dealing with more referrals but with fewer staffing resources to adequately cope with them.

It is perhaps a useful exercise to reflect on how each one of us are placed for dealing with safeguarding concerns by completing the practice reflection task.

Practice reflection point

What would I do and how would I respond?

As an early years professional there will be several occasions throughout your career when safeguarding is a concern to you. Attempt to answer the questions as a starting point for your practice; this will help you to address any areas that need further development later.

- What would you do if you had an initial concern about a child?

- Who could you consult with in your organization?

- What guidance is available to you?

- What sources of support are available to you if you suspect abuse?

- What could you do if you felt your concerns were not being taken seriously?

Safer cultures

The discussion so far has raised questions regarding how practitioners develop a context in which parents and carers may feel more supported and less on trial or under surveillance for their childcare, at the same time maintaining a clear focus on the well-being of the baby and young child. The examples mentioned earlier referring to the experiences of Victoria Climbié and Peter Connelly show how important it is to remain vigilant with the child at the centre of practitioner considerations.

When concerns are raised by practitioners about a child, they usually arise from the perception of parent–child relationships becoming negative, which becomes apparent in the interactions and attitudes that may be expressed publicly and directly. There are also times when you might observe negative parental or carer reactions to a child's conduct, such as at the nursery reception area or school at either the start of the day or when parents collect their children at home time. There may be other circumstances where you may believe that a child is unhappy because something is going on at home, perhaps because of something the child has said or because of their mood or general demeanour. For such circumstances we suggest that the concept of 'safer cultures' can be used as a framework to help to address any negativity by emphasizing the real contributions that are made by parents and carers through positive expressions of care they make to their child. Most parents can expect to go through difficult times with their child, but these difficult moments are usually balanced by times when they feel more positive. Of course it is important to monitor the situation to see if there is any real improvements in the relationship and whether it is sustainable for a reasonable time. Safer cultures recognize that a practitioner needs to have a view about what she or he might do that could lead to improvements taking place in the parent–carer–child relationship and this picture will emerge from information about the relationship and what is likely to impact on it.

The concept of safer cultures links to the systems model expressed by Bronfenbrenner (1979), which highlights an ecological approach in which individuals are affected by interactions between a variety of different overlapping ecosystems (see Figure 3.1). This can be utilized by you as an early years professional to develop a deeper assessment of the needs of a baby or young child to determine the positive and negative factors possibly impacting on their well-being. In relation to safer cultures its application should consider the relationship that the different systems have on the life of the child and how the parent or carer can be supported in developing enabling strategies that will overcome areas of difficulty that otherwise can lead to a more negative relationship being experienced.

The focus for practice starts at the centre of Figure 3.1, with the individual factors that impact on the child: in fact the child is at the heart of all the systems, including their genetic make-up, disposition and the way this manifests in social contexts. At a personal level the individual is recognized as belonging within a microsystem which includes the immediate and [some members of] the child's extended family, as well as carers and friends. In addition to this group those early

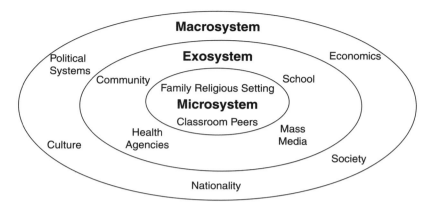

Figure 3.1 Bronfenbrenner's ecological model based on Bronfenbrenner, U. (1979). *The Ecology of Human Development.* Cambridge, MA: Harvard University Press.

years professionals who have direct contact with the child on a regular basis such as children's centre workers, crèche workers and teachers from early years settings. It could also include religious and cultural groups who may have regular contact with the child. The model then moves through meso, exo and macro levels to reflect the community and environmental influences on a child's well-being. We have translated Bronfenbrenner's model into Figure 3.2.

- *Individual child:* the centre is the child, where at an individual level there may be factors such as inherited genetic conditions, illnesses or premature birth that could impact on the child's needs and well-being. These in turn could impact on the ability of the parents to give adequate care.
- *Local:* this next level is made up of the child's immediate carers and those people he or she relies on to maintain their well-being. This could be parents, siblings, extended family or other carers; it could also include the local community if significant, such as through community religious involvement. It could also include sources of comfort for the child such as pets.
- *Professional:* this is where services may be involved, such as those universal services all children may access, e.g. health visitor, GP, midwife and early years and educational provision. It can also include more targeted and specialist services according to need.
- *Sociocultural, political and environmental:* this outer circle refers to wider factors that can impact on a child's well-being such as the political climate's influence on service provision, geography or location which can influence what is available in the community. There may be specific health risks depending on where the child lives; there may also be other sociocultural factors relating to the child's social and cultural identity and the child's position in relation to ethnicity, religion or poverty and deprivation and disability.

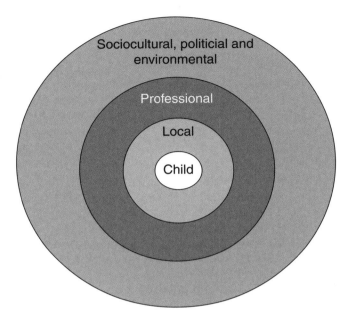

Figure 3.2 Ecological safeguarding model (Powell and Uppal) based on Bronfenbrenner, U. (1979). *The Ecology of Human Development.* Cambridge, MA: Harvard University Press.

A systems approach

Healy (2005: 136) argues that a systems theory approach (second wave) places an emphasis on transactions (Wakefield 1996a, 1996b; Kemp et al. 1997; Payne 1997) as part of an ecosystem. 'The ecosystems perspective encourages [social workers] to recognize that problems arise because of a poor fit between the person's environment and his or her needs, capacities, rights and aspirations' (Germain and Glitterman 1996: 8).

The systems approach recognizes the potential of sharing expertise through the personal knowledge of the parent(s) with the practitioner's professional knowledge. They are both viewed as potentially working together towards an improvement in the 'fit' that the parent or carer has with other aspects of the system that might support the outcome for the child. For example this could mean that a problem of not having a break from childcare might lead to more stressful behaviour and potential loss of control unless grandparents or friends, identified in their own rights as being part of the family system, may be able to give support and thereby alleviate the parental pressure. Domestic arrangements such as getting the grandparents involved might be something that the parents could arrange themselves, the intervention of a practitioner might be helpful if there are already difficulties in that relationship to broker a new set of arrangements. The aim of the systems approach is to develop a clear set of objectives to be worked towards and preferably achieved. This means that regular discussions during which detailed information sharing about progress relating to each objective can take place.

Practice that is aimed at pragmatic and positive outcomes as suggested above help the development of an ongoing safer culture which has identified and then settled around a set of principles that convey practitioner and parental or carer values so that they can be applied as a working agenda that may support any caring moments that parents share with their child. This means always placing the child at the centre of a set of attitudes that attempt to demonstrate that *the child is the valued focus of both practitioner and parent interactions*, which always needs to link to the aims of safeguarding. To reiterate what was said earlier, safeguarding is determined as:

> The process of protecting children from abuse and neglect, preventing impairment of their health and development, and ensuring they grow up in circumstances consistent with the provision of safe and effective care that enables children to have optimum life chances and enter adulthood successfully.
>
> (DCSF 2010: 27)

This idea of protection and prevention of impairment can be related to developing safer cultures. This may then be included as a professional technique in ensuring that a positive focus remains on the baby or young child. Safer cultures has a tenuous link to safer recruitment, which was a proposal arising from the Bichard inquiry (2004) into the deaths of Jessica Chapman and Holly Wells, the Soham schoolgirls who were murdered by the school caretaker Ian Huntley. Safer recruitment has resulted in the development of a regulatory framework to screen potential abusers out of the system. Safer cultures, however, as discussed in this chapter is concerned with identifying and wherever possible producing a values ethos that actively views and reviews babies and young children as part of a shared community where they are seen to be highly significant and valued and where the environment and interactions taking place within it are critically determined in the way that the above values are evident.

You are likely to be doing something along these lines already but what we propose is that this should be followed through a more formalized procedure, particularly where concern is felt to be present. It is important for practitioners to guard against stereotyping and operating in hierarchically powerful ways that relegate parents' and carers' views and therefore run the risk of not acknowledging the significance and closeness of their relationships with their children. As Furedi (2009) suggests, this can potentially create 'paranoid parenting' as a result.

Principles for a safer cultures approach

The following are a set of principles to guide you in understanding what a safer cultures approach may be likely to include:

- A proactive ethos regarding safer cultures should be at the forefront of practitioner considerations.
- This ethos should facilitate the promotion of a positive community ethos that has the best interests and the well-being of the baby and young child at the forefront of any considerations.
- There should be a sharing of understanding of any issues relating to safer cultures with carers and/or colleagues.
- A common position regarding establishing ground rules for a safer culture needs to be developed within any context felt to be problematic for the baby or young child.
- Procedures need not be implemented directly unless the situation is concerning enough to do so. However, partnership and cooperation should be agreed that is linked to an agreed set of values articulated possibly in an action plan and reviewed as an ongoing conversation.
- The processes and procedures that are relevant to safeguarding should be visible and clear and understood by all parties involved as being there and available if and when required.
- Recommended agreed areas of work should be negotiated with all parties involved particularly including the carers and child or children and practitioners from different disciplines.

Promoting safer cultures

The development of sets of principles concerning developing a safer culture should help you to be clearer about what matters for the baby or young child to be able to thrive, when you consider the caring practices on display in the contexts that a child can experience. This could include any of the following:

- The baby or young child's home context – is it a suitable and rich environment where the child is able to develop and grow? Is there a suitable place in the home where the child can play? Are there suitable materials and toys available? Do parents and carers have a positive attitude to children's play or not?
- The baby or young child with close carers – does the relationship appear to be a caring and loving one? Clarify what the strengths and weaknesses of the relationship appear to be. How exactly do the parents and carers relate to their babies or young children? What appear to be the moments when they are able to relate easily and positively and when are such moments

noticeable by their absence? Try to be as detailed as you can when applying this to a real-life case.

- Importantly comment in a consistent manner on any positive behaviour with approval and encouragement. The attitude of the early years professional is highly significant in establishing, through such moments of encouragement and approval, a shared sense of values around what might be considered to be positive and help to shape parenting skills without the practitioner having to articulate this specifically.

- Consider the baby or young child within their local community and what resources are available in the locality to facilitate the child's well-being and support parents and carers to promote the well-being of the child. It is important for any assessment focusing on safer cultures to take into account the importance of significant people within the local community and their potential influence on the well-being of the child and the parent–child interaction. These include a range of people such as neighbours, friends, and voluntary, religious or cultural groups.

- You should also review on a fairly regular basis the agency context and practices performed by you as an individual as well as the work of immediate colleagues. Is the establishment a suitable and rich environment? Are children responded to with care and consideration? Is foundation level practice in evidence? Do parents and carers appear to be welcome and encouraged to participate? Do you examine and reflect on your own practice with parents, carers and other practitioners? We must not make assumptions that establishments, even if they are well equipped, are necessarily always accessible to parents and inclusive towards all children. Sometimes it may appear that children might be included within specific activities such as group play at the encouragement of the early years professional.

- You should always be alert to act in a creative and inclusive manner and wherever possible encourage parents to participate at the same time. It is sometimes surprising how effective this can be as a practice and how much our own childhoods and the incorporation of play within them is assumed to be the norm when this may not always be the shared experience of the parents and carers.

- Wider agency involvement – consider the ways that other practitioners operate. Is it clear to all practitioners what each one does? Are there formal and informal agreements relating to working practices between practitioners? This area is important in identifying values that underpin practices that are agreed across professional and disciplinary boundaries and those that are more disputed. As more practitioners get involved in supporting a family, it is reasonable to expect the focus to differ according to agency priorities. Any such shift should be noted by you if you are to sustain the child within the developing safer culture.

- The influence of society – are there wider social, cultural, political or environmental factors impacting on the care of the child? What is valued by society in terms of promoting safer cultures?

Central to the development of any working arrangement therefore, you need to have at the forefront of your mind as clear a view as possible of the ways that the environments where you are responsible for children reflects clear values that support the baby or young child's well-being and best interests. In the practice reflection point we invite you to consider what you believe to be important in developing and ensuring a 'safer culture' where babies and young children as beings with rights can flourish.

Practice reflection point

Establishing a safer cultures framework for practice

Consider what you believe should be present in the contexts below that would make you feel that the child was being appropriately valued and cared for. Apply this to a family you are currently working with or if you are a student, relate it to one of the main cases that have been referred to in Chapter 1.

- The baby or young child's home context

- The baby or young child with their close family and carers

- The baby or young child in their local community

- The local practitioners' contexts and practices

- Wider agency involvement

- The influence of society such as politics, media and so on

Key messages

- You need to recognize the importance of clear communication in cases concerning safeguarding and child protection.
- Any concerns that you have raised relating to a child and possible child abuse need to be treated as a priority and followed through, until you feel satisfied that each concern has been addressed properly.
- Full discussion should take place as a matter of priority, with as many practitioners as is deemed necessary, or who have already

become involved, where a child has been identified as causing concern in relation to safeguarding and child protection.

- You should keep records through clear note taking, which should relate to your observations of a child, where safeguarding concerns are being considered. In addition relevant statements made by parents, carers or children should be recorded verbatim to aid any assessment process later.
- When working alongside parents and carers, you should develop a safer culture that can be monitored and reviewed together with the parent or carer.
- You must draw conclusions objectively from the evidence before you, maintaining a clear focus on the needs of the child, rather than being distracted by the needs, demands or actions of the parents or carers.
- The opinions of others should not sway you if you still have a strong feeling that something isn't right. This may require challenging more senior staff both within and external to your organization.

4 Acting ethically: developing ethical practices in safeguarding contexts

Chapter Overview

This chapter considers the importance of developing and maintaining a series of ethical issues at the centre of professional practice to inform appropriate action on behalf of babies and young children. The chapter offers the opportunity for reflection in relation to power dynamics and argue that an anti-discriminatory ethical practice is essential in this area of work. Anti-discriminatory practice helps to develop the discussion surrounding reflexivity and the part that we play as social practitioners in influencing the outcomes of interventions.

Ethics and safeguarding: important aspects of practice

Ethics refers to the ways in which early years professionals engage with safeguarding practice, guidelines and wider policy and legal frameworks. This engagement is in response to the demands of a number of competing concerns and priorities present within the context of a safeguarding situation. As an early years professional you will already attempt to be ethical by weighing up the needs and rights of carers in relation to their babies and young children in their care and the expectations and functions of all agencies involved, while relating them to the expectations and requirements of social policy. This presents you with practical dilemmas about what to do for the best in a safeguarding situation each time you are involved in one.

It is necessary to consciously integrate an ethical approach into ways of thinking to help you to face the complexities relating to the well-being of a baby or young child. Ethical issues arise out of the identification, referral and investigation of child ill-treatment and the impact on personal values, attitudes and any training in this field that may be brought to bear in the safeguarding contexts.

It is important for you to make yourself aware of the codes of ethics that your agency relates to. For social work, the British Association of Social Workers (BASW 2011) code of ethics refers you to key principles of recognizing human dignity and worth, promoting social justice, supporting people in developing their potential, behaving with honesty and integrity while ensuring that you remain competent in fulfilling your role. Health visitors, teachers and early years professionals also reflect similar ethical standards for practice. For example, the code for nursing and midwifery professionals is the foundation for practice, acting as a tool to safeguard and protect the public from harm (Nursing and Midwifery Council (NMC) 2008). The *Code of Conduct and Practice for Registered Teacher* is available from the general Teaching Council (GTC 2009).

Clarifying the possible meanings of ethics in safeguarding contexts

Banks (2006: 4) suggests that there are three types of ethics distinguished by philosophers, as follows:

- *Metaethics* comprises critical and analytical thinking about the meaning and use of moral terms such as 'right', 'good' or 'duty', about whether moral judgements can be justified.
- *Normative ethics* attempts to give answers to moral questions and problems regarding, for example, what the morally right course of action in the particular case is, whether someone is a morally good person or whether lying is always wrong.
- *Descriptive ethics* studies what people's moral opinions and beliefs are and how they act in relation to these. For example, whether people in Britain believe abortion is always morally wrong.

The above definitions provide a framework for thinking about ethics which can be applied in real-life situations.

Ethical decision-making

Whenever concerns are raised about a child that lead to the need to implement safeguarding procedures, practitioners are met with a range of complex situations that may require painstaking decision-making, which should be transparent, and in the perceived best interests of the child. Often this is done without much time for detailed or in-depth reflection or supervisory discussion to help inform practice. However you need to ask the question about how decisions have been made and what has informed them as well as the nature of them.

As this statement suggests, there are a number of potential difficulties immediately likely to be encountered as you attempt to make sense of a safeguarding situation and responsibly interpret what the best interests of the child may be. The concern for an ethical approach to safeguarding immediately raises a question of whose perceptions count most when deciding what the best interests of the child are. There will usually be several professional and community contacts likely to be involved in the process of noticing and following up concerns. Each of them may identify a diverse set of factors that may offer ways of understanding the situation better. In the case of an unexplained injury, such as a bruise found on a baby or young child, concerns felt by the practitioners involved may depend on the site and size of the bruise and the explanation given by the parent or carer. In cases such as this, practitioners are likely to view the child as dependent for her or his daily care on the parents or carers and they will need to find out as much as possible through a process of assessment. This assessment process may reveal clues about the nature of the relationship between the baby or young child and their immediate carers. Often when there are no obvious concerns noted, practitioners may act proactively by introducing a more preventative strategy such as provided through the model of the Common Assessment Framework (CAF). The CAF offers a forum to carers and parents with practitioners so that they can share views and identify any common difficulty which through no fault of the parents or carers may result in a deterioration in the well-being of a baby or young child. The CAF is quite clear in the way that it has to operate and is dependent on the voluntary involvement of parents and carers as well as practitioners who may represent a wide range of disciplines.

It is clear that safeguarding as a practice faces several fundamental difficulties. First, any ill-treatment or abuse usually takes place in private and attempts to understand what may have happened to a child is dependent on the ability of practitioners to care for children and what happens to them. Second, the practitioner needs to be observant in order to identify when a child seems injured or behaving in a way that does not reflect their usual mood but one that seems relatively unhappy compared to the ways the child presents usually. The early years professional, following discussion with colleagues, may feel that a referral should be made to another agency such as a social worker being contacted by a school's designated child protection coordinator. The articulation of a suspicion may be fraught with difficulties as the practitioner strives to be as accurate and objective as possible.

Once a visit to the home takes place the desire to uncover the truth may be perceived as unwelcome and intrusive by parents and carers and cooperation may not be forthcoming. Rather than parents and carers joining with the outside agencies and forming a cooperative view of how to proceed, this is often not the case as both sides struggle to assert themselves.

Ethical issues and social work

Banks (2006) explores ethics and values and offers some useful discussion in relation to ethical issues in connection with social work. While this book is clearly not solely about social work, it is undoubtedly one of the key areas of practice likely to be involved with babies and young children in relation to safeguarding. In this respect, the points that Banks (2006) makes are extremely relevant when she asks: 'What are the ethical issues in social work?' This question could be applied slightly differently to ask what the ethical issues are for practitioners working with children in a number of different types of contexts representing health, social care and education, thus what are the ethical issues for their work?

Banks (2006) goes on to discuss four types of issues occurring representative of ethical problems and dilemmas:

- **Issues around individual rights and welfare:** a service user's right to make her own decisions and choices; the social worker's responsibility to promote the welfare of the service user.
- **Issues around public welfare:** the rights and interests of parties other than the service user; the social worker's responsibility to their employing agency and to society; the promotion of the greatest good for the greatest number of people.
- **Issues around the quality, difference and structural oppression:** balancing the promotion of equality, with due regard to diversity; the social worker's responsibility to challenge oppression and to work for changes in agency policy and in society.
- **Issues around professional roles, boundaries and relationships:** deciding what role the social worker should take in particular situations (counsellor, controller, advocate, assessor, campaigner, ally or friend); considerations of issues of boundaries between personal, professional and political life.

(Banks 2006: 13–14)

The above points raise a number of considerations that need to be at the forefront of thinking around any practices. First, concerning the rights and obligations of all the participants in safeguarding a child, what are they and where are they likely to conflict? Second, who in Banks' terms is the service user? Third, are you clear on whose behalf you are acting as the early years professional? Fourth, who should make decisions about the child and how clearly up front can you be as a practitioner with the parents and carers about the roles of different practitioners and will the way that information is imparted show that a hierarchy of power exists? Finally, where would you place parents and carers in relation to each other and the power they appear to have in safeguarding? It is likely that when hierarchical power is perceived, it will be responded to, not necessarily by parents bowing before it but by acting in other ways, such as attempting to manipulate or resist it. Neither is it likely that all practitioners will work comfortably together – apart from the positioning that they may make in relation to power, there might be other factors of a more personal nature present such as likes and dislikes, or whether the other practitioner is considered effective or conscientious.

The position of the practitioner to their sense of public welfare is also an influential argument for practitioners to cooperate with each other in a child's best interest. Banks (2006) is also reminding her audience that we as practitioners may have our own prejudices about different groups in society and therefore may represent if we are unthinking about it an establishment position that may reflect discriminatory attitudes of others. Discrimination may be hard to own up to, but as Thompson (2003) argues, discrimination and oppression are closely related concepts: 'a fundamental source of oppression is the set of processes by which certain social groups are discriminated against and thereby disadvantaged' (Thompson

2003: 11): this can be experienced economically, socially, politically, ethically, ideologically and psychologically. It is likely that when we are acting out of concern for a child's welfare that we are at risk of introducing the prejudices and oppressions present within society through the process of introducing questions that go to the core of the relationship between babies and young children and their closest carers. We have to remain effective and not lose sight of our need to act on behalf of the potentially abused child, we also need to develop our own reflective and reflexive internal radar in an attempt to detect possible moments when we are likely to be acting out of prejudice and not solely in the interests of the child.

Setting the scene for ethical practices

When a practitioner becomes concerned and enters into a discussion with a parent or carer about a child, a number of responses can be experienced including denial, emotional distress or anger. As Munro (2007: 41) argues, 'prevention and early intervention services also seem more appealing than the current state of child welfare services in many developed countries. They have become dominated by reactive services for serious problems'. At the moment when concerns are raised regarding a child's well-being that leads to the implementation of safeguarding procedures, practitioners are likely to be met with a range of accounts that may require painstaking unravelling to help better understand the power dynamics present within those interactions and the degree of risk that a child might be experiencing. This means those interactions are likely to focus on the relationship between a child's parents or carers and of course the child.

Confidentiality

Maintaining confidentiality and appropriate information sharing are often of concern to professionals, particularly in relation to the Data Protection Act 1998. Ultimately in cases where the safety of an individual is compromised the right to privacy (Article 8 of the Human Rights Act 1998) is overridden by the protection of the rights and freedoms of others (Article 8(2)). The Children Act 2004 adds weight to this culture of information sharing between agencies by authorizing the creation of an electronic file on every child in England so that those at risk of abuse, neglect, or deprivation could be helped before they reach crisis point. Agencies could share information about any suspicion of abuse or neglect in the family. This electronic Information Sharing Index database was subsequently named Contact Point, but it was heavily criticized by a wide range of groups, mainly on privacy and security issues. The UK coalition government announced plans to scrap Contact Point and the database was switched off on 6 August 2010. The legal basis for sharing information suggests that there are some clear circumstances where it would be the professional's duty to act in the best interest to protect a child or young person from significant harm. Indeed a failure to share information even at the level of 'niggling concern' (DH 2003) may have serious welfare consequences, if not considered together with the shared concern of others. This is often referred to anecdotally as putting the pieces of a jigsaw together, where one piece can provide the last vital clue, with the sum of the individual parts being greater than the whole (Adair 1987). The importance of accurate record keeping cannot be over-emphasized. This is particularly true of child protection practice where records may be scrutinized in a court of law. Jones and Jenkins (2004) emphasize the importance of professionals viewing record keeping in a positive light as being necessary for the welfare of mother and child rather than merely 'to cover their back'.

One situation that can take place is that the child, parent or carer may attempt to tell you something that you are asked to treat confidentially. To remedy such a situation many practitioners prefer to *forewarn*:

> ethical and practice contexts encourage a wide range of human service workers worldwide, including Social Workers, to report or refer any reasonable suspicions/beliefs that a child is at risk of harm to their respective Child Protection agencies, regardless of any pre-existing confidentiality arrangements they may have made. Even for legal practitioners, where 'privilege' traditionally exists, 'confidentiality is abrogated ... by mandatory child abuse reporting laws'.
>
> (McLaren 2007: 23)

It is clear from this that *child protection and safeguarding issues have priority over issues of confidentiality*. McLaren (2007) puts the case that in her research 'Social Workers and their organizations use standardised client consent forms and/or a variety of verbal procedures to state their child abuse reporting obligations when commencing the worker-client relationship. This practice is known as "forewarning"' (McLaren 2007: 23). It is worth commenting that the inclusion of statements within agency documentation is an important means of clarifying the position of each agency and the likely position it will take towards confidentiality in relation to any safeguarding context.

Forewarning is not an undisputed practice and can be viewed as potentially capable of undermining the relationship between the early years professional and the parent or carer. However, referring back to McLaren (2007), it is clear that to collude with the idea that the practitioner can keep confidential whatever they will hear, before they hear it, places them at risk of being party to an offence against a child. McLaren (2007) sums up her thoughts in the conclusion of her article in which she lists the various ways in which practitioners may view forewarning. For instance, it might scare parents or carers, resulting in avoidance of the practitioner and reticence (McLaren 2007: 30), which is clearly not ideal at a time when the process of assessment is pushing for more information not less. Additionally, once a situation appears to be one of safeguarding and child protection, the number of early years professionals tends to grow in relation to the family or carers in question, and then the ethical standards referred to earlier should be triggered. The more transparent that relationships appear to be, and the more discussion that accompanies decision-making, then the clearer the values, attitudes and standards that are held by different professionals can be appreciated better. In this kind of situation, it is more likely that the perceived best interests of the child are able to be met. For instance, there should be more clarity regarding how decisions have been made and the nature of any concerns. It is clear that from the moment that safeguarding concerns are raised, a careful assessment reflecting on the complexity of interactions and the child's well-being, and a proper plan can be developed. In addition to this, we will place emphasis on the concept of reflection as an important means of examining the key features that appear to be presented in any safeguarding situation.

Tensions between practice and policy

For many early years professionals, policy, with its external set of rules driven by a legal framework created by particular government concerns arising from particular times and contexts, can raise sets of aims and objectives that can feel constraining. This reduces the degree of choice and flexibility that practitioners might feel is necessary to carry out their role to its fullest potential.

Policy, introduced to aid practice, can undermine and hinder practitioners, leading to them feeling unable to function to the full extent of their professional discretion. The external pressure generated by policy and legal framework may tend towards the development of a more official line of inquiry as the norm when communicating a concern relating to safeguarding to a parent or carer. This over-emphasis on process has been highlighted by the Munro review (2010), meaning that practitioners have less time to focus on building relationships with children and families in order to complete what Laming (2009: 3) claimed were over-complicated assessments and procedures. Additionally because of the way in which practitioners have to work in safeguarding, they can become symbols of the organization. Parents and carers may see practitioners as agents of officialdom rather than human beings with social obligations and positions.

The ethical approach recommended by this book is for practitioners to attempt to balance the demands of social policy and legal framework with the sensitivities of the interactions they are likely to get involved in with parents and carers. While practitioners must always be cognizant of safeguarding guidelines and the supporting legal framework, they must also be able to be flexible in relation to the contexts in which they find themselves and adapt their practice accordingly.

Banks (2006: 144) points out that: 'In child protection, [these trends] have been given added impetus by the series of public enquiries into child abuse cases where the children died in their homes or they were taken away from home unnecessarily and it was said that Social Workers should have acted differently'. Banks (2006: 146) also points out that 'to regard child welfare and protection purely as a technical exercise ignores the ethical questions about how much "*abuse*" society is prepared to tolerate, balanced against how much interference in family life is thought to be justified'.

The stance assumed by the practitioner, including the one that you might take, can reflect a number of different positions where safeguarding is concerned. Banks (2006) covers three particular options concerned with practice. They are, first, the notion of defensive practice where practitioners play by the book; second, reflective practice where practitioners consider ethical dilemmas and analyse their practice for future situations; third, the position identified as reflexive practice, which refers to the practitioner developing a sense of personal awareness towards the stance they take within any interaction and the degree to which the practitioner is involved in influencing the situation at particularly important moments (Banks 2006: 150).

Initiating an intervention where there is a concern relating to safeguarding is one where the child appears to be at the centre of your thinking and where the focus of your interest is clarifying around a particular human being – that of the child. It is at such moments when consideration of the parent(s) and carer(s) as being 'for' the child is placed in doubt, and replaced by the possibility that they are 'against' the child might be considered. At such a moment it is reasonable for you to believe that you might make the difference between the child's unhappiness and his or her well-being. This of course suggests that everything from this point on depends on you and the actions now taken – or not!

What might the practitioner's rationale be if they are to act ethically at such a critical time? What are their concerns likely to be? Singer (1993: 323) argues that 'conscientiousness (that is acting for the sake of doing what is right) is a particular useful motive from the community's point of view'. The moment when we each develop a sense of concern raises the question of how to act responsibly reflects on the practitioner in a personal as well as professional way and the ways that the community of colleagues will consider it. Perhaps the first likely emotions when concern is felt for a child's welfare is that of feeling defensive and making sure that we have covered our own back. The second feeling is that we have acted in line with the community of practitioners where we feel we belong. Wenger (1998) states that:

> in a community of practice, we learn certain ways of engaging with other people. We develop certain expectations about how to interact, how people treat each other, and how to work together. We become who we are by being able to play a part in the relations of engagement that constitute our community.
>
> (Wenger 1998: 152)

As Banks and Gallagher (2009: 216) argue, '"professional ethics" can be regarded as a discourse that is created and enacted through social relations'.

Practitioners are concerned that they might be blamed if anything terrible happened to a child that they were concerned about while at the same time the child for whom you are worried somehow benefited from your actions. This is the defensive position referred to earlier by Munro (2010: 5), who provides some useful considerations to reflect on. To consider the notion whether indeed there is a safeguarding issue requires reference to personal and professional awareness and understanding of legal and policy frameworks that are concerned with safe-guarding. Alongside this, early years professionals need to contemplate personal values and attitudes, not only towards the child, but also to give attention to the stance they might be taking towards the carer or parent, while remaining clear in any planning that the purpose of intervention is to offer support to the child often by supporting the primary care context. To put this another way, most early years professionals will be operating in a system of surveillance or watchfulness pertaining to the types of relationships and their accompanying behaviours that primary and secondary carers may exhibit towards children in their charge. Being watchful requires a framework against which concerns can be identified and then acted upon in some way. These will be the statutory requirements set down for the safeguarding and protection of children.

Practitioner's framework of watchfulness

The framework is likely to include a number of key points of reference, such as:

- The legislative framework, including some understanding of the Children Act 1989 and Children Act 2004.
- Government policies such as *Working Together to Safeguard Children* (DCSF, 2010) and *What To Do If You're Worried a Child is Being Abused* (DfES 2006b). *Every Child Matters* (DfES 2003b) is another important point of reference and within that sections relating to aspects of childcare such as well-being and the five outcomes.
- Advice relating to safeguarding issued by Local Safeguarding Children Boards.
- Advice arising from training such as how to recognize potential signs that may suggest that the child is being abused and/or neglected.
- How to initiate meetings with colleagues or managers to share your concerns and initiate an appropriate response, if it is felt appropriate to take some form of action in protecting the child.

All of the above impact on each interaction with children and their parents and carers.

Developing watchfulness through an ethical lens

Early years professionals by the very nature of their intervention emphasize in the early stages of their involvement degrees of separation between themselves and those others who are the carers and parents. Consequently a set of power dynamics is activated and in play from the beginning of the relationship. If there is a concern relating to child protection issues right from the start, the power dynamics will tend to be far more noticeable and one-sided as early assessments are initiated and an attempt to develop an understanding of risk is undertaken. On the other hand, if an intervention is initiated to attempt to respond to an emergency in the family through the process of the Common Assessment Framework, there may be a reliance on the inclusion and cooperation of the primary carers and without it the process cannot continue. In this type of situation the power dynamics between the practitioner and the primary carers will often be more uneven and favour the practitioner. There is always the ever present dilemma for early years professionals of needing to feel in control of the situation while at the same time potentially being hoodwinked because parents and carers seem to be compliant with practitioner demands. However it might well be the case that the carer is actually intent upon resisting the efforts of the practitioner, who may be perceived as trying to take control of the running of family relationships.

It is therefore essential that the early years professional enters into a relationship with the parent or carer so that a clearer understanding of relationships can be exchanged and the potential for negotiation and improvement developed. This should support a sense of working together towards developing a set of common outcomes that are shared and formally agreed with the welfare of the child as the focus. It is not only the child and the parents or carers who will be scrutinized in safeguarding but also the practitioner and her or his line manager backed up by agency policy and safeguarding practices. There is also the wider community of practitioners from other agencies and the legal framework that is there to guide practitioners, including the ways it relates to the courts system.

Maintaining an ethical focus on the child

It is undoubtedly important for negotiation and communication to be a primary concern to practitioners during their interactions with parents and carers within safeguarding contexts, while at the same time remaining mindful of policy and guidance and the legal framework. The early years professional should remain vigilant about the child that they are involved with, keeping safeguarding practice in the foreground and trying not to let their attention become distracted by concerns relating to the parents and carers. Feelings arising from general concerns about children include a core regard for their well-being which can produce a sense of heightened sensitivity on the part of early years professionals, which might result in overreaction and occasional moments of panic. At the other end of the spectrum there might be a situation where there was a lack of interest shown by the early years professional. In either case practitioners are constantly involved in a situation of attempting to understand and assess risk, and at the same time making decisions in relation to whether they trust the apparent normal appearances and reassurances offered by carers and parents. Professional judgement needs to be exercised in matters of trust which must be relied on to a great extent. Practitioners should, while engaging in the development of trust with parents and carers, continuously reflect on progress and identify and be aware of any clear evidence to substantiate any sense of improvement.

Developing a reflexive radar in ethical practice

Giddens (1991: 129) argues that 'in modern social conditions, the more the individual seeks reflexively to forge a self-identity, the more he or she will be aware that current practices shape future outcomes'. What Giddens (1991) appears to be concerned with is the relationship between developing self-awareness and the impact that this can have on future situations. Personal awareness impacts on the professional practices of each individual practitioner, which then has an impact on the manner and style of future interventions and forms of interactions with carers and parents. In other words, the more focused on themselves as a practitioner that early years professionals become, the greater the impact this will have on their abilities to develop safeguarding skills. The immediate question this raises is why should this be so? Of course no one can be certain that this will be the outcome but it is reasonable to assume that if professional awareness is raised, then a clearer and stronger focus can be developed in relation to understanding the daily practices of safeguarding children.

Practitioners, parents and carers tend through their interactions with each other to position themselves in relation to the other person, often in ways that seem acceptable to that other person. This can support a sense of maintaining the status quo and the appearance that everything is fine when both practitioner and parent may not believe it is. It is at times like this when trust again can be seen to be an important factor in the relationship between parents and carers and early years professionals. An ethical approach to intervention in safeguarding situations may lead to the development of more trusting relationships. It is however important to first clarify what ethics might mean in situations where safeguarding is the main concern of the practitioner. Returning to the earlier question, how can trust be developed between practitioners and parents and carers within the contexts relating to safeguarding? If we refer to the ethical typologies mentioned above, it is clear that discussion around issues to clarify meanings and understandings are an important feature of an ethical approach. Practitioners should therefore reflect and question moral terms and see how the ways they are used can be justified.

When discussing relationships between practitioners and carers and parents of babies and young children that are the focus of safeguarding concerns, remember that these relationships are clearly connected to dynamics of power and influence, with babies and young children usually the most disempowered and dependent on the actions of the adults nearest to them.

Power and ethics

If babies and young children are the focus for safeguarding concerns, they also can appear to be the least powerful actors within these contexts. Although they have rights of participation, this will be difficult for them to assert, especially if they are very young. In this respect, ensuring babies and young children are safe and well tends to be the responsibility of their parents and their daily carers – for instance grandparents, relatives, family friends, childminders, children centre staff and (depending on the age of the child) nursery nurses, crèche workers, childminders or early years teachers. When care is shared throughout the day with a number of different carers, there can be a number of views as to what counts as appropriate in terms of adequate parenting or caring skills. It is in this area of sharing care of the child that perspectives may develop about whether a child is being adequately cared for or not and where any problems might be located. It is important that children should be given the chance to be spoken to privately by the practitioner so that the child's voice can be included wherever possible.

Ethics clearly will have something to say concerning what is felt to be acceptable treatment to a child as well as helping to understand ways of determining thresholds of acceptable care. From these positions, conversation can be developed which should help to open up what actually happened and to consider whether that is acceptable in relation to cultural and national expectations in childcare practices.

Safeguarding situations reflect potentially difficult relationships based upon sometimes conflicting values between practitioners, carers, parents and other key adults who are concerned with how children experience their lives. Ethical clarification can legitimately be sought at a number of different levels, as follows:

- Personal and professional practices with particular reference to developing reflection and self-awareness and how practitioners might be involved in the construction of stereotypes and certain types of social prejudice.
- Practitioner self-awareness and the construction of personal values, attitudes and beliefs.
- The understanding and appreciation of the lives of primary carers and the way that they may construct values, attitudes and beliefs.
- The ways that primary and secondary carers construct values, attitudes and beliefs and the potential cultural impact that has influenced these constructions.
- Ways of developing an acceptable, clear and open method of communication between practitioners and carers about their childcare practices and the impact that this might have on their children.
- Ways to develop communication with babies and young children to ensure that their voice as part of their participatory rights can be incorporated into any discussion about their future.

Ethical dilemmas in the safeguarding context

Protecting a vulnerable child is of paramount importance, yet this concern for the child can be seen as detrimental to the parents or carers if they are stigmatized as being neglectful as abusive, particularly if the concern proves to be unfounded.

Table 4.1 Ethical terminology explained

Ethical principles	
Autonomy	Self-determination, control of decision-making, respect for individual's choices
Beneficence	To do good
Non-maleficence	To avoid hurting/do no harm, or do the least harm where it is not possible to do good
Justice	To act fairly with a logical basis underpinning the action
Philosophies underpinning ethical responses	
Deontology	Duty or rule-based, acting in the right way according to a moral code, focuses on intention rather than consequences
Act Utilitarianism	Concerns doing the greatest good for the greatest number, focuses on consequences rather than intention

This raises the prospect, not of abandoning the concern or excusing inaction, but of dealing sensitively with parents and carers when concerns are raised about the welfare of a child, and dealing professionally and directly with parents and carers to raise and if necessary act on concern. This may involve direct communication with the parents and carers and liaison with other professionals and agencies, it is crucial that explanations are given to parents and carers to explain the concern and any subsequent referral or actions. While consent of those involved is ideal, the early years professional should proceed with information sharing if there is a concern regarding the welfare or safety of a child or if you are legally obliged to do so (e.g. for a court report, witness statement, or access to records in a criminal investigation). However this must be on a 'need to know' basis and 'proportionate', meaning only share information relevant to the case.

A lack of child-centredness is a common failing in safeguarding practice (Laming 2003; DfES 2003b, 2004a) with a focus on the parents, carers and processes, arguably to the detriment of the child's needs. Ethical principles of autonomy, beneficence, non-maleficence and justice (Beauchamp and Childress 2001) can be applied to child protection practice in that it is important to act in the best interests of the child, to act fairly, do good and avoid harm (see Table 4.1). Non-maleficence is based on the concept that one should not inflict evil or harm (Beauchamp and Childress 2001). There are different philosophies that can be used to explore ethical responses; for instance deontological theorists such as Kant support the principle of non-maleficence, forming the basis of rules and respect. Act Utilitarianism would support non-maleficence or beneficence, so long as it provided the greatest good for the greatest number. However, Act Utilitarianism may support maleficence if it contributes ultimately to the greater good. For example in some countries the death penalty is seen as acceptable, undoubtedly on principle a maleficent action: however, if society is rid of a killer, who could take more lives, justice is being served and maleficence is potentially thus acceptable.

Kant's deontological theory is admirable in its intention to treat everyone with the same considerations. However, humans are influenced by their emotions and rarely act in such a pure way, as this theory demands. Kant deontology offers little scope for individual considerations, suggesting that if we act for one person then the same act must be undertaken for all. Arguably Act Utilitarianism is simpler to understand, although it could be criticized as discriminatory in relation to the greatest good for the greatest number, particularly if the party negatively affected is a minority. This is potentially in contravention of Article 14 of the Human Rights Act 1998, which prohibits discrimination on any grounds, particularly in relation to enjoyment of the rights set out in the convention. Act Utilitarianism is unpredictable in its outcomes as it can be difficult to predict the consequences of one action, and whom it will affect. 'When we try to pick out anything by itself, we find it hitched to everything else in the universe' (Muir 1911).

With regard to service provision, it could be inferred that there has been a paradigm shift from a deontological to a consequentialist stance, particularly where the benefits of spending large sums of money on the needs of those who don't appear to help themselves can be questioned. Indeed in relation to healthcare, media reports have highlighted that the National Institute for Health and Clinical Excellence (NICE) had suggested to doctors who consider a particular treatment might not be effective because of the lifestyle of the patient, may be entitled to withhold it (Hawkes 2005). The policy context promoted in *Liberating the NHS* (DH 2010) highlights improving choice and outcomes, yet was set within the context of challenging times financially, resulting in likely service cuts and higher resultant social need for the population. While few would argue against children's services and safeguarding practice as essential services, we are still faced with resource shortages, including staff, resulting in choices regarding priorities having to be made. This has perhaps been reflected in increasing targeting of services at the most vulnerable in society, rather than providing universal services (Hall and Elliman 2003). A concern of this trend with regard to safeguarding practice is that opportunities for risk assessment may be missed, while acceptability of services may also be questioned by families if they are considered to be at risk, rather than routine.

Negligence

Negligence is more commonly referred to with regard to clinical practice, particularly concerning a breach of the duty of care, with harm resulting. The burden of proof lies with the complainant on the balance of probabilities in a civil court, or beyond reasonable doubt in a criminal court, which would suggest proof is more likely within the civil arena, depending on the case. The standard of competence regarding negligence is measured by the Bolam Test (Bolam v Friern Hospital Management Committee 1957) which means that a professional is not negligent if acting in accordance with acceptable practice as judged by a responsible body of like professionals. Further weight was added to this premise by Bolitho v City and Hackney HA (1997) which reaffirmed Bolam, but also modified it to ensure that in addition to being supported by a responsible body of professional opinion, that the care or information provided must be reasonable, responsible and capable of withstanding logical scrutiny. This not only suggests that professionals must act according to common practice, but also heightens the awareness of individual accountability, particularly with regard to information giving and consent.

While we may be comforted by vicarious liability (where an employer or professional organization will cover the insurance regarding any claims against their employees or members), nevertheless hounding and scapegoating of individual professionals involved in child protection cases is a now a relatively common occurence, often resulting in trial by media. It could be argued that organizations also need to take responsibility for failings, particularly where factors such as lack of resources and pressures on services mean that a comprehensive service is not being provided. Unfortunately, those in most need often appear to get the least services, resulting in an inverse care law (Hart 1971). This can be due to a number of factors including difficulty recruiting staff to deprived areas and better articulation of need by those in more affluent areas. Despite the optimism regarding future policy and practice direction following the Victoria Climbié case (Laming 2003), it would appear that vulnerable children are subsequently still being failed (Commission for Social Care Inspection 2005; Laming 2009), particularly with regard to recognition and response to child abuse; weaknesses in procedures, suitability, recruitment and retention of staff (Ward 2005). This is reinforced by the Munro review (2010).

Risk management

While the potential for blame regarding false accusations is undoubtedly real, this must be balanced with the possibility of missing a true case of abuse or potential harm, raising the importance of issues such as risk assessment, record keeping and confidentiality. Mason et al. (2002) raise the prospect of branding parents, through misdiagnosis of non-accidental injury and the distress this would cause (R v Norfolk County Social Services Department 1989; R v Harrow London Borough Council 1990). Unfortunately, professionals sometimes do not act appropriately through fear of upsetting parents or even due to the rule of optimism (Dingwall et al. 1983) that all parents love their children and would not deliberately harm them. Parents or carers, if informed appropriately, may understand why investigations or assessments are being undertaken. However the accountable professional needs to be able to back their decision-making process with excellent record keeping, peer and clinical supervision and appropriate information sharing and referral if necessary. This is exemplified in a case of wrongly suspected parents (P v East Berkshire Community Health Trust 2003). Ultimately this appeal ruled that the health professionals responsible for investigating the suspected abuse did not owe the person suspected of having committed the abuse a duty if they carried out the investigation in good faith but carelessly, despite the alleged interference with family life. Health professionals acted in good faith in what they believed was in the best interest of the child, Sullivan v Moody (2001) considered. Defence to the claim of breach of duty due to negligence would include acting in the person's or public's best interest, however this disclosure would need to be to appropriate authorities and in the presence of a real risk (W v Egdell 1990).

Ethical practice

Practitioners face potential conflicts in relation to legal and ethical considerations; indeed professional practice is not always underpinned by the appropriate moral rationale. There is a dichotomy within child protection practice concerning the conflict between simultaneously caring and supporting families on the one hand and monitoring or policing on the other (Oberle and Tenove 2000; Marcellus 2005). This may affect the therapeutic relationship between practitioner and client if trust is not developed, particularly if the family feels threatened, powerless and under surveillance. Peckover (2002) highlights the importance of maintaining a non-hierarchical relationship, particularly in the professional discourse of the social arena in which we are potentially invading clients' personal space. Now consider the following scenario in which ethical questions will be raised and seen to be integral to practice.

Case study 1: Ben and Suzie

Jack and Millie are both 18 years of age, and have lived together for two years. They have two children, Ben and Suzie. Ben is nearly 2 years old, and Suzie is 2 months. During a visit to the home the health visitor noticed a small linear bruise on Suzie's neck – just below her right ear. On inquiring how the bruise occurred, Millie says that she has no idea and until the health visitor pointed it out, she hadn't noticed that there was a bruise. This is not the first time that there have been suspicions about the level of care being provided by the parents; three months ago Jack had been seen by an early years professional from the Sure Start children's centre where Ben attends nursery, because Jack had shouted at Ben, who had wet himself as he waited for his dad to collect him. On that occasion the centre head asked to speak to the parents to express her concern, but had felt that a referral to children's services was not appropriate. However the incident was recorded and when the health visitor called into the children's centre, the centre head had a chat about what she had observed, being aware that there was a baby in the home. The earlier situation between Jack and his son Ben has put staff on a heightened state of vigilance. On returning to her office at the children's centre, the health visitor called children's services to make an immediate telephone referral. After a brief discussion, a social worker is despatched to the home to carry out a risk assessment and to start a child protection investigation.

Ethical considerations arising

What are the central ethical concerns of the early years professional?

- The needs of the children need to be of paramount consideration; however, the parents need to be informed directly of concerns.
- The practitioners involved so far include the children's centre staff and the health visitor. Now a referral has been made by the health visitor to children's services advice and assessment based on Suzie's unexplained and potentially non-accidental injury. The picture following the previous incident with Ben and concerns expressed by the children's centre are building up to a pattern where these children are potentially not thriving, are experiencing or are at risk of neglect, significant harm and actual physical abuse.
- There is still the potential for a positive relationship to be maintained with the family if they are communicated with sensitively. Referrals should not be made to a social worker without informing the parents or carers unless it is felt that this could result in more risk of harm to the child.
- The importance of communication between different professionals and agencies is clear in this scenario. It should also be clear that the family are aware that this communication is taking place.

How can positive well-being be developed for both the children and their parents?

- Maintaining a positive relationship with the parents is important, but it is often difficult for practitioners to get this balance right. The practitioner's role is balanced between support and monitoring the situation. If they are perceived as too authoritarian there may be resistance to professional involvement. Equally the relationship needs to maintain professional boundaries to avoid being fooled by deceptive techniques to cover up abuse, as in Peter Connelly's case. Professionals can be accused of collusion with abusive parents or carers if they perpetuate the abuse by reinforcing non-engagement as in Victoria Climbié's case, where social workers were reported to be afraid of her carers, or conversely accepting carers' accounts without question.
- The focus of professionals' concerns need to be what will improve the lives of the children. The parents' needs should not be acknowledged to the detriment of the needs of the children, but it must be recognized that supporting the parents can reduce factors that hinder while introducing factors that promote positive parenting.

What may the early years professionals introduce that may support or hinder well-being?

- Early years professionals often have significant contact with young children as in this scenario with a crucial role in ensuring safety, well-being and promoting psychosocial development.

- Assessment tells us what factors help or hinder the achievement of development goals. Basic objectives are to remove factors that hinder and to introduce or promote factors that aid.
- This includes assessment of the strengths and needs of the children, the resources available to them within the immediate and wider family, community resources and services available that could support the family, particularly focusing on parenting skills. A service directory could be accessed by any professional involved with the family or by the parents or carers themselves (e.g. Help4Me).
- While this scenario has resulted in a formal referral to a social worker for investigation (this process will be discussed in Chapter 8), there was also an option before this injury took place for practitioners involved to consider a child in need or child action meeting. This process and levels of prevention will be discussed in Part 2.
- With appropriate support, families have the potential to provide caring adults with whom the child can attach; continuous contact with significant adults; gradually changing relationships over a lifetime; safety and security; stimulation and encouragement for growth; reasonable expectations; experience in identifying and expressing emotions; support in times of crises; others with whom to share successes. All children have the right to experience a positive environment.
- Babies and young children are more vulnerable due to the following factors: basic need dependency on adults; little or no language; significant and rapid development; limited experience of adult parenting or care relationships; they are often unseen and can be hidden from society; and they have limited social experience. Due to this lack of exposure there may be an acceptance of their experience as the norm; they also have increased health risks and increased health and safety risks – they are easier to harm in effect, either deliberately or through neglect.
- The early years professional role is extremely important for the following reasons: they have access to and see babies, young children and their families; they understand development needs of babies and young children; they can listen to and observe babies and young children; indeed for some they provide significant primary care. They are also in a position to share positive parenting; offer direct support to parents experiencing stress; and provide assistance and information regarding services and support.

Key messages

This chapter has considered ethical practices within the safeguarding context, so that you can explore competing priorities, particularly between the rights and needs of children and their parents or carers, as there is often a requirement for complex judgements to be made.

- You should recognize the importance of transparent relationships and direct communication with parents and carers regarding concerns and actions.
- Policy and process, while introduced to aid practice, can sometimes undermine and hinder you, leading to you feeling unable to function to the full extent of your professional role.
- While you must always be cognizant of safeguarding guidelines and the legal framework which supported them, you should also be flexible in relation to the contexts in which you find yourself, and adapt your practice accordingly.
- You need to be aware of the influence of power dynamics, in terms of you being perceived as more powerful by parents and carers. Although this can result in compliance, it can also result in, sometimes covert, resistance potentially resulting in collusion between you and the parent or carer.
- The needs and concerns for the child must remain your paramount concern, bearing in mind that the child is the most vulnerable and least powerful within the power relationships.

5   The development of community involvement

Chapter Overview

This chapter explores the important development of community involvement which has been rediscovered recently through policies such as Sure Start and Every Child Matters. The chapter describes a wider historical context in which communities are discussed as being either helpful or unhelpful in supporting vulnerable babies and young children in relation to safeguarding concerns.

What is a community?

A community is often perceived as a group of people living in close proximity; it can also be seen as sharing common values (Frazer 2000: 76). Communities can be national or even global if they share a common identity or shared set of interests, values or beliefs, based on culture, religion or lifestyle for example. Cohen (1985: 12) proposes the concept of similarity and difference within a community, in that members of a community are likely to have similarities with each other that simultaneously distinguishes them from other groups. He later expands this to suggest that commonality need not mean uniformity (Cohen 1989: 21), therefore individual behaviour may vary to some extent within the boundaries of a community.

Communities of practice

Is it possible to be a member of more than one community simultaneously? You may be a member of a local geographical community or a particular cultural group with shared meanings and goals; however, you are also a member of a community of practice with particular reference to your professional role and organization. In a community of practice various members are brought together by common activities and by 'what they have learned through their mutual engagement in these activities' (Wenger 1998), providing a sense of joint enterprise and identity. Each agency and the practitioners within have their own identity, boundaries, shared meanings and goals. In safeguarding practice there are several agencies which need to interact and work together effectively in the interests of children and young people, who are also members of a family and wider community. Yet professional and organization barriers can prevent this from happening.

Practice reflection points

Thinking about your organization or team

- What is your organization or team about? What is its *joint enterprise* as understood and continually renegotiated by its members?

- How does it function? Does it have a *mutual engagement* that bind members together into a social entity?

- What capability has it produced? What is the *shared repertoire* of communal resources (routines, sensibilities, language, achievements, etc.) that members have developed over time (Wenger 1998, 1999)?

- How well does it communicate with other agencies working with children?

Organizational culture and communication

Different organizational procedures, ways of dealing with issues, even different geographical boundaries and protocols for accepting referrals can all impact negatively on inter-agency working relationships. Each agency has its own culture, ethos, hierarchy and language, with a resultant lack of understanding about the roles and responsibilities of others. Assumptions ensue concerning level of knowledge, information and actions. When services are busy, omissions can occur if it is wrongly assumed other workers are involved.

Even when agencies do communicate, misunderstandings can occur. Reder and Duncan (2003) outline numerous incidents in Victoria Climbié's case where meanings attributed to information was misinterpreted, suggesting that both participants in communication should monitor the content of their own message for clarity of meaning. This should be extended to check their interpretation of the other person's message; this is particularly true of consultation in safeguarding practice and subsequent recording. Different professional language, particularly jargon and abbreviations, can worsen this situation. Laming (2003: 13) called for a common language to ensure better identification and response to concerns. Timing of response and messages was also highlighted as an area of concern (Laming 2003; Reder and Duncan 2003). In addition to practical problems, Reder and Duncan (2003) outline psychological barriers to communication, concerning processing information, shared meanings and interaction. Brandon et al. (1999) added issues around lack of respect or professional mistrust.

Reder and Duncan (2003) introduce the prospect of overt and covert communication, often a source of negativity within relationships. This can relate to identity issues in terms of perceptions of self as a professional within an agency or organization and perceptions of other professionals and their own organization or agency. It could even be extended to cover what you perceive their perception to be of you. Reder and Duncan (2003) relate this concept to purpose of communication in terms of what the overt reason for contact may be and the perhaps hidden agenda or more covert reason, often involving referral or even to discuss a completely different unrelated matter. This is further compounded if the other person does not pick up on hidden cues, with both potentially leaving the conversation with the perception that the other person is taking responsibility for instance.

Context is also cited by Reder and Duncan (2003) and by Brandon et al. (1999) as an influencing factor in communication episodes in terms of workload, resources, atmosphere, supervision and individual factors such as confidence, experience and level of seniority of the practitioner. This was particularly pertinent to Victoria Climbié's case where in one instance a customer services receptionist took messages and referrals on behalf of one of the social care team (Laming 2003: section 5). Powell (2005a) discusses the influence of power and status where it may be difficult for some practitioners to develop perspectives that may challenge more highly considered 'expert' positions, potentially resulting in the swinging of any professional group perspectives towards a single agency viewpoint such as health, social work or education. Thus some professionals' voices, such as early years for instance, may not be easily heard or valued, resulting in a hierarchy that undermines a key aim of *Every Child Matters: Next Steps*, that:

> all professions share a common language and core of training, and encourage professionals to work together to share professional insights, while retaining and enhancing the specialist skills that health professionals bring.
>
> (DfES 2004b: 40)

Understanding and application of sensitive issues such as confidentiality and consent can hinder working together. Practitioners are wary of breaching legislation such as the Data Protection Act 1998 and the Human Rights Act 1998. Even if practitioners feel concerned about a family, they may be unwilling to contact other agencies or unsure of the response they will receive. Sinclair and Bullock's (2002) review of serious case reviews identified inadequate sharing of information and knowledge directly related to this issue further compounded by lack of understanding of referral process. However, Laming (2003: 17.103) identified this as a dangerous major concern in terms of responses to Sections 17 and 47 of the Children Act 1989.

Despite numerous cases and recommendations, some of which have been discussed here, it would appear that failures in practice keep recurring. Reder and Duncan (2003) suggest that the issue of communication is more complex than inquiries or reviewers can envisage. Indeed the interpersonal nature of communication involving human beings without the benefit of hindsight could also be cited. A common information-sharing problem would appear to be that a wealth of assessment data is gathered, but not subsequently processed or shared (Reder and Duncan 1999, 2003; Munro 1999) meaning that the jigsaw is often incomplete. Rather than merely changing procedures a change in communication mindset is required.

Inter-agency relationships

Reder and Duncan (2003) outline factors impacting on inter-agency relationships including territorialism and role identifications; status and power; competition for resources; professional and organizational priorities, stereotypes; value systems, unfulfilled expectations; and disrespect for others' expertise (Blythe and Milner 1990; Morrison 1998; Stevenson 1998). Such dissonance is not unique to any profession and a common feature of human groups. Indeed Bion (1961) would recommend the following measures to encourage good group spirit: a shared purpose; shared recognition of boundaries; flexibility – especially in response to new members; absence of cliques; a sense of the worth and freedom of each individual; and a readiness to acknowledge discontent among members.

Application of team-building principles could contribute to improved working relationships, especially in the current climate of integrated teams and collaborative working. Team building can be considered an essential component of organizational development whereby the needs and roles of the individual group members, and team objectives, are identified and clarified and responsibilities negotiated and assigned. A degree of conflict can be not only an inevitable part of social and organizational life to some extent, but also a necessary element of a group, creating the ability to challenge and innovate. Similarly, if the make-up of the group is too similar, there is a danger of being restricted. A lack of leadership can result in lack of purpose in a group task. A popular analogy of a team would be Winnie the Pooh and his friends, with too many Tiggers or Eeyores not conducive to a sense of purpose (Hoff 1982).

Robinson et al. (2004) explored the implications of joined-up working within a multi-agency team. Barriers encountered included use of jargon to exclude team members, quality of leadership and loss of professional identity. Positive facilitating factors highlighted to resolve dilemmas included the development of mutual respect, personal relationships and shared language. Less positive strategies were also mentioned, such as displacing blame to past working practices or other agencies, diverting problems to individual processes such as supervision or masking problems with 'group speak'. This research drew attention to useful strategies at structural, ideological and procedural levels, such as common purposes and goals, team building, and transparent lines of communication. Analysis of professional beliefs and values is particularly pertinent, with a clash between previous work experiences and creating new meaning for the 'greater good' of the new community of practice, the danger here being that dominant groups or individuals could prevail. Knowledge exchange is also a crucial factor, ranging from informal corridor and coffee chats to more formal training mechanisms and dissemination at team meetings. The necessity of a leadership style to establish a culture of celebrating diversity together with valuing knowledge and expertise must be emphasized.

The unique nature of safeguarding practice means that teams form, re-form and change all the time. Team-building principles (Adair 1987) can be applied to the process of working together, recognizing that the sum of the parts can be greater than the whole.

Indeed in safeguarding practice not everyone has or even needs the same knowledge, expertise, information or pieces of the jigsaw puzzle. The Common Assessment Framework encourages each practitioner involved with the family to consider the strengths, needs and resources available to support a child. This assessment considers individual factors such as the health and development of the child, but it also considers the parents' and carers' capacity to care for the child effectively and the wider family and community factors that may enable or hinder their ability to undertake this. The knowledge each practitioner and their agency can contribute and share with others working with the child and their family can provide a fuller picture of strengths and needs.

Community involvement in safeguarding children

Jack (2006) suggests that in the past, mainstream services for children in the UK have largely been reactive and individualistic in their response to safeguarding children. Numerous reports have criticized services for a lack of inter-agency response and poor communication. In focusing more on the 'area and community components of children's well-being' (Jack 2006), we can meet the shift in emphasis towards promoting well-being in children's lives in a more holistic manner, based on the Every Child Matters outcomes of 'being healthy, staying safe, enjoying and achieving, making a positive contribution and economic well-being' (DfES 2003b: 5). Measures to remove barriers to inter-agency working included an emphasis on early intervention, information sharing and multiprofessional working, using the Common Assessment Framework (CAF). The introduction of Local Safeguarding Children's Boards coalesced services with an increased focus on co-ordination of local services and measures to improve children's lives, rather than the more reactionary assessment and monitoring which had been a strong feature of safeguarding practice before. This was perhaps due largely to resourcing issues and a lack of power on the part of the previous Area Child Protection Committees to influence planning and enforce allocation.

A greater emphasis on prevention and community involvement was needed to harness information to create a fuller picture, for instance members of the public have a strong interest in safeguarding children fuelled by the desire to protect their own and society's children. Indeed in Victoria Climbié's case, key information was received from a neighbour and a taxi driver. Professionals often do not live in the communities where they work and need to listen to and act upon positive suggestions and concerns expressed by the public. This has always been possible where the public have been engaged in community initiative or parents have been consulted in schools, for example. However policy initiative is now encouraging and facilitating this in Sure Start children and family centres.

Sharing information between agencies can also highlight overlap or hotspots of concerns. The example of the jigsaw puzzle has been used in the past with each agency providing an important piece of information that may not be important or constitute a cause for concern alone. The CAF endeavours to promote sharing of information about a family in terms of a child's needs, emphasizing both positive and negative factors and including assessment of both the barriers and resources available within the family and wider community to address issues and promote well-being. Additionally community profiling can identify area factors beyond the individual factors if there is a culture of sharing information between agencies. This could include details of known offenders, drug use, crime on a negative level; however, conversely it could also include sharing of information regarding preventative and support services. The service directories are a good example of sharing information, where professionals, members of the public, voluntary and statutory services can look for and post information about services available to support children and families.

It is known that parents under stress are more likely to harm their children, therefore removing factors that hinder, and promoting factors that help support families in need, can undoubtedly influence child well-being. Examples include drug use, domestic abuse, very young or unsupported parents, and parents with learning difficulties, physical or mental health problems. While it cannot be said that all parents or carers living in all these circumstances will harm their children, research suggests that without support they are known to be at a higher risk. This is where preventative measures can help, identifying and adding to existing strengths and removing factors that may lead to abuse. A coordinated approach to targeting and supporting families in need can make a difference in the form of individual support visits or access to statutory and voluntary services within the community. A bottom-up approach to community engagement can result in a better investment in social capital than a top-down approach managed by professionals who may be perceived as lacking in local knowledge at best and interfering and didactic at worst.

Policy initiatives

Sure Start programmes, introduced in more disadvantaged communities in the late 1990s, represent an attempt to assess what local communities want and need and provide services to promote the well-being of children in partnership with the communities in which they were situated, investing in children aged 0–4 years and their carers. Since 1997 and the launch of the National Childcare Strategy a more integrated approach has been evident, building on the view that joining up education, care, family support and health is the key to good outcomes for children, both short and longer term. Measurable outcomes have included increases and improvements in services and number of childcare places.

Funding was initially targeted at the needs of children under 5 years old, although centres may offer services to a wider age range using alternative funding. By 2006 children's centres were expected to reach at least 650,000 pre-school children in the 20 per cent most disadvantaged areas; initially developed from Sure Start local programmes, neighbourhood nurseries (new and planned), early excellence centres, schools and other existing local provision are in the maintained, private and voluntary sectors. They were designed to serve children and families in disadvantaged communities by providing integrated care and education for young children; child and family health services; family support; a base for childminders and foster carers; and services for children with disabilities and children with special educational needs. They were also crucially designed to facilitate the return to work of unemployed parents, with additional financial benefits in the form of tax credits.

Health services included antenatal and postnatal advice and support for parents; information and guidance on breastfeeding, hygiene, nutrition, home safety; identification, support and care for those suffering from maternal depression (both antenatal and postnatal); speech and language and other specialist support; and smoking cessation services. A key role of children's centres was to act as a service hub, bringing together locally available services; integrating management and staffing structures; providing a base for childminder and foster carer networks; providing services for children with disabilities and children with special needs; and providing links to other day care provision, such as out of school clubs or links with local training and education centres, Job Centre Plus and childcare information services.

The future? Coalition government policy

The UK coalition government remains committed to Sure Start services, but does highlight the need to increase its focus on the neediest families, to investigate ways of paying providers by results and to take Sure Start back to its original purpose of early intervention. Free nursery places also remain, with 15 hours' provision for all 3 and 4 year olds, and disadvantaged 2 year olds will also receive an additional 15 hours. While Sure Start funding was not cut in the government comprehensive spending review of October 2010, it is no longer ring-fenced funding (local councils have absorbed the budgets) and there is an expectation to save money in administration and 'back-office functions' in order to focus more on frontline services. While the coalition government highlighted targeting the neediest families through measures such as means tested tax credits and child benefits, this is set alongside cuts in Department for Education non-school budgets (12 per cent). Preventative services such as family support services and children's services could be hard hit by proposed cuts (28 per cent). This perhaps will lead to more pressure on schools to provide services and support, with monies set aside for this, perhaps highlighting a shift away from early years provision and prevention strategies. A combination of job losses following the impact of spending review cuts and the prospect of parents finding it difficult to not only find work, but also fund childcare costs following a reduction in the childcare element of the Working Families Tax Credit from 80 per cent to 70 per cent of total cost, results in difficulties for families and early years provision. Parents now also need to work for at least 24 hours per week to claim this credit.

The coalition government announced a childhood and families taskforce, in which they both made the 'welfare of the next generation central to their political identities' in terms of issues such as parental leave, supporting families with a disabled child, definitions of poverty and promoting life chances. Additionally the Munro (2010) review of children's social work and frontline child protection practice considers how communication between social work teams and universal children's services can be strengthened to improve early intervention processes. Barriers to best practice are explored together with simplification of regulation and bureaucracy. The initial consultation included the views of professionals, children, young people and families with a wide variety of experience to gather evidence of local innovations and new approaches to child protection and identify good frontline social work practice. This included measures to enhance identification of children in need, improving practice, developing skills, shared learning from practice such as critical incidents that recognize accountability but counteract potential tendencies towards scapegoating or a culture of blame, approaches to case discussions and measures to enhance transparency and clarity of responsibility to improve public engagement and confidence.

The aim of the report is to consider why previous reforms of safeguarding services have not led to improvements in provision or outcomes; rather they have resulted in an increasingly bureaucratized and target-driven service, with less time subsequently spent in direct contact with vulnerable children and families at risk. The review considers three main areas: early intervention and prevention; frontline practice; and transparency and accountability.

Problems identified in the report include the following:

- Professionals being too focused on complying with rules and regulations, therefore spending less time assessing children's needs.
- Target-driven culture meaning social workers are unable to exercise their professional judgement.
- Too much emphasis on identifying families and not enough attention to putting children's needs first.
- Serious case reviews concentrating only on errors when things have gone wrong, rather than looking at good practice and continually reflecting on what could be done better.
- Concerns about the impact of delays in the family courts on the welfare of children.
- Professionals becoming demoralized over time as organizations fail to recognize the emotional impact of the work they do and the support they need.

Working with children and families is not an exact science and while professionals should take responsibility when things go wrong, Munro (2010) argues that frontline staff require more freedom to make decisions, more support and understanding, and less prescription and censure.

> Child Protection work involves working with uncertainty: we cannot know for sure what is going on in families; we cannot be sure that improvements in family circumstances will last. Many of the problems in current practice seem to arise from the defensive ways in which professionals are expected to manage that uncertainty. For some, following rules and being compliant can appear less risky than carrying the personal responsibility for exercising judgment.
>
> (Munro 2010: 5)

Indeed Munro (2010) argues that fear of missing a case leads to too many referrals, with lengthy assessments that conversely do not always add up to more service input when need is identified. Services are thus concentrated in identification rather than prevention and provision. The report draws on evidence produced by Laming's (2009) review of progress and reform since his Victoria Climbié report (Laming 2003), with subsequent cases such as Peter Connelly highlighting a lack of improvement and impact on children's lives. Laming (2009) suggested that progress on key reforms were too slow, strongly criticizing social services departments, which he said suffered from 'low staff morale, poor supervision, high caseloads, under-resourcing and inadequate training'. These difficulties are undoubtedly added to by resultant high staff turnover and recruitment and retention issues.

Areas included from this report in Munro's (2010) analysis are grouped under the three main headings as mentioned above: early intervention and prevention; frontline practice; and transparency and accountability. Early intervention and prevention issues include a lack of early specialist assessment and comprehensive family support for vulnerable children due to a lack of expertise in frontline universal services such as children's centres. Lack of consistency in referrals and responses was highlighted, early years professionals need to know when and how to respond and knowledge of referral processes. Frontline practice can be negatively affected by an overemphasis on process, rules and regulation rather than interaction and relationship building with children and their families or carers. ICT systems can cause more problems than they solve if they add to the time spent on report writing and non-contact activities. Additionally systems may not be fit for the purpose such as assessment, for example the CAF can promote insufficient assessment that is not driven by professional judgement, chronologies are not easily created, and the child and family's voice may be lacking.

The Signs of Well-Being tool developed by Gateshead Children and Young People's Partnership (2009) can be useful to some extent as an exercise prior to more formal CAF processes' for example, by focusing more on child, family and professional's goals particularly in early intervention strategies (see Table 5.1). Derived from a Signs of Safety risk assessment tool devised by Turnell and Edwards (1999) in Western Australia, it is designed to be used with young people and their families, focusing on key current issues, highlighting positive factors

Table 5.1 Signs of well-being

Worries		Strengths and resources
What is happening with the child/young person that is worrying you?		What relevant resources and strengths are already in place?
Here the practitioner is invited to document his/her worries in a clear, concise an factual manner, keeping these concern in perspective		Here practitioners are asked to note through discussion with the family, relevant strengths and resources which are already in place

Child/young person's goals	Parent/carer's goals	Professional's goals
What does the young person want to change and what are their ideas fo achieving this?	What does the parent/carer want to achieve and what are their ideas for achieving this?	What changes do the professionals need to see to be confident about the young person's well-being?
Here children and young people are invited to share their thoughts on what need to be different and what might help to bring that about	Here there is an opportunity for carers to say what they are aiming for as a good outcome along with thoughts on what might help to bring this about	Here the practitioner has an opportunity to be explicit about the changes they need to see happening for them to be confident that the child or young person can manage without extra services

Well-being scale	Service user evaluation
Given the above information, rate the young person' well-being on a scale of 0–10 0 – your worries about the child are bound to continue 10 – the young person is doing well enough that no extra professional involvement is required	Rate this completed form on a scale of 0–10 0 – this has not captured what you said 10 – this has completely captured what you said

and facilitating progress. The consideration of the perspective of the child, parent or carer and practitioner perspectives and goals can facilitate exploration of concerns, priorities and likely actions and thus result in a more thorough assessment of need, with potential for better cooperation and a consensus on the way forward. Goals for change and ideas for how to achieve them are clarified in a partnership approach.

The third theme examined by Munro (2010) focuses on accountability and transparency, with a need to focus on what works for children and families rather than what is detrimental. A system similar to the Centre for Maternal and Child Enquiries (CMACE) on maternal and infant deaths could be a more positive way forward. Features of this programme include anonymous reporting that reduces scapegoating and blame cultures. The reports consider all maternal and perinatal deaths reporting all cases within a triennial period. Details of cases are then altered or made into composite case studies so that lessons can be learned through recommendations for future practice. This may include guidance on how to avoid substandard care, treatment recommendations and so on. The public and media focus on key figures in high profile child protection cases can be detrimental, not only to the individuals being scapegoated, but also mean that future practice becomes more defensive and process led.

While Munro's (2010) review focuses on social care provision to some extent, there are clear indications that all agencies and staff working with children need to take responsibility for their actions and respond to concerns appropriately. However, this work is set within the context of increasing regulation, frameworks for assessment, increasingly delayed and complex guidance and processes. The practical element of building relationships with complex families who can be resistant to service input and developing skills and knowledge regarding underlying issues that impact on parenting such as domestic abuse, drug and alcohol use, parents who are very young, have mental health problems or learning difficulties and are unsupported by families and/or service are more difficult to address. Indeed serious case reviews are highlighting weaknesses such as an overemphasis on parent or carer needs and voice; invisibility of vulnerable children in need with a lack of assessment and support when needed. Practitioners need support and training not only to work with resistant families, but also to avoid distorted relationships with families that could result in collusion. For instance a mother can engender sympathy from the practitioner, resulting in attention to her needs rather than remaining child-focused. Brandon et al. (2009) reiterated Dingwall et al.'s (1983) seminal work regarding the rule of optimism, with a reluctance to make negative professional judgements and rather see the best in families. While it is important to focus on strengths and positive features in any assessment, this should not leave the child exposed unnecessarily to avoidable risk and harm. Building positive relationships with families needs to be balanced with attention to monitoring and assessment, remaining child focused. This is particularly relevant in early years practice where the voice of the child can be even less evident. The practitioner must practise empathetically, considering the perspective of the child at all times, maintaining 'respectful uncertainty' and 'healthy scepticism' (Laming 2003). This can ensure concerns about a child's welfare are not over- or underestimated.

Overall Munro (2010) advocates a holistic systems approach that focuses on a learning culture with enabling management styles for frontline staff. She proposes a requisite variety in responses focusing on meeting children's needs with appropriate pathways for beneficial outcomes. An important aspect of the review was consideration of how social workers and all those involved in child protection can be better helped to handle uncertainty – how they can be assisted in making appropriate evidence-based assessments and interventions that will be more likely to protect vulnerable children. But the review also considers 'how the media and the public can be supported in understanding that tragedies will often not be the result of unprofessional practice but rather will occur in the context of uncertainty about unpredictable families in unpredictable circumstances' (Munro 2010: 20).

Agency responses and information sharing

An advantage of multi-agency working within children and family centres is the potential for a greater emphasis on working together. This is particularly relevant for child protection practice. Historically there have been some good examples of inter-agency working; however the barriers and problems have perhaps been emphasized more both in professional publications and research and in the media generally. Lessons from serious case reviews have taught us that we need to work together effectively and highlight poor practice. Perhaps refreshingly Munro's (2010) review aims to highlight what measures may help by providing evidence and best practice examples. Multi-agency child protection training provided by local safeguarding training also aims to reduce some of the barriers highlighted, such as understanding of roles and definitions of abuse, communication and applying thresholds for intervention.

While it was clear from the outset that the UK coalition government planned to scrap Contact Point, the information-sharing tool that recorded every child's data, there will still be a national signposting database system to record details of vulnerable children. Indeed there is still a strong emphasis on sharing meaningful information between professionals and agencies. This means that early years professionals must consider their role within a wider inter-agency network, not only exchanging information and facts, but also considering our part in the jigsaw – what we can contribute and what other agencies or practitioners may know and be able to contribute. This means that assessments must become more than a paper exercise or mechanism for referral, but a means of sharing a variety of perspectives on a child and their family life, including resources available to them.

Failure to share information is cited as a contributory factor in most child death inquiries. It is therefore essential that professionals working with children have a clear understanding of their duties and how they can fulfil them. Many professionals are still unclear about what information they can share and when. There are many laws that govern confidentiality and the sharing of information. These are just a few of the most relevant:

- The Children Act 2004 states clearly that we have a duty to share information when we have concerns about a child's welfare.
- Common Law Duty of Confidence relates to the confidentiality expected in a professional–client relationship, most notably within the legal profession. Nurses, midwives and health visitors are bound by a code of conduct (Nursing and Midwifery Council (NMC) 2008) that includes a confidentiality clause. Employees are also usually bound by confidentiality regulations within their employment contracts.
- Article 8 of the Human Rights Act 1998 concerns everyone's right to privacy for his private and family life, his home and his correspondence (Article 8:1); further stating that

> There shall be no interference by a public authority with the exercise of this right except such as is in accordance with the law and is necessary in a democratic society in the interests of national security, public safety or the economic well-being of the country, for the prevention of disorder or crime, for the protection of health or morals, or for the protection of the rights and freedoms of others.
>
> (Article 8:2)

- Data Protection Act 1998 concerns the protection and processing of personal data.
- Caldicott Guardian is a senior person in health and social care organizations, responsible for protecting the confidentiality of patient and service-user information and enabling appropriate information sharing.
- Freedom of Information Act 2000 introduced a public 'right to know' in relation to public bodies.

The Every Child Matters framework helpfully provides support through the *Information Sharing: Guidance for Practitioners and Managers* (DCSF 2008), which includes seven Golden Rules for sharing information:

1. Is there a clear and legitimate purpose for sharing information?
2. Does the information enable a living person to be identified?
3. Is the information confidential?
4. Do you have consent to share?
5. Is there sufficient public interest to share information?
6. Are you sharing information appropriately and securely?
7. Have you properly recorded your information sharing decision?

Concern about welfare and safety overrides all other considerations and you must disclose information whether you have consent or not. However, the age of consent can be lower than 18, depending on the understanding of the child. The *Information Sharing: Practitioner's Guide* (DfES 2006a) suggests 12 as a lower age limit for consent, but this is not a legal limit. A key legal case regarding consent was the Gillick case, now referred to as the Fraser competency concerning the child's level of understanding (Gillick v West Norfolk and Wisbech AHA 1986). You must also provide information if there is a legal obligation to do so, such as a request from a court for a report. 'Need to know' and 'proportionality' are also important considerations. The person who needs to know could be your manager and the duty officer at referral and assessment. However, the information they need is only that which is immediately relevant to the child.

Agency roles and early years professionals

There are a wide range of practitioners working with babies and young children who are often the most vulnerable. These include nursery workers, childminders and foster carers, outreach and family support workers, social workers, midwives and health visitors. They work in a range of settings including the home, private, voluntary and service settings such as children, family and Sure Start centres (see Table 5.2). Consider the children and families you work with: there are universal services that all children should have access to, such as a midwife, health visitor and GP. Later, children are all entitled to early years and school education. There may also be services working with families with additional needs. Consider which agencies and practitioners you work with. There may be adult services in addition

Table 5.2 Agency roles and responsibilities

Social care advice and assessment	Sports and leisure, library and youth services	Police
Investigating all allegations of child abuse: children at risk of protection are immediately safeguarded via safeguarding procedures, implementing Section 47 enquiries Accommodating children at risk (where an immediate safeguarding plan within the family cannot be established) Undertaking Initial and Core assessments Initiating child protection conferences Assessing children in need, and convening child action meetings Attending child in need meetings Offering advice and consultation Private fostering assessments	Well placed to pick up possible abuse and need to know how to report concerns, due to nature of direct contact with children and young people	The police have a responsibility to investigate the criminal element of child abuse. They work in cooperation with advice and assessment (e.g. they are part of the strategy meeting) and are responsible for gathering evidence and prosecuting adults or young people who have committed a crime, e.g. neglect, physical abuse, sexual abuse. The police keep records of children who have protection plans and are often the first point of contact in domestic abuse cases. They have a responsibility to keep and share relevant information and to contribute to multi-agency meetings. The police can receive direct referrals regarding child abuse and have emergenc powers (Police Protection Order) to enter premises and remove children (72 hours)
	Housing	
	Housing staff have an important role in 'recognizing child welfare issues, sharing information, making referrals and subsequently managing or reducing risks' (DCSF2010: 43). They have close contact with children and families and may be the first person to identify a need. They may assist families, e.g. by • referral for support • providing appropriate housing/ adaptations • providing support for victims of domestic abuse. Environmental health may identify unsuitable conditions for children	
		Probation
		In addition to supervising offenders, probation officers: provide a service to child victims of serious sexual or violent offences, supervise 16/17 year olds on community punishment, staff youth offending teams and support victims of domestic abuse. (DCSF 2010: 62–3) Contribute to MARAC (monitors sexual offenders living in the community)
Health		
Responsibilities for protecting children in community and hospital settings. They support children in need, Identifying abuse. They assess, plan and respond, contribute to assessments and child in need meetings about children/young people. Routine health and development surveillance and advice and support for families. Additional specialist services targeted based on assessment of need, e.g. speech therapy, hearing assessment, orthoptics, behaviour management, biomechanics and referral to hospital services such as community paediatric nurses and hospital doctors. Hospital services in direct contact with children include Maternity, Paediatrics, Neonatal Unit and Accident and Emergency	**Early years professionals**	
	Wide range of people working with babies and young children who are arguably the most vulnerable. These include nursery workers, childminders and foster carers working in a range of settings including the home, private, voluntary and service settings such as children, family and Sure Start centres	**Youth offending teams**
		Multi-agency team who supervise young people 'subject to pre-court interventions and statutory court disposals (DCSF 2010: 65). Work with young people who are in need and some who will be the victims of abuse
	Schools	
	Responsibility to ensure that children are safe in school and are well placed to identify abuse and children in need. Need to be familiar with all aspects of the safeguarding process and will be expected to contribute to that process, e.g. by referral, sharing information, providing support	
Voluntary and private sectors	**Connexions**	**Faith organizations**
Provide a wide range of services, including preventative interventions, specialist support, information, advocacy. Need to be fully aware of the safeguarding process and able to refer appropriately. Note: NSPCC is the only organization (other than social services and police) who can initiate proceedings to protect children, and who can receive referrals about child abuse	Provide advice, counselling, advocacy, referral to specialist agencies, for young people. Need to be aware of safeguarding issues and able to refer appropriately	Well placed to identify need and abuse (cf. Victoria Climbié). Need to be fully aware of the safeguarding process and able to refer appropriately. Should ensure that they have internal codes of practice and procedures to guide staff

to children's services if the parents, carers or older children within the family have issues to resolve.

This section leads into Part 2, where we consider the responses of a variety of agencies and professionals with reference to particular case studies. You are also encouraged to reflect on particular cases from your own experience to consider questions, such as what may raise your level of concern? Who would you consult with? What would or should your actions be?

Key Messages

- You need to be aware of the context of the families you work with. This may include geographical or cultural factors relevant to the lives of the babies and young children.
- Remember that professionals themselves belong to a variety of communities influencing their values and judgements, including their upbringing, their own cultural, family and living circumstances, and the professional and organizational influences on their working practices.
- This variety of experiences and perspectives can influence your relationships with families and other professionals and agencies.
- Efforts must be made by all practitioners working with families to avoid making assumptions, not only about the behaviour of families, but also regarding the knowledge and actions of other professionals and agencies who may be in contact with the family.
- Effort is required for you to communicate effectively, build positive working relationships and share responsibility for assessment and support of families.
- These positive working relationships can be facilitated by developing a shared understanding of roles and perspective through joint training and meetings, while co-location and integrated teams are sometimes recommended to achieve this. It is not always necessary to be in the same building to work together well – indeed the opposite can be true, while professionals can equally communicate and work together effectively while retaining separate roles and responsibilities.
- The benefits to the family cannot be overemphasized such as seamless provision of services; avoiding overlap while ensuring that services are actually being provided (misunderstandings can occur when everyone thinks someone else is involved); for the client, avoiding repetition of their story to a number of different professionals; and avoiding contradictions and conflicting advice.
- Effective communication between all professionals involved with a family can result in appropriate support being provided at the right time, with a focus on prevention rather than dealing with the results of abuse. Delay and drift can also be avoided in dealing with issues as they arise.
- While following procedures and process is important, this must not be at the expense of direct engagement and interaction with families, professional judgement and quality assessment of need, or indeed timely and appropriate action.

Part 2

Practical considerations

Exploring the actions and roles of early years professionals in safeguarding babies and yound children

6 Raising concerns and identifying abuse

Chapter Overview

This chapter introduces the practical concerns surrounding the early moments when the practitioner begins to suspect or believe that a baby or young child may be being abused. Considerations and dilemmas surrounding the recognition of abuse are explored within the safeguarding framework and linked to a case study. The focus for the discussion provided by the case study invites you to examine and explore possible actions or inactions and their likely consequences. A general formula for personal reflection is based around feelings and emotions, anxieties and the social, physical, intellectual impact that abuse may have on a baby or young child.

The starting point

We start again with the five outcomes from *Every Child Matters* (DfES 2003b) as a means of assessing and identifying the difficulties and problems that children may be encountering. We are also interested in exploring the strengths which parents and carers offer to babies and young children. From the beginning we are able to identify and relate to children who appear to be thriving and equally to those who are not. This is in effect an initial observational assessment taking place through the vigilance and watchfulness of the early years professional. We all want better lives for children. Most children do well, and we need to remind ourselves of this. Many of the children and young people we work with may have additional needs and issues in their daily lives, and we sometimes forget what it is that we are working towards in terms of a safe, healthy and thriving child. This means making sure that their basic needs are met; they can use the medical, educational, leisure and welfare services necessary for a healthy and positive childhood; they live in an environment protected from exploitation, abuse and harm; and they feel loved and supported by a network of reliable and affectionate relationships.

Practical concerns

No matter what your role is in working with children and families, as an early years professional, your daily routine will include occasions when you begin to feel that the well-being of a young child is not being achieved. At this point you want to engage in a dialogue with the parents and carers to see whether it is possible with their cooperation that the well-being of the child can be improved. Following this you may notice a change for the better in the child's well-being as your agreed plan with the parents and carers delivers results. Unfortunately in many cases the results may be short lived and you may have to think of other means of intervening so you can improve the child's well-being. In your professional role you will be aware of the guidelines that you are expected to follow in such an event.

What is the guidance?

Children who are defined as being 'in need' under Section 17 of the Children Act 1989 are those whose vulnerability is such that they are unlikely to reach or maintain a satisfactory level of health or development; their health or development is likely to be significantly impaired or further impaired without the provision of services; or they have a disability. Concerns about children are usually categorized according to levels of need as outlined below:

- *Every Child:* This has previously been referred to as Level 0. Every child should have access to universal services, including a midwife, health visitor, general practitioner, school and pre-school early years provision.
- *Level 1*: This includes children with additional needs, whose health and development may be affected. They may need a referral to services such as a dietician, behaviour management service, home support service, or speech and language therapy for example.
- *Level 2*: This covers children with additional needs, whose health and development is at increased risk of being affected. You may have exhausted the resources in your agency and/or several agencies are involved and need coordinating. At higher levels of need, a child in need or child action meeting is likely to be held and it is at this meeting that the lead professional will be agreed. It is important to note that the lead professional will not take responsibility for providing all the care, but will perhaps be the person or agency in most contact with the family and will be in a position to coordinate care, thus avoiding omissions and overlaps in service provision.
- *Level 3*: This includes children who have complex needs, whose health and development are being affected as a result. Specialist assessment would be required, such as Initial and Core assessments by social workers from advice and assessment children's services, substance misuse, youth offending team or child and adolescent mental health services.
- *Level 4*: This covers children at risk of or suffering significant harm, and therefore in need of protection or substitute care.

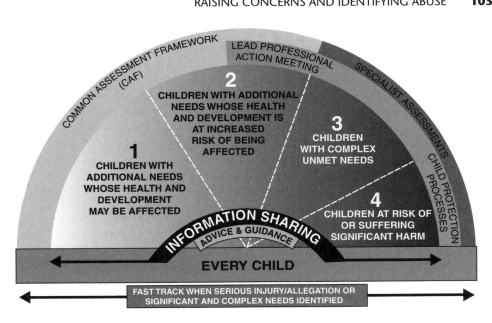

Figure 6.1 Framework for action for all children, young people and families

The majority of children have needs that can be met by their parents or carers and universal services or by a single agency. However, some children have additional needs that require the support of several agencies working together with parents and carers to promote positive outcomes. A very small number of children and young people will have complex needs that require a planned package of support by agencies to meet the identified needs, and address and manage risk. A smaller number will still be at risk of significant harm and will require a coordinated child protection plan.

The Bolton Safeguarding Board's (2007) *Framework for Action* (see Figure 6.1) is an example of how to ensure that professionals work together to support children to achieve their full potential and children at risk are properly protected. This promotes the use of a common language, understanding and consistency across all services for children, young people, families, workers and volunteers from all organizations. The *Framework for Action* provides a consistent approach for workers to identify and respond to children's needs. The *Framework for Action* is underpinned by the following principles:

- The child's welfare and safety is paramount.
- Assessments of need will be child centred and holistic.
- All organizations are committed to the duty to safeguard and promote the welfare of all children.
- All organizations demonstrate commitment to integrated processes for all children.
- Integrated working will avoid duplication and unnecessary intrusion into family life.

In early years settings all staff must be aware of guidelines for action if they suspect a child is being abused. It is the responsibility of all childcare providers to inform appropriate agencies if they suspect a child is at risk of harm or has been harmed. In situations where you suspect a child or children may be at risk of abuse within their own family environment, you must consult your local guidance and/or consult with someone within the early years and childcare teams within your area (this could be from the local authority, Local Safeguarding Children Board, or your social care children's services advice and assessment team). Also read the *What To Do If You're Worried a Child Is Being Abused* guidance (DH 2003; DfES 2006b).

All childcare providers must keep a record of any concerns they have about children in their care in an 'Incidents and Concerns' book. Information kept is confidential to individual families. Records should be kept on separate pages, and the book kept in a safe place. It should be accessible only to named staff. Parents should be aware of the existence of the book and informed if a record is made that concerns their children. The parent or carer should be asked to sign to confirm they have seen the record and that it has been discussed with them.

All carers of children, including childminders and foster carers, have a responsibility to keep records. It can, however, be difficult to have these conversations with parents or carers and then document and/or share your concerns. Many early years professionals worry about maintaining a relationship with the parents or carers. This is particularly worrying for some early years care providers who may feel that the parent or carer is effectively their employer. It must be remembered that the needs of the child are paramount and that by discussing concerns and actions with parents and carers, particularly if this is done at an early stage, the professional relationship can be maintained in a positive manner. It is often when parents or carers feel that the provider or professional is 'going behind their back' that the relationship with parents or carers can perceptibly deteriorate. The 'Incidents and Concerns' book records routine types of event where a child is noted to have a bruise that is likely to have been caused by accident, depending on its shape and location on the child. However, if abuse is suspected, a confidential record may be kept, particularly in situations where concerns have been already raised and monitoring is taking place. Records under these circumstances may be confidential and shared between appropriate practitioners. Often the rationale for keeping a confidential record relates to concerns that knowledge by the parent or carer may place the child at greater risk, may lead to the child being withdrawn from the nursery or school to prevent further official action, or may suppress abusive activity or make it a more covert activity.

Individual early years establishments should have a designated person responsible for leading on child protection issues and ensuring that child protection guidelines are understood and kept. This designated officer should be a manager (or senior staff member) within the setting. In cases of allegations against those in a position of trust, where you suspect child abuse has occurred during the time a child has been attending a childcare setting registered with Ofsted under the

Childcare Act 1989, you must contact the appropriate person or agency such as your line manager, designated person for child protection, a more senior colleague, an educational social worker, or children's services. There must be a section in child protection policy on how to deal with professional abuse or abuse by staff in your setting. If an allegation is made to a member of staff concerning a manager or owner, these concerns should be raised with a deputy manager or person in a senior position. If you do not work in a more formal childcare provider setting, perhaps being home based as a childminder or foster carer, you will still have someone you can discuss your concerns with – this may be a designated social worker or relevant early years contact.

If following initial discussions with parents or carers the agreed plan is unsuccessful, you must continue to discuss your concerns with your manager, named or designated health professional or designated teacher. If you still have concerns, you or your manager could also, without necessarily identifying the child in question, discuss your concerns with your peers or senior colleagues in other agencies – this may be an important way of you developing an understanding of the reasons for your concerns about the child's welfare. If, after this discussion, you still have concerns, and consider the child and their parents would benefit from further services, consider which agency, including another part of your own, you should make a referral to. If you consider the child is or may be a child in need, you should refer the child and family to the relevant social services advice and assessment team. This may include a child whom you believe is, or may be at risk of, suffering significant harm. Concerns about significant harm may also arise with children who are already known to social services. Information about these children should be given to the allocated social worker within social services. In addition to social services, the police and the NSPCC have powers to intervene in these circumstances in the form of an Emergency Protection Order.

Alerts and warnings

Now we introduce you to the idea of the alerts and warnings as ways in which you – through the use of observational techniques and your knowledge of either children in particular or of children in general – leads you to the situation where your concerns for a child is heightened and enhanced. What are alerts and when do they develop into a warning sign? For example, perhaps one particular day you notice a child's slight bruise or alternatively you observe some difficulty with the child's behaviour or demeanour. It is important to try to hold on to the concern and what it is about the child on this particular day that is raising the concern with you. First reflection: what is it that is noticed by you – can you recall or pin it down? Reflect on any incident that relates to this type of situation, it may be helpful to use a cyclical reflective model such as Gibbs' model of reflective practice (Gibbs 1988). Gibbs' model can be simply represented by Figure 6.2.

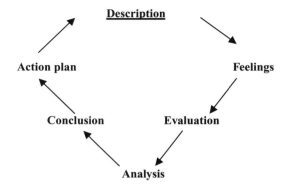

Figure 6.2 Gibbs' model of reflective practice

In order to maximize the use of this process, the stages can be explained as:

- *Description:* What happened? Tell the story . . . uninterrupted.
- *Feelings:* What were you thinking and feeling? Even consider how you are feeling now as you retell it.
- *Evaluation:* What was good and bad about the experience? Additionally, why was it good or bad and what are you basing this upon?
- *Analysis:* What sense can you make of the situation? Think about what this means to you. This can be supported with evidence from literature.
- *Conclusion:* What else could you have done? And why didn't you? Maybe you didn't have to?
- *Action plan:* If a similar situation arose again, what would you do? Would it be the same or something different? How could you prepare yourself for this? Is it a situation you expect to deal with again? If not how could your reflections be applied to other situations?

Another useful model is Johns' model of structured reflection (Johns 1994) where you would write a description of the experience and then respond to cue questions as outlined in Table 6.1. Both models can be helpful in allowing you to think through your concerns systematically.

What is abuse?

Definitions of abuse can be subjective and changeable over time within society and differ between agencies, in terms of what is often referred to as thresholds of abuse. A simple definition of child abuse from the Oxford English dictionary is 'maltreatment of a child, especially by beating, sexual interference or neglect'. Yet legal terminology as reflected in the Children Act 1989 would define child abuse in terms of primary justification for the state to initiate proceedings seeking

Table 6.1 John's model of structured reflection

Aesthetics	• What was I trying to achieve?
	• Why did I respond as I did?
	• What were the consequences of that for the patient or client, others or myself?
	• How was this person or persons feeling?
	• How did I know this?
Personal	• How did I feel in this situation?
	• What internal factors were influencing me?
Ethics	• How did my actions match with my beliefs?
	• What factors made me act in incongruent ways?
Empirics	• What knowledge did or should have informed or guided me?
Reflexivity	• How does this connect with previous experience?
	• Could I handle this better in similar situations?
	• What would be the consequences of alternative action for the patient or client, others or myself?
	• How do I feel now about the experience?
	• Can I support others and myself better as a consequence?
	• Has this changed my ways of knowing?

compulsory powers where there is actual or likely harm to the child, in which case harm would include ill-treatment (including sexual and emotional abuse) and impairment of health or development (health meaning physical or mental health; development including physical, intellectual, emotional, social or behavioural development). (See Chapter 1 for full list of categories.)

'If, from a list of behaviours, ticks could be put against those which are abusive and crosses against those which are not, the task of practitioners and researchers would be made easier' (DH 1995). For example, hitting children might be ticked, indicating that such behaviour is abusive, but this is an ongoing area of debate for legislature. Some might argue that in certain contexts it is good for children to be smacked and, as at least 90 per cent of children have had this experience at some time, the behaviour could be said to be 'normal'. The tick might be replaced by a cross or, at best, a question mark.

Definitions of abuse often refer to concrete abusive incidents, especially beating, sexual interference or neglect. Yet policy-makers, practitioners and researchers are more likely to consider the context in which such incidents occur before they will define them as abusive; however, the needs of the child must remain central. Evidence on what constitutes normal behaviour within families is important in defining what is abnormal or abusive. Different generations and social contexts can have different views about issues such as sending children to boarding school, or levels of nakedness within families for example.

Similarly, just because a lot of parents do something doesn't make it acceptable, it could be argued that smacking is a good example in this case. Clear parameters for intervention are difficult to determine but necessary if professionals are to act with confidence to protect vulnerable children. Thresholds (this can be described as an upper limit or trigger for response) which legitimize action on the part of child protection agencies appear as the most important components of any definition of child abuse. The research evidence suggests that authoritative knowledge about what is known to be bad for children should play a greater part in drawing these thresholds (DH 1995), perhaps in terms of the point beyond which a behaviour or parenting style can be considered maltreatment and action is required. Maltreatment is seldom a single event or serious incident; however, a single event can be very dangerous and may still require a strong immediate response. A continuum of concern is often mentioned with a chronology of events and incidents useful, however other factors such as the context of the abuse and what the child may think about it could also be considered.

One of the difficulties in assessing the effectiveness of child protection interventions is determining causative factors. Browne and Saqi (1987) provide an account of the various theories put forward since the Second World War illustrating the relationship between definitions and perceived causes of abuse. They identify five different models which explain why children are maltreated: psychopathic; social or environmental; special victim; psychosocial; and integrated model – the latter reflecting the variety of factors within the perpetrator, the victim and the environment that can combine to result in abuse.

Families overwhelmed and depressed by social problems form the greatest proportion of those assessed and supported by agencies. Studies have been undertaken in a variety of disciplines including psychology and sociology; however, there is often more than one reason for the occurrence of child abuse. Increasingly studies have recognized the impact of several factors and various levels of causation, through adopting an integrative approach (Sameroff and Chandler 1975; Brofenbrenner 1979; Cicchetti and Rizley 1981). Macdonald and Winkley (1999) summarize four core elements of the integrative approach. These provide a framework for developing an appropriate research process and using the findings to develop suitable social responses:

- Dynamic contribution of the different disciplines and perspectives and their cumulative impact over time.
- Some factors increase the risk of abuse, while others have a protective effect, the cumulative factors approach.
- Some factors have an enduring effect and some are circumstantial or transient.
- Understanding abuse requires that we examine the interplay of factors at different levels of analysis – the ecological approach.

It is increasingly evident that child abuse is not down to a single factor but is the result of multiple circumstances, event or perhaps a series or continuum of events – stress, poverty, psychological problems, parents own poor childhood experiences, or a lack of social support (Olds and Henderson 1986).

Child protection within a context of prevention

It is critical that all our endeavours to foster the safety and well-being of babies and young children occur within a context of prevention of child abuse that recognizes risk factors, protective factors and maintaining safety. Risk factors include child factors, family factors, social context, life events and community and cultural factors. It is important that those working with babies and young children have an appreciation of both the existence and influence of these factors. Their significance should be duly recognized in any planning aimed at the prevention of child abuse. Munro (2010) suggests that preventative services can operate at different points in the development of a social problem, later going on to discuss the child's journey or experience of intervention (Munro 2011).

Levels of prevention

Primary prevention is targeted at one or more stress factors that are known to have the capacity to provoke abuse. Tackling these stress factors, or enabling parents to cope with them in order to promote the general well-being of children, are the characteristics of primary prevention. This may involve social support, use of family centres and community networks. General strategies to tackle poverty or social exclusion can also promote factors that aid and reduce factors that provoke family stress and thus reduce the prospect of child abuse. Primary prevention seeks to improve conditions that create problems in the first place, targeting stressors that can cause abuse. When applied to child protection, primary prevention programmes target families and the whole community with the aim of stopping abuse before it occurs.

Secondary prevention aims to respond quickly when a problem starts to arise and prevent deterioration. It may also seek to identify and intervene in situations where children are at high risk of abuse and provide programmes for children and young people who are at risk, for example peer support or positive parenting programmes.

Tertiary prevention concerns a response when the problem has become more serious, targeting families, groups and individuals where abuse has occurred and attempts to stop it recurring. A fourth level of prevention identified by Hardiker et al. (1991) within a safeguarding context involves providing therapy to victims so that they do not suffer long-term harm. This fourth or quaternary level refers to minimizing or preventing long-term harmful effects.

Primary and secondary levels of prevention may involve individual or more likely community action and responses. Tertiary and quaternary levels are more likely to be targeted on a specialist and individual level, by for instance at

Table 6.2 Four levels of prevention

Type of prevention	Definition	Activities
Primary prevention	Taking universal action to promote conditions so that problems do not arise	• Supportive visiting • Recognition and response • Assessment framework • Child-centred focus • Community development • Inter-agency collaboration • Education and training
Secondary prevention	Focusing on individuals or families who are at high risk, but may not yet have problems	• Intervention for children who are at risk • Child in need or action meetings
Tertiary prevention	Targeting individuals or families with problems to minimize the adverse effects	• Child protection legislation and procedures • Community services • Inter-agency support
Quaternary prevention	Optimizing the prospects for children where family problems have resulted in their placement in substitute care	• Counselling of victims • Supportive environments • Monitoring substitute care

tertiary level by addressing causal factors within the family, usually by seeking to improve competency and parenting skills. Quaternary prevention may involve individual psychological support or specialist treatment, together with supporting and monitoring the environment of substitute care (see Table 6.2).

Munro (2010) proposes a dichotomy regarding the 'early' in early intervention because it can refer to intervening early in a child's life and conversely early in the genesis of problems, which may emerge at any point in a child's life. Early years intervention has been a feature of UK social policy for some time, seeking to offer support for parents and carers of young children and provide opportunities for young children to thrive in positive and stimulating environments through early years education and schemes such as Sure Start. Community level support is a duty for local government to provide under the Children Act 2004. This remained a key priority for the UK coalition government, and Graham Allen MP was commissioned by the government in July 2010 to undertake an independent review investigating how children at greatest risk of disadvantage can get the best start in life and which delivery models can provide the best early intervention. However the government was subsequently criticized for not protecting key services from inevitable financial cuts with ring-fenced funding.

Case study 2: Kyle and Sami

Jo works in a children's centre baby room with Sandra and notices that one of the babies, Sami (9 months old), seems to be very upset, crying loudly, when she arrives at the centre. However, her mother Angela, who has brought her, seems to ignore her for most of the time before walking over to Jo and thrusting Sami into her arms saying, 'Take her. I've got to get out of here before I hurt her – I can't stand her'. Before Jo can say anything, Angela has left the centre virtually at a run.

Jo knows Angela well because Sami is her second child, her first child Kyle also attended the children's centre from a very early age. Angela is in a long-term relationship with Ged, who works in the building trade. Ged has a problem with alcohol and has been violent towards Angela in the past. During a particularly difficult time in their relationship, Angela had confided to Jo that she was often 'beaten up' by Ged. On one occasion she had left her home with Kyle after a very nasty attack while she was three months pregnant with Sami. On that occasion Angela was happy to discuss her problems, but was very worried when Jo suggested contacting the police or a social worker – 'He will kill me if he thought I was talking to anyone about this,' she had said urging Jo not to discuss her concerns with anyone else. Jo had said that she didn't feel able to keep the information to herself but would talk it over with her line manager.

Alerts and warnings for Case study 2

Considerations	Possible responses	Useful agencies and contacts to support the family or you as a professional
Initial alert – what concerns you about this scenario? What have you noticed? Why is it of concern to you? How can you respond immediately? How do you believe the child is experiencing this moment? What is he or she likely to be feeling? How do you feel at this stage?		
Applying definitions of safeguarding and child protection: • Is this child being ill-treated? • Is it easy to recognize in this instance?		

(Continued)

(Continued)

Considerations	Possible responses	Useful agencies and contacts to support the family or you as a professional
• What is the child's understanding of this situation likely to be? • Are there any factors within the context of the scenario that may add to your concerns? • Are there any existing strengths you can identify in terms of existing factors or possible sources of support?		
How would you feel about initiating any action? Possible actions? What can you do? How will this impact on the child and the family, including the parents or carers?		
What is already known? What else do you need to know? Where could you get the information you need?		
Risks and benefits of action: consider the needs and impact on • the children, Kyle and Sami • the mother, Angela • the father, Ged • you as a professional • the service setting you work in		

Developing a line of thought that may lead to action

What are the risks? Is this abuse?

It is important to focus on the child's needs first, although of course providing support to parents under stress will impact on the child's well-being. As there are two of you in the baby room, one (perhaps Sandra) can focus on receiving Sami and calming her down, giving her a cuddle, assessing any immediate physical and emotional needs. It is important to consider if there are any signs or suggestions of any form of ill-treatment: refer to *Working Together to Safeguard Children* (DCSF 2010) and *What To Do If You Are Worried a Child Is Being Abused* (DfES 2006b). This could be a physical injury, or signs indicating neglect or emotional abuse.

What makes you feel concerned?

Thoughts from well-known cases such as serious reviews may raise a concern. Messages from research should also be considered. Local and national guidelines and training regarding signs of abuse may trigger action.

What actions might you consider?

This may include immediate actions, telling someone, telling no one and writing a report, making a referral – how and to whom? It is important to consider where the buck stops. While Sandra is assessing Sami's immediate needs and perhaps seeking assistance from other members of staff if there are additional duties or children to focus on, this gives Jo the opportunity to consider Angela's needs. You would need to consider when would be a suitable time to discuss the situation with Angela, bearing in mind that she is upset and trying to leave. She may be unwilling to speak to you at this time; however, it is important to acknowledge that both she and Sami appear upset, with questions such as 'Would you like to tell me about it?' Or 'Is there anything I can do to help you?' This is where a private room away from the hectic environment of the baby room would be helpful, together with the obligatory cup of tea. If she feels unable or is unwilling to talk to you at this stage, it is important to let her know that you will need to speak to her later when she collects Sami, ensuring that other staff are aware in case Angela tries to avoid the discussion. You need to establish if there are any explanations that the mother Angela may be able to offer about her feelings generally, and about Sami in particular. It is important to establish what the practitioner may ask Angela and in what tone of voice about her feelings towards Sami. General questions about her well-being and if there is anything upsetting her could be a good start, being more specific about any recent events that contribute towards her feelings may also be useful.

Bearing in mind the child's journey now (Munro 2011) it is important to focus on the needs of the child, who has a right to be cared for, not only in terms of their basic physical needs, but also in terms of their emotional well-being. Ethically it is crucial to focus on the best outcome for the child as the paramount consideration; however, this will also include the well-being of Angela, as addressing her needs and those of the family as a whole will impact positively on the children. This is where your prior knowledge of the family and the background can be helpful. It is important to document current events contemporaneously in the records you hold on the child: this may be on a separate more confidential record. You may also have a specific place to record safeguarding concerns, which also gives you the opportunity to reflect on prior contacts and any previous concerns documented. This process may help you to make an assessment about what is making you feel concerned. Thoughts from well-known cases, perhaps serious case reviews, and messages from research may help you to establish if this is a case of abuse in terms of the categories of neglect, physical, sexual or emotional harm.

What further actions might you consider?

It may be that your initial discussion with Angela communicates to her your concerns about Sami's needs being addressed, she may provide an explanation and calm down. It is still important to document and follow up the incident with Angela, continuing to monitor the situation. This simple intervention may be enough, but the continuum of abuse needs to be acknowledged, particularly if there have been other concerns noted previously.

In addition to immediate intervention and support as outlined above, it is important to discuss the events with a more senior colleague, such as your line manager or designated safeguarding officer. Angela would need to be informed that you are documenting the events and sharing information. Even if she is not happy about this, you would need to explain that it is your duty to put Sami's needs first. This is where an open and honest dialogue about the reasons for this, while still maintaining your support of Angela's needs could result in a positive relationship being maintained. If this is not the case and resistance develops, that could add to your concerns about the well-being of the children within the family.

In addition to telling someone within your organization, you may consider sharing information, verbally in the first instance, with other agencies to establish if they have any concerns about the family. This is also useful as a means to consider what other services are in place, to assess if the needs of the family are being met, and if any additional service may be helpful. A formal assessment of needs can be undertaken using a Common Assessment Framework (CAF) form, if one is not already in place. The CAF can establish the strengths and resources available to the family, in addition to identifying concerns and needs. Again, openness with the family about this assessment can allow them to input into the assessment and maintain a positive relationship with service providers. If this is not possible, you would still need to keep them informed, providing a copy of the assessment and any referrals made. This also allows them to voice any concerns about the process or the assessment findings.

This sharing of information may raise the level of your concern, resulting perhaps in a child action meeting with professionals or a formal referral to social services advice and assessment team, resulting in a Section 17 inquiry and/or child protection plan. It can be seen from this scenario where preventative services could impact positively with all members of the family, avoiding escalation of the initial concerns.

Key messages

- Sometimes you may feel that the well-being of a young child may not be being achieved within their current context or circumstances.
- As an early years professional you are one of the key practice workers with access to babies and young children. Therefore you are in a position to assess well-being, monitor any concerns and support parents to care effectively for their children.
- You must follow local and national guidance and legislation regarding child protection, maintaining a focus on the child's journey, rights and ethical practice.
- Effective open and honest communication with parents or carers about any concerns may help maintain positive relationships. However, if resistance to intervention is evident, further advice and support should be sought from key people such as your line manager or designated safeguarding contact.
- If the child is likely to be exposed to more risk by communicating concerns with parents, referrals can and should be made without consultation.
- You may find it difficult to define abuse and interpretations may differ between individuals and professionals within and between agencies. Thresholds for what constitutes abuse may be at perceptibly different levels.
- Causative factors can be complex and difficult to determine. It is accepted that a range of factors may contribute to abuse and that it is not always deliberate.
- Early prevention practice such as support of parents, particularly those suggestive in research of being at increased risk of harming their children, is undoubtedly useful.
- There are additional levels of prevention: secondary, tertiary and quaternary; these should still be employed even if early responses have not been initiated or have been unsuccessful.

7 Providing support for 'at risk' babies and young children

Chapter Overview

This chapter discusses the real and effective ways that practitioners are able to support children who may be being abused at the point before which any referral to an outside agency has been made. The chapter considers ways of supporting babies and young children in abuse situations after these initial referrals have been made, including dealing with the feelings that parents and carers may have in relation to the practitioner who made the referral. The chapter also considers how babies and young children may be emotionally sustained following abuse and describes important practices that may be applied.

Supporting children and families

While primary prevention is undoubtedly the ideal, crisis intervention or early referral when initial need arises can prevent escalation of the problems within families, meaning that children may not subsequently need to be cared for within the looked after system and removed from their primary carers. This does not mean keeping children with their carers at all costs; however, efforts need to be made by the multidisciplinary team to facilitate the development of relevant parenting skills.

This raises the importance of not only working with parents and carers in these early stages, but also liaising effectively with other agencies to share information and provide seamless services. Effective inter-agency communication and working together can prevent escalation of problems. This can range from an early referral related specifically to the child or targeted parental support to facilitate better responses and management of childcare. At the more serious end of the scale it could mean crisis intervention services, such as those provided by Action for Children (ACH 2008) where situations can be diffused with targeted support and intervention, including liaison with relevant other agencies. However, this is likely to be more successful in an acute rather than chronic or longer-term history of safeguarding concerns.

In the context of child protection, secondary prevention is targeted at families at higher risk of abuse who are sometimes identified through universal supportive visiting and screening processes within health services. It is important to utilize knowledge of risk factors for abuse, to identify problems before they can deteriorate further, in order only to prevent a single serious incident of abuse or a declining continuum of harm. This secondary level of intervention can be more effective than tertiary prevention. Not only does secondary prevention reduce the potential for abuse and maltreatment, but also it maximizes the chances of better outcomes for children. Macdonald and Winkley (1999) also highlight the prospect of better engagement through increased acceptability of services that are universal and thus not stigmatized as child protection services.

A number of interventions can be effective in supporting parents who may be at increased risk of harming their children, through lack of knowledge or support. These include assessment of need and supportive home visiting by professionals and voluntary organizations in the antenatal and postnatal period. Macmillan et al. (1994) suggest that long-term home visiting programmes for parents with one or more risk factors such as single parenthood, poverty or being teenage parents was effective in the prevention of child physical abuse. A large randomized control trial by Olds et al. (1997) provides an example of an effective long-term home visiting scheme for first-time mothers, comparing antenatal care and screening with a home visiting service. The study reported significantly higher rates of abuse among poor, unmarried, teenage mothers, compared with the similar group who had received the intervention. There was also 40 per cent less chance of a visit to a doctor as a result of a physical injury or ingestion of poisonous substance, perhaps highlighting the potential for supportive intervention to prevent abuse through reducing factors that harm and promoting factors that help, such as parent capacity and knowledge through education. It could also be proposed that additional monitoring was evident in this study intervention.

Tertiary levels of prevention within the context of child protection can involve action taken within families where abuse has already taken place. Oates and Bross (1995) highlighted a lack of evidence to support the effectiveness of specific interventions targeted at both children and parents or carers. The complex nature of work at this level, and the difficulty of working with families who may be resistant to intervention, highlights the importance of primary and secondary prevention. It is perhaps difficult to determine whether the lack of success of interventions is a result of the abuse itself rather than the measures taken to address the impact of the events. An overemphasis on formal processes such as investigations, legal proceedings, case conferences, and child protection plans is potentially reducing the opportunity to provide effective therapeutic interventions focusing on parenting capacity and behaviour management for example.

Quaternary prevention can be seen as the last resort for a child where significant abuse has taken place. This is likely to be when a child has been removed from the abusive situation and requires ongoing support and treatment, perhaps in the form of counselling and ongoing monitoring of their health and well-being.

Child protection within a context of secondary prevention

In the context of child protection, secondary prevention is targeted at 'high-risk' families who are sometimes identified through screening processes within health services. As a result of the increased knowledge around risk factors and the cumulative effect these have on families, it is believed that secondary prevention is an important facet of child protection, and can be more effective than the limited success that has been experienced with tertiary prevention. Not only does secondary prevention act as a preventive strategy to abuse and maltreatment, but also it maximizes the chances of good developmental outcomes for children. Effective intervention lies partly with the ability to identify groups or individuals at increased risk of abuse. Such groups could include teenage mothers, parents who have mental health problems or who are misusing drugs or alcohol, and parents who have been abused themselves. It is also known that domestic abuse impacts negatively on children, even if they are not physically harmed. This identification of risk is important so that interventions can be provided to them in order to promote factors that may help and reduce factors that hinder.

A number of interventions have been identified as effective in providing support to parents thought to be at risk of abuse/maltreatment. In particular home visiting by professionals and volunteers antenatally and postnatally to women in high-risk groups has been found to be effective with respect to child protection. Although there are a number of studies in this area, some are more methodologically rigorous than others and the strength of their findings varies accordingly (Olds and Kitzman 1993; Macmillan et al. 1994; Clémant and Tourginy 1997). Macmillan et al. (1994) found that long-term home visiting programmes for parents with one or more risk factors (single parenthood, poverty, teenage parent status) was effective in the prevention of child physical abuse. However, the available evidence regarding the provision of short-term home visiting schemes was inconclusive.

The impact of a study by Olds et al. (1997) provides a good example of an effective long-term home visiting scheme. It was specifically designed to improve particular aspects of maternal and child functioning and therefore provided interventions that were directly related to known risk factors. The study consisted of 400 predominantly white women, all first-time mothers. Those allocated to the control group received antenatal care and screening only, and the intervention group received home visiting. Children aged 1–2 years in the intervention group were 40 per cent less likely to have visited a physician for a physical injury or ingestion of a poisonous substance. While no change occurred in the number of referrals for child maltreatment in the two years following the study, overall the children in the intervention group had 87 per cent fewer visits to the physician for physical injury or ingestion of poisonous substances compared with the control group. The intervention group children also lived in better family environments, which were more conducive to safety and intellectual and emotional development.

Although the study proved effective in a number of ways, it was evident that no change occurred in the rate of referrals for child maltreatment. As Olds et al. (1997) indicated, this may be partly because child abuse could be over-reported in the intervention group as they were under closer scrutiny than the comparison group. Olds et al. (1997) suggest that a longer period of intervention is perhaps required to make any impact on this issue, because different problems emerge as children get older, which parents may not have the capacity to deal with. In addition the environmental and socio-economic problems already faced by such families are long standing and may need constant attention over a longer period of time.

Now we consider a situation in which there may be at a higher level of concern, where perhaps more than one agency may be involved with a family or you as an early years professional may be thinking of consulting with or referring to other agencies as you are concerned that a child may be at risk of harm.

Case study 3: Katie and Amelia

Amelia is 5 months old; she has an older sister Katie, who is 2 years old. Their mother, Suzanne, who is 19 years old, has recently moved into the area to be nearer to her extended family, and to move away from the girls' father, who has been abusive towards her in the past. He does not know their current address. Her sister and mother live in a nearby town.

Suzanne brings Amelia to the drop-in baby clinic where you notice that Amelia has a plaster on her index finger and ask Suzanne about it. However Suzanne does not know how the injury happened and has not taken Amelia to the hospital or GP. She removes the plaster and shows you what looks like a fingertip burn extending around the fingertip completely: it looks inflamed. You ask her to see the doctor and arrange an appointment for later in the afternoon. When you telephone the surgery later, they report that Suzanne did not attend the appointment.

Alerts and warnings for Case study 3

Considerations	Possible responses	Useful agencies and contacts to support the family or you as a professional
Initial alert – what concerns you about this scenario? What have you noticed? Why is it of concern to you? How can you respond immediately? How do you believe the child is experiencing this moment? What is he or she likely to be feeling? How do you feel at this stage?		
Applying definitions of safeguarding and child protection: • Is this child being ill-treated? • Is it easy to recognize in this instance?		

(Continued)

(Continued)

Considerations	Possible responses	Useful agencies and contacts to support the family or you as a professional
• What is the child's understanding of this situation likely to be? • Are there any factors within the context of the scenario that may add to your concerns? • Are there any existing strengths you can identify in terms of existing factors or possible sources of support?		
How would you feel about initiating any action? Possible actions? What can you do? How will this impact on the child and the family, including the parents or carers?		
What is already known? What else do you need to know? Where could you get the information you need?		
Risks and benefits of action: consider the needs and impact on • the children, Katie and Amelia • the mother, Suzanne • the father and Suzanne's extended family • you as a professional • the service setting you work in		

Developing a line of thought that may lead to action

What are the risks? Is this abuse?

There may be a perfectly plausible reason for this injury. However the mother, Suzanne, either cannot explain what happened or could be covering up a deliberate injury. You may be inclined to go with your instincts in terms of what you already know about this family and the relationship you may have formed with the mother; however, in this case an unexplained injury in a child under

6 months who is unlikely to be mobile is of concern. Therefore the case should be referred to a social worker and the child examined by a medical practitioner. These should both be arranged simultaneously by the person who has the initial concern, although if a social worker from children's services agrees to investigate, she or he is likely to make arrangements with a medical practitioner for a medical examination. In Amelia's case, from a development perspective, she is not walking or crawling, although she may be able to make some attempt to roll; therefore the chances of her injuring herself are quite unlikely. The practitioner should consider how this injury occurred, for instance is it likely to be accidental or a deliberate injury? It is worrying that the mother, Suzanne, cannot recall an injury taking place. This creates some suspicion that information is being withheld, or she may genuinely not know how it happened. There is also a toddler in the equation of this case study; could Katie have caused the injury? If an incident or accident happened while Suzanne was out of the room, this could raise concerns regarding adequate supervision and boundaries. Therefore, even if parents or carers do not deliberately cause physical injuries, it can be categorized as abuse if there is evidence of neglect.

What makes you feel concerned?

We know from past cases such as Victoria Climbié and Peter Connelly (see Chapters 1 and 3) that concerns are not always acted upon appropriately. While this is easy to say in retrospective examination of cases such as these that have a poor outcome, it does perhaps highlight the need to have a healthy suspicion. This is achievable while still maintaining a positive relationship with parents and carers if communication channels and openness regarding concerns and actions are maintained. Alarm bells that could have been heeded in these historical cases were Victoria's demeanour and incontinence in the presence of her great-aunt; similarly Peter Connelly's fractiousness was not picked up on as a baby in significant pain and his facial injuries were covered by smearing with chocolate. The carers in these cases were manipulative and intimidating towards professionals; however the rights and needs of the child should be the paramount concern of the practitioner. Thus if the practitioner avoids the rule of optimism and cultural relativism highlighted by Dingwall et al. (1983) due to a change in circumstances, then concerns will be responded to, and appropriate action taken to safeguard the child's needs and promote optimum well-being. Where the concern is not substantiated, then if the situation has been handled sensitively and honestly, most parents and carers will understand.

The case of Peter Connelly highlights the difficulty for practitioners to always 'get it right': they are to a great extent dependent on the parent or carer and are unlikely to hear if there is someone else hurting the child, as indeed was the case with Peter. Practitioners are therefore urged to be sceptical and open minded as well as supportive to prevent an overenthusiastic reading of the situation.

The balance of potentially feeling like you may have 'accused' a mother unnecessarily and damaged the professional relationship formed with her needs to be balanced with an objective view about potential for the child to be at risk in terms of this injury and the possibility of further abuse taking place. Thus recognition of what could be a potentially non-accidental injury needs to be taken into consideration; you may be concerned by the lack of explanation and the type of injury being plausible as an accident. In this case study, not only is the injury unexplained but also the mother has not taken appropriate action such as seeing a GP about the injury. This is where messages from research and serious case reviews have informed processes and guidelines in the safeguarding arena, suggesting that an unexplained injury in a young child who is immobile warrants further investigation. In terms of what makes a practitioner feel concerned, thoughts from well-known cases may raise a concern, local and national guidelines and training regarding signs of abuse may trigger action. Even if deliberate abuse has not taken place, the mother may benefit from some advice and support regarding childcare practices, risks to young children, accident prevention, and access to local services.

What actions might you consider?

Actions may range from doing nothing, to telling someone, telling no one and writing a report, or making a referral. Do you know how to do this and who to refer to within your context? This is a question of where does the responsibility lie? It is not, for instance, acceptable to ask another practitioner to make the referral if you have noted the initial concern. In the past, some practitioners may have passed the concern on to the health visitor because 'they know the family', or the GP or paediatrician to make the physical assessment to determine if an injury is non-accidental.

What further actions might you consider?

Safeguarding intervention in this case should be initiated by the person who saw the baby first (this could be you), with a referral to a social worker via the advice and assessment team. Amelia should be seen by a paediatrician at the hospital. This may be through Accident and Emergency or direct to the Children's Department at the hospital. You would therefore need to seek supervision, advice and support from your line manager or a more experienced colleague to liaise directly with the paediatrician on call. The health visitor would also need to be contacted to discuss the response. Other practitioners and services involved with this family would need to share information, to support the initial investigation by the social worker. In this case the result was that a joint visit was carried out by the social worker and health visitor to look at the location and potential circumstances of the injury. A wall-mounted metal electric fire (without a fireguard) in the lounge was determined to be the source of the injury. The mother

Suzanne had heard Amelia cry out while she was in the kitchen: it was thought that Katie, the 2 year old, had moved Amelia by dragging her on her changing mat, putting her in a position where she was able to touch the hot metal surround of the fire.

Suzanne needs to be advised of the serious nature of the injury: despite it seeming like a small area, fingertip burns are potentially very serious in young children. The need for safety measures such as a fireguard and supervision were also highlighted to the mother. Communication between various agencies resulted in some additional childcare support to allow Suzanne to attend college. Ongoing supportive visiting was provided to Suzanne by the health visitor, her family also tried to help more, recognizing her social and emotional isolation.

This is an example of how supporting the mother can impact on the well-being of the children; however, care needs to be taken to avoid focusing more on the carer than the child. The children need an advocate to promote their well-being if the parents or carers either can't or won't do this. Evidence from previous cases shows that parents can distract professionals from focusing on the needs of the children as the paramount concern. This may be unintentional, particularly in chaotic families where the parents or carers themselves have many problems. However, it can also be a deliberate act on the part of the parents or carers to cover up abuse (such as Baby Peter's mother, Tracey Connelly). If the professionals do not maintain their focus on the child's needs or journey, then this is a form of collusion.

In Suzanne's case she appears to be socially isolated, having moved into a new area, although her extended family were not too far away geographically. Through a joint assessment by the social worker and health visitor, risk assessment of the living space and care provided was undertaken.

In addition to accident prevention advice (specifically regarding supervision and use of a fireguard) childcare options were explored to allow Suzanne to attend college. She was also offered voluntary family support visiting schemes in addition to the supportive visiting and postnatal depression screening offered by some health visiting teams. Information about local services and groups was provided. This can be easily accessed by clients and professionals through local service directories such as 'Help4Me' (www.help4me.info/). Secondary prevention in this case meant that appropriate inter-agency support and parent education was coordinated and targeted to prevent further incidents or escalation of parental stress. This would of course have been better employed before the incident occurred.

Any intervention offered to parents and carers to improve their skills will have an effect on their children, particularly pre-school children who are likely to be spending longer periods with their main carers. The Sure Start initiative represented an attempt to target young children through input with their carers. Similarly the pre-school education provision for all young children has provided opportunities for young children to experience routines, social and educational opportunities that not all children would otherwise be exposed to.

Key messages

- While prevention of abuse is the ideal, you may not always achieve this. However, early intervention can prevent escalation of concerns.
- Providing support involves working with families effectively to assess strengths and need and monitor concerns, together with supportive measures. This may result in you having a more successful engagement with parents and carers.
- Effective inter-agency working to share information and provide seamless services is also essential.
- As the level of need rises, you may find it more difficult to achieve better outcomes for children, particularly if families are stigmatized by service involvement and the labelling that safeguarding provision can imply.
- This chapter raises the importance of early prevention through universal service provision. If you know the causative factors of abuse, this can facilitate screening and targeted support, identified through universal services such as health and early years provision.

8 Assessment and referral: passing on concerns

Chapter Overview

This chapter examines the procedural requirements relating to assessment and referral. The involvement of a multiprofessional and multidisciplinary workforce and its purpose in supporting this particular stage of information gathering are fully considered. A case study exploring the likely dynamics of a multiprofessional group involved in assessment will identify key strategies for developing a coherent approach to understanding the nature of safeguarding concerns relating to an abuse case and then explore likely and appropriate responses to it.

What is assessment?

An assessment is a key practitioner method of gathering information and insights relating to a particular child who is suspected or likely to be suffering from significant harm. The point of the first development of insight and information will probably be with the practitioners who know the child best. This could be you in the case of a baby or a very young child with a crèche or nursery worker. If there is some involvement with the family in the community, this could be a Sure Start outreach worker or a family resource worker. It can in effect be almost any of several practitioners who have from time to time direct contact with families, carers and children. The child will represent at this point to the early years professional, as potentially being harmed or having experienced some aspect of ill-treatment as defined through the physical, sexual, emotional or neglect indicators of abuse. There might be a bruise that appears to be in an awkward place or one that could reflect the use of an object including a hand, that may have left the impression of a handprint. An apparent injury that appears non-accidental or circumstantially questionable, or some aspect of the child's appearance, demeanour or behaviour to indicate areas of abuse such as neglect, failure to thrive, sexual abuse or emotional ill-treatment may have been the trigger for the practitioner to develop a sense of concern for the child.

Assessment has increasingly focused not only on identifying instances of abuse and potential for harm, but also on identifying the needs of children and the strengths and weaknesses within their current context, in order to determine the next course of action for you as the practitioner. This process has been initiated by key documents such as the *Framework for the Assessment of Children in Need and their Families* (DH 2000) and later supported by processes such as the Common Assessment Framework (CAF) in order to target integrated support at more vulnerable children.

Within a safeguarding context Holland (2004) outlines assessment and decision-making processes, highlighting a range of approaches that have been utilized, including diagnostic, predictive, and broader social and bureaucratic assessments with a considerable amount of overlap between these categories. However, according to Smale et al. (1993), there are three types of assessment processes:

- The questioning model
- The procedural model
- The exchange model.

The exchange model relates closely to Parton and O'Byrne's (2000) notion of constructive assessment, which although formal and procedural to some extent, needs to consider strengths as well as identifying problems and needs within families. This is all set within the context of uncertainty and the knowledge that your judgement and actions as an early years professional are potentially so crucial to a child's well-being.

O'Hanlon (1995) pays considerable attention to the distinction between emotions, thoughts and actions (cited in Parton and O'Byrne 2000: 73). This is particularly relevant when considering rational decision-making (Allison 1971, cited in Holland 2004) or cost-benefit (Hall 1982) models for the assessment of needs while balancing risk. Holland (2004) suggests that there is potential for irregularity of parameters within the assessor (irrational behaviour or decisions), or the potential variables within the context for example, resulting in a lack of rationality or objectivity within the decision-making process. Parton and O'Byrne (2000: 146) highlight that a more positive approach is required when considering risk assessment. This could mean that rather than considering the worst case scenario, that is what could go wrong, that we should instead focus on aspects such as potential certain versus uncertain gains (or losses). An overemphasis on risk does not necessarily result in better outcomes for children; this can be seen clearly in cases where children have died despite the apparent involvement of services.

Munro (2008) introduces the concept of risk within assessment processes, potentially shifting the emphasis not only from the 'here and now' but also to the future well-being of a child. A risk assessment makes a prediction about what may happen to the child (Munro 2008: 59). It can be considered relatively easy to assess a child's current risk of harm within an immediate safeguarding scenario, particularly if the event is serious in nature, such as a sudden physical injury or evidence of several cumulative events relating to severe neglect. Even in serious incidents such as these, the future well-being of the child could be secured given appropriate support, whereas it is commonly accepted that minor incidents often precede more serious episodes of abuse. The reason risk assessment can be so complicated is that it involves uncertainty.

Munro (2008: 58) outlines risk as a new concept in child protection practice, perhaps representative of an increasing focus on child abuse cases and practitioner responses to these in the media. There can be varying perceptions of risk depending on the culture and experiences of the individual and the organization (Douglas 1992), with the resultant discourse potentially downplaying or normalizing some risks, while others are overemphasized. The calculation of risk depends on the creation of an 'average' individual based on the average of the whole population, meaning that danger can then be moved from something completely unpredictable and unpreventable to a schedule of probabilities and predictabilities. If we use statistics to explain this further, a one in four risk of harm can also be interpreted as a three in four chance of no harm occurring. This link with statistical analysis potentially moves safeguarding practice away from intuition and experience to processes and probabilities, Munro (2008: 58) terms this 'the conflict between the analytic and intuitive approaches'. Furthermore this overemphasis on process rather than intuition has been criticized in the Munro reviews (2010, 2011) with a need to avoid predictive practice, focusing rather on the assessment of need within the family context and emphasizing the child's journey not only to minimize risk but also to maximize well-being. This brings to mind Sinclair et al.'s (1997) representation of the child's passage through childhood as a snakes and ladder board; where the ladders represented supportive factors and the snakes the factors that hinder. Therefore when determining the best course of action, you need to consider the strengths and weaknesses within the situation and family context, in conjunction with any immediate and longer-term risks of harm. An overemphasis on the potential for immediate harm in safeguarding practice could also divert attention from earlier preventative intervention.

Although adopting a risk approach can be seen as having some negative consequences, it can provide good results in genuinely high-risk cases, where an assessment has highlighted concerns based perhaps on evidence from research, serious case reviews and your personal experience as a practitioner. Indeed objecting to a risk approach is difficult because the idea of risk is a product of the culture in which we live, where we continually try to reduce risks in order to prevent harmful events such as accidents. Classic examples would include increasing health and safety legislation and parental tendencies to restrict adventurous activities.

Is risk assessment easy to implement and how does it relate to a practitioner's feelings of concern?

Feelings are important, but they can be subjective rather than objective assessments of the strengths and needs evident within a child's particular circumstances. Assessment can provide a formal structure for exploring what you know about a child and their family; it can also facilitate documentation of your concerns and allow a full assessment of events through a chronology.

Key questions to ask yourself could include:

1. What is there about the child that causes me to feel some degree of concern?
2. What is already known about this child?
3. Are my concerns reasonable or might I be overreacting?
4. Are there any immediate notes to make?
5. Who can I share this information with?
6. Any initial actions to take?

The Signs of Well-Being tool and CAF discussed in Part 1 can be useful to explore your concerns together with the child and/or their family. When utilized by all the practitioners working with a child following the same template, the various pieces of the jigsaw puzzle can be put together, providing a fuller picture of the strengths and needs within a family. More formal assessments would be utilized once a referral and investigation has been commenced by a social worker from the children's services advice and assessment team. These will now be outlined to give you as the early years professional insight into the process.

Purpose of Initial Assessment (Section 17, Children Act 1989)

The focus of the Initial Assessment should be the welfare of the child, the purpose being for the social worker to ascertain during the course of an Initial Assessment whether the child is 'in need' (Section 17, Children Act 1989) or if there is reasonable cause to suspect that this child is 'suffering, or is likely to suffer significant harm' (Section 47, Children Act 1989). The Initial Assessment should be done following or in accordance with the CAF, thus the information from the CAF can inform the Initial Assessment.

Timescale of Initial Assessment

The Initial Assessment must be completed within a maximum of ten working days of the date of the referral, while the referral may initially have been via telephone contact. There is an expectation that this would be followed up with a written CAF within 24–48 hours. If the timescales are not met, where it becomes apparent that a timescale will require extension, the team manager within the children's social care duty and investigation team must review the file, record the reason for the extension and agree the new timescale. In reality most are undertaken within seven working days. If the scale of concern is high it could be undertaken on the day of the referral and the decision made to conduct a strategy meeting with the various agencies and professionals involved with the family, followed by a Core Assessment as part of a Section 47 enquiry.

Who carries out the Initial Assessment?

The Initial Assessment must be led by a qualified and experienced social worker. The social worker should, in consultation with their manager and the other agencies involved with the child and family, carefully plan action with clarity about who is doing what, including:

- Whether the child or children should be seen and spoken to with or without their parents.
- When to interview the child or children (within an appropriate timescale).
- When to interview parents and any other relevant family members.
- What the child and parents should be told of any concerns.
- What contributions (historical and contemporaneous information) to the assessment from other agencies should be and who will provide them. This may include each of the professionals involved requesting information from equivalent agencies abroad if the child has lived outside the UK.

Seeing the child

The child must be seen within a timescale that is appropriate to the nature of the concerns at the time of referral, according to an agreed plan. This includes observing and communicating with the child in a manner appropriate to his or her age and understanding and ascertaining the child's wishes and feelings about the provision of services. Interviews with the child should be undertaken in the preferred language of the child. For some children with a disability, interviews may require the use of non-verbal communication methods. This can of course present difficulties when working with very young children. However as discussed in Part 1, the child's perspective can still be considered by observing their responses and considering what is appropriate for a child's stage of development.

Agency checks and information gathering

Personal information about non-professional referrers should not be disclosed to third parties (including subject families and other agencies) without consent. The parents' or carers' permission should be sought before discussing a referral and Initial Assessment about them with other agencies. However, there are circumstances where information can be shared without consent. If the manager decides to proceed with checks without parental knowledge or permission, they must record the reasons why, such as doing so would:

- prejudice the child's welfare
- aggravate seriously concerning behaviours of the adult
- increase the risk of further significant harm to the child
- prejudice a criminal investigation.

The checks should be undertaken directly with involved professionals and not through messages with intermediaries. The relevant agency should be informed of the reason for the enquiry, whether or not parental consent has been obtained, and asked for their assessment of the child in the light of information presented. All discussions and interviews with family members (which may include the child) should be undertaken in their preferred language. Where appropriate for some people, non-verbal communication methods may be used. The social worker should make it clear to families (where appropriate) and other agencies that the information provided for this assessment may be shared with other agencies and contribute to the written form completed at the end of the assessment. Consent to do so is of course preferable. However, the family should be made aware that it is legally possible to do so without their consent if the child is considered at risk of harm.

Notifying the police

It will not necessarily be clear whether a criminal offence has been committed, which means that even initial discussions with a child should be undertaken in a way that minimizes distress to them and maximizes the likelihood that they will provide accurate and complete information, avoiding leading or suggestive questions. The police must be informed at the earliest opportunity if a crime may have been committed. The police will then be able to decide whether to commence a criminal investigation.

Outcome of Initial Assessment

Following an Initial Assessment, the social worker should decide on the next course of action, following discussion with the child and family, unless such a discussion may place a child at risk of significant harm. If there are concerns about a parent or carer's ability to protect a child from harm, careful consideration should be given to what parents should be told, when and by whom, taking full account of the child's welfare.

The possible outcomes of this Initial Assessment include no further action; an initial plan for immediate provision of child in need services to promote the child's heath and development (this would be in the form of a child action meeting); instigation of a Core Assessment or a more in-depth assessment of the child's needs and circumstances; instigation of a strategy discussion or multi-agency meeting and a Section 47 enquiry alongside a Core Assessment; or emergency action to protect a child. The outcome of the Initial Assessment should be discussed with the child and family, and provided to them in written form; exceptions to this are where this might place a child at risk of harm or jeopardize an inquiry. Other considerations include taking account of the confidentiality provided to both lay and professional referrers.

A team manager within children's social care must approve the outcomes of an Initial Assessment and must record and authorize the reasons for decisions, future actions to be taken and also that the child has been seen or there has been a recorded management decision that this is not appropriate. Other necessities include that the needs of all children in the household have been considered; that a chronology of events (usually at the front of the forms) has been completed and updated as required; written feedback has been provided to the family, other agencies and referrers about the outcome of this stage of the referral in a manner consistent with respecting the confidentiality and welfare of the child. However, if the criteria for initiating a Section 47 enquiry are met at any stage during an Initial Assessment, this Section 17 assessment should be regarded as concluded.

Core Assessment

Core Assessments must be completed within a maximum of 35 working days. Social care staff are responsible for the coordination and completion of the assessment, drawing upon information provided by other agencies working with the family. Core Assessments commence when an Initial Assessment recommends that a further complex assessment is required; a strategy discussion meeting initiates a Section 47 enquiry; or if new information obtained on an open case indicates a Core Assessment is required.

During the course and upon completion of Initial and Core Assessments, it will be necessary to decide what services should be provided. The services will be appropriate depending on the needs of the child or children. A child in need plan should be agreed with family and other agencies, usually a child in need or child action meeting would take place. If further action or investigation is not instigated, the Core Assessment should be monitored and reviewed regularly at maximum intervals of six months.

Section 47 enquiries

Where a child is suspected to be suffering, or likely to suffer, significant harm, the local authority is required by Section 47 of the Children Act 1989 to make enquiries in the form of a Core Assessment, to enable it to decide whether it should take any action to safeguard and promote the welfare of the child. This usually takes place after the Initial Assessment and strategy meeting. Section 47 enquiries are usually conducted by a social worker, sometimes jointly with the police, and must be completed within 15 days of a strategy discussion. Where concerns are confirmed and the child is judged to be at continued risk of significant harm, a child protection conference should be convened.

Responsibility for undertaking Section 47 enquiries lies with the local authority in whose area the child lives or is 'found'. For the purposes of these procedures, the local authority in which the child lives is called the 'home authority' and the local authority in which the child is found is the child's 'host authority'. 'Found' means the physical location where the child suffers the incident of harm or neglect, or is identified to be at risk of harm or neglect, for example day nursery or school, boarding school, hospital or one-off event, such as a day trip or holiday home.

Whenever a child is harmed or concerns are raised that a child may be at risk of harm or neglect, the host authority is responsible for informing the home authority immediately and invited to participate in the strategy discussion or multi-agency meeting to plan action to protect the child. Only when the home authority explicitly accepts responsibility is the host authority relieved of the responsibility to take emergency and ongoing action. Such acceptance should occur as soon as possible and should be confirmed in writing.

We now explore a case study where a variety of agencies are involved in a more complex scenario.

Case study 4: the Khan family

Sameer, 35 years old, is a taxi driver who has lived in England from a very young age. Farhat, 33 years old, is a housewife who does sewing work at home; she speaks very little English. They have two boys, Sajid, 8 years old, and Hamid, 6 years old, who attend the local primary school; their daughter Aisha, 3 years old, attends nursery at the same school in the afternoons. The family live with the paternal grandparents in a privately owned, three-bedroomed terraced house.

Farhat has asked for help with behaviour management strategies in the past. There are few toys in the house. Aisha often goes into visitors' handbags and work bags to find trinkets and playthings; she is a lively little girl. There is an unguarded boiler-type fire in the main living area with a naked flame. Despite repeated reference to safety advice, this remains a hazard. All the children's immunizations are up to date.

Farhat has reported domestic abuse in the past on numerous occasions. She left once with the children, but was brought back by her husband. She has no family in England: she left them in Pakistan when she married Sameer. She is now reporting that the abuse is continuing, her husband and his family do not want her to go out to work, and there are loud and violent arguments involving the children. Farhat reports that both she and the children are hit by her husband and his parents. They are critical of her parenting and housekeeping skills.

Sajid and Hamid are in trouble at school for bad behaviour, including swearing, bullying and looking at girls' underwear. Sajid has poor concentration in class and frequently forgets his glasses. On this particular day the headmistress phones home to ask someone to bring them in for Sajid. Aisha answers the phone and says mummy is not there: she appears to be alone in the house. When Aisha comes to nursery the next day she is more subdued than usual and you notice a linear lesion across the palm of her hand.

Alerts and warnings for Case study 4

Considerations	Possible responses	Useful agencies and contacts to support the family or you as a professional
Initial alert – what concerns you about this scenario?		
Applying definitions of safeguarding and child protection: • Are the children being ill-treated? • Is it easy to recognize in this instance?		
How would you feel about initiating any actions? Possible actions? What can you do? How will this impact on the child and the family, including the parents or carers?		
What is already known? What else do you need to know? Where could you get the information you need?		
Risks and benefits of action: consider the needs and impact on • the children, Sajid and Hamid • the mother, Farhat • the father, Sameer • the grandparents and extended family • you as a professional • the service setting you work in		

We now consider Case study 4 within the context of the five chapters in Part 1 of the book.

History: what can it teach?

There are two kinds of history to consider in this case. The first is a contemporary history of child protection cases and what they may have to show in relation to this case study. The second historical area is the family and its position within the local community.

If we consider the particular aspects of family history that the case study suggests to us, we can identify a number of historical features which we will articulate as brief points:

- Sameer has been in England since being a small child.
- Farhat has not been in England very long and speaks little English, and therefore she appears more dependent on Sameer as a result.
- Parenting issues: there are some safety problems in the house. Farhat has asked for support with behaviour management. There are no toys perhaps indicating lack of stimulating play.
- Extended family living together: do the parents-in-law have any input into childcare arrangements? Do they enhance or worsen family relationships?
- There is a history of domestic abuse which seems to be recurring. There are connections between domestic and child abuse generally in terms of the potential impact on the children, even if they are not physically abused or present when the abuse takes place.
- The two boys are demonstrating behaviour problems at school.
- Aisha has been left home alone unsupervised. Her behaviour indicates that this may have happened before and she now has a physical injury.
- Is there a history of non-attendance at school or nursery?
- Are there any other community influences on the family such as religion and work, for example taxi drivers typically work long and unsocial hours.

How are the child's rights being recognized?

The needs of the children should be of paramount concern; however, the family dynamics suggest that the children's basic physical and emotional needs are not being fully met due to several factors. In particular Aisha's right to be kept safe and free from abuse is in question. There are issues around supervision and boundaries, in that Aisha is left alone inappropriately and the boys are displaying age-inappropriate behaviour, suggesting they are not being protected and could be in danger of exploitation.

While the cultural identity of the family should be recognized and acknowledged in any assessment and proceedings, it should not be considered a means to explain the abuse. Cultural relativism is highlighted by Dingwall et al. (1983), where abuse can sometimes be minimized through cultural explanations of behaviour. Victoria Climbié provides a pertinent example of this where her subdued demeanour was attributed to culture rather than fear of her great-aunt. Thus signs of abuse must be viewed objectively rather than through a cultural lens.

Ethical practice

The needs of the children in terms of assessing their well-being need to be of paramount concern; however, the impact of family dynamics and the well-being of the mother are also of concern. Farhat may have little access to family or community resources due to her isolation from her relatives through geographical location; she is also isolated from the wider community and services due to language and cultural barriers.

Focusing in on the child: what is the child experiencing?

All of the children would be assessed and/or interviewed by the social worker. Some of this information would be gathered from the various practitioners working with the family through discussion and on the CAF forms provided by each agency. It is important that these assessments remain child focused by speaking to the children about any difficulties they are experiencing or considering what effects the events are having on the children. If the child cannot articulate what has happened or how they feel, the likely impact on them should be explored. This could be based on evidence from research or the normal development expectations of children.

Community involvement

In this case there is direct involvement of the extended family; there is also potentially a wider cultural and possibly religious affiliation. The school community is directly involved with the three children, with the headmistress, school teachers and nursery staff able to provide assessment of strengths and needs and offer support. In terms of professional communities, there is likely to be involvement from the school nurse, GP and health visitor. From a social care perspective, the social worker from advice and assessment would perform an initial investigation in terms of a Section 17 assessment. There could also be input from support services such as family support or behaviour management.

Local statutory and third sector or voluntary services may also be able to offer some input. These can be found on a local service directory such as Help4me (www.help4me.info/) by the family themselves or any practitioner working with them. The police were also called into this situation by the headmistress when Aisha was found to be alone. They have the power to issue an Emergency Protection Order and arrest Aisha's mother for child abandonment.

What have the carers to say about the concerns?

All members of the family would be interviewed, including the mother, father and grandparents. Their understanding of the potential impact of events and their behaviour towards the children would be crucial in the assessment. Their willingness to engage with practitioners, services and the assessment process would also be taken into consideration, recognizing also that carers can be manipulative and devious. The needs of parents and carers is important in terms of how they impact on their ability to provide care, however this should not supersede the needs of the children which are of course of paramount importance.

What actions might be considered by the practitioner?

This may range from doing nothing, to telling someone, telling no one and writing a report, or making a referral. In this case the police were called as it is illegal to leave a child unattended. The police (along with the NSPCC) have the power to initiate an Emergency Protection order and take the child to a place of safety if required. For this they would need to liaise with the children's social care team to identify temporary foster care or place the children with family or friends in some instances.

In this case the mother returned before Aisha was removed and the father was contacted to return home from work. Farhat was arrested and charged, resulting in designation as a Schedule 1 offender according to the Children and Young Persons Act 1933, which lists a wide range of offences against children and young persons under the age of 18. These include sexual assaults, various forms of abuse, and other forms of maltreatment including murder, cruelty, neglect, and offences resulting in bodily injury to the victim. Schedule 1 status is for life, meaning that Farhat will remain on the local authority register of Schedule 1 offenders, with her details being passed on should she move to another area. It also means she can never work with children. Where a Schedule 1 offender is known to be living with children, like Farhat, a child protection investigation ensues, thus a Section 17 enquiry was initiated. This involved gathering information from the school staff for each of the three children. Health staff who have contact with the family would include the health visitor, school nurse and GP.

While this may feel negative, a single incident (leaving Aisha home alone and the subsequent injury) effectively focused services more clearly on the needs of the children, facilitating a full assessment of their needs and drew attention to a continuum of incidents that as a single event may not have caused safeguarding intervention. All the agencies involved with the family were able to contribute to the assessment through reports to a child protection conference. Services were effectively coordinated resulting in several interventions:

- Farhat received family support to explore and develop her parenting skills.
- Sameer was encouraged to attend anger management classes.
- The grandparents were found to be adding to the deterioration in family dynamics, punishing the children in an inappropriate physical manner and restricting and criticizing Farhat's parenting. This resulted in them leaving the home to live with their daughter.
- School staff members were able to work with the children more effectively knowing the background to their behaviour.

- Services became more seamless, with the health visitor and nursery nurse from health services coordinating the supportive visits with the work being done by family support services.
- It was made clear that the supportive visit included a monitoring role, with regular core group meetings following the child protection conference, which had registered the children under a child protection plan due to actual physical harm (in Aisha's case), neglect and potential for further harm.

It is important to see registration, or what is now termed being on a child protection plan, not as an end, but rather as the start of a process requiring intervention, monitoring and regular review to ensure progress is being made. Decisions can range from not registering the children (with clear follow-up in the form of child in need/child action proceedings); registering under a child protection with regular core group (key people working with the family and the parents or carers attending) meetings; or a decision to remove the children to alternative care.

Key messages

- Assessment of the strengths and needs within a child's situation is crucial for all children. It allows factors that may impact on a child's well-being to be identified at an early stage and preventative measures to be put in place.
- This may take the form of a Common Assessment Framework where any practitioner working with a child can provide information to assess levels of need or refer to another agency.
- This process may also be utilized in a child in need context or as part of conference proceedings following a Section 17 inquiry by a social worker.
- The uniform nature of the assessment means that key information is shared effectively building a fuller picture of a child and their family and social context.
- Section 17 and 47 inquiries are more formal investigations undertaken by a social worker once concerns are expressed by a practitioner or member of the public and a referral has been made.
- Risk assessment needs to focus not only on the potential for the child to be harmed but also on what will reduce those risks.

9   Teamwork and safeguarding

Chapter Overview

This chapter explores the recent and current legislation which emphasizes the importance of coherent teamwork practice, particularly in relation to safeguarding babies and young children. The chapter considers the nature of teams and the ways in which by working together effective safeguards may be afforded to vulnerable or abused babies and young children. A case study is presented for you to examine the aims and objectives as well as the roles and functions of teamworking in relation to a specific case.

Working with other practitioners and agencies

It is important to be aware of the importance of working together and crucially to understand *why* it is important. This includes knowing what agencies and organizations exist within the community and their role in the safeguarding process. Understanding your responsibilities as an early years professional and being able to work together with staff from other agencies and organizations will enhance the individual and collective ability to safeguard children and promote their well-being. The constructive impact of positive attitudes, particularly towards other people, groups and agencies will facilitate mutual respect, challenging sensitively, listening to each other and care and support.

Policy direction supports inter-professional working (Laming 2003; DfES 2004a; DH 2004). This has been spelt out clearly by the government in legislation through the Children Acts 1989 and 2004), and in policy guidance: 'The safety and welfare of children is the responsibility of the Local Authority, working in partnership with other public organizations, the voluntary sector and service users and carers' (DCSF 2010).

Yet a review of frontline safeguarding practices by Munro (2010) has found that there is an overemphasis on processes and procedure rather than meaningful relationships between agencies. While it is important to understand the difference between agencies in terms of what they can contribute to assessment, support and monitoring of families, it is timely to remember that we are all working towards the same outcomes in terms of a healthy child who can thrive and achieve. There are many similarities in common responsibilities identified in *Working Together*

Figure 9.1 'General's family' by Octavio Ocampo. flatrock.org.nz/.../can_this _be_true.htm

to Safeguard Children (DCSF 2010) such as clear priorities; commitment of senior management; clear lines of accountability; safe recruitment procedures; procedures for dealing with allegations against staff; staff training; child protection policy; arrangements to work with other agencies and a child-centred culture.

Consider the agencies and professionals you work with. Who else works with the children in your care? Are there other professionals and agencies working with children that you are not in contact with? These may be working with other members of the family such as older children and parents or carers. Consider the image in Figure 9.1: how many people can you see?

You should have found nine people (or just faces), perhaps not easily, and you may not have found them all. This highlights that there may be many people who work with children, but some may not be easily apparent. Case study 5 will help you to explore who else you may need to consult or work with to make a difference for a family. Start perhaps by making a list of professionals and agencies you have had contact with in your dealings with families. Then consider are there others you have not worked with yet? These may be universal services that all children should have contact with, such as a midwife, health visitor, GP, schools and so on. There are other agencies that deal with more specialist services, such as speech and language therapy, orthoptics, dieticians, family support, behaviour specialists, psychologists, social workers, and special educational needs, to name but a few.

If you are not sure what agencies or services are available in your area access your local service directory, which is easily searchable by both families and practitioners, providing information about a broad range of services both mainstream and voluntary, thus facilitating direct access by families and better, more informed referrals by practitioners. For instance Bolton has commissioned its Service Directory solution from a company called Help4Me (www.Help4me.info), together with seven other authorities from the North West of England who also use this product, so the information provided in the directory is available across a wider geographical area. By understanding what services are available, what their eligibility criteria are and mechanisms for accessing services, families should have improved access to the most appropriate services. Practitioners also have a time saving if they are able to access information from one source rather than chase around for information. However, it is reliant on services providing current information about their provision.

Before considering the role of other professionals within the case study it is useful to think first what you can individually provide as a practitioner and what your agency can provide. Ask yourself the following questions:

- What are the key aspects of my role?

- What is the structure of my team and organization?

- What are my responsibilities for safeguarding children?

- What is a 'day/hour in the life' of my team working in safeguarding?

- What happens in my team when there is a concern?

- What aspects of safeguarding work do I find easy and difficult?

- Where do I usually come into conflict with other agencies and why?

Case study 5: Kylie and Louise

The people involved in this case study are:

- Susan Oxley (mother, 31 years old)
- Dave Smith (father of Louise, 42 years old)
- Jamie Oxley (15 years old)

- Kylie Oxley (4 years old)
- Louise Smith (6 months old)
- Brian Oxley (Jamie and Kylie's father, 38 years old)

You are an early years professional working in a children's centre where Kylie attends the pre-school class five mornings a week and Louise has attended the crèche while Susan completes a childcare course, as she wants to be a childminder.

Kylie's attendance is usually reasonable, although she is often brought by her older brother, Jamie. Recently her presentation is poor in terms of cleanliness, wearing the same clothes for a few days, and she is always hungry. She is underachieving and struggles to concentrate on activities. Kylie should wear glasses and have regular check-ups. She never has her glasses with her and she has missed her last two appointments. You have tried to see her mother about this but she has avoided you, and has now stopped attending the childcare course. Louise has also not been in the crèche, where members of staff raise the concern that she appears underweight and slightly delayed in her development.

Practice reflection points

Case study 5

- What are your concerns?

- Who else would it be useful to talk to?

- What further information would you need?

- What action would you like to take?

Health visitor

You ring the health visitor first as you know her from the regular drop-in sessions she does in the clinic. She is also concerned about Louise. Her mum Susan did not attend for antenatal and postnatal appointments and she agrees that she is underweight and developmentally delayed. She has not been brought for her immunizations. When she talked to the mother, Susan, about this, she assured her she intends to come to the next clinic but she never does. Louise also seems quiet and withdrawn during visits.

Practice reflection points

Case study 5

- What action could you agree upon?

- Is there any other information you might need?

- Who could provide it?

You both agree to try to see Susan and the children to discuss your concerns. The health visitor will do a visit, while you will try to see Susan at the centre when Kylie is being dropped off or collected. When you ask Susan to come in for a few minutes to speak with you, she is very reluctant to stay, she looks unkempt and keeps her head down; however, you notice a bruise on her temple.

Practice reflection points

Case study 5

- What would you say to Susan about your concerns regarding the children?

- What would you ask her about the bruise?

Susan dismisses the injury when asked about it and says she hasn't got time to discuss the children as her husband is waiting for her. Dave arrives as you are speaking to ask what is going on and why she is still there.

At this stage you should document your concerns and speak to your manager and/or senior person responsible for child protection. You agree that it would be useful to ask for a consultation with social services advice and assessment as they may have more information about other members of the family, including any concerns about Dave. When you ring the health visitor to share your progress, she explains that she has had no access visits and that she has received a domestic violence information slip from the police to say they had been called to an incident at the home.

You agree to call a child action meeting as the children appear to be at risk of harm – including potential for physical injury due to the domestic abuse, risk of emotional abuse and possible neglect due to the delayed development, poor basic care, and lack of attention to medical needs.

Practice reflection points

Care study 4

- Who would you invite to a meeting about this family?

- What information and support could you offer?

- What information and support could other agencies offer?

- What level of need would you say this family met on the Child Concern/Framework for Action model (see Chapter 6)?

Professionals involved with the family could include the following people, although not all of these may necessarily attend the meeting; some may send a report or one representative from the agency who has the most involvement with the family may attend. The important practice point to note is that the information and action from each agency could create a fuller picture and more effective collective response.

Education	Teacher – secondary school; head of year or child protection lead
Early Years	Teacher – pre-school; crèche leader; head teacher, nursery manager or designated person child protection
Health	Health visitor; school nurse; nursery nurse; orthoptist; general practitioner
Social care	Advice and assessment social worker; education social worker; learning disability social worker; family support
Police/Probation	Domestic Violence Unit police officer; probation officer; youth offending team member
Voluntary sector	Youth worker; Home Start

Child action meeting

Susan and Dave attend with the children, the meeting is held in the children's centre at 4 pm so that Jamie can attend after school; the younger children are cared for in the children's centre while the meeting takes place. All reports should have been shared with the parents or carers prior to the meeting in a spirit of openness. Jamie and Kylie's father, Brian, has also been invited to the meeting.

Health

The health visitor attends representing her agency; she has a brief report from the school nurse. The GP also sends a brief report; he has known Susan Oxley for 12 years. She suffered postnatal depression after the birth of Louise and she is being prescribed antidepressants; she has refused to be referred to the mental health team. Health services have wide-ranging responsibilities for protecting children both in the community and hospital settings. They may be involved in supporting children in need and identifying abuse. They need to be able to assess, plan and respond, and contribute to assessments and meetings about children and young people. Universal child health services are provided to all children by health visitors, school nurses, nursery nurses, general practitioners and community paediatricians in the form of routine health and development surveillance and advice and support. Additional services are targeted based on assessment of need. More specialist services are provided including speech therapy, hearing assessment, orthoptics, behaviour management, biomechanics and referral to hospital services such as community paediatric nurses and hospital doctors. Hospital services in direct contact with children include Maternity, Paediatrics, Neonatal Unit and Accident and Emergency departments.

If a professional has a concern they may seek clinical supervision from more senior peers or the 'designated/named professionals' who can advise on the safeguarding process and contribute to serious case reviews. They can call child action meetings, refer to other agencies, or consult and refer to the children's social care advice and assessment team by telephone, following this referral up in writing with a CAF form.

Education

The head of year from Jamie's secondary school attends; staff members are concerned about Jamie, his attendance is poor and he is underachieving. His appearance is usually poor and he sometimes smells. As a result he is ostracized by the other children and a victim of bullying. He also bullies younger children occasionally. He has been suspected of stealing food and small amounts of money from the other children on occasions. He has previously been charged for shoplifting. Professionals involved with Jamie could include the teacher: this could be his form teacher, head of year or the named professional with responsibility for safeguarding), school nurse, educational social worker or youth offending team, a multi-agency team who supervise young people 'subject to pre-court interventions and statutory court disposals' (DCSF 2010: 65). They work with young people who are in need and some who will be the victims of abuse.

Schools have a responsibility to ensure that children are safe in school and are well placed to identify abuse and children in need. Staff need to be familiar with all aspects of the safeguarding process and will be expected to contribute to that process, e.g. by referral, sharing information, providing support, etc. Additional support for Jamie could also be offered by Connexions services, providing advice, counselling, advocacy, referral to specialist agencies, for young people. All staff must be aware of safeguarding issues and able to refer appropriately.

Other attendees at the meeting

From the children's centre your manager agrees to chair the meeting and you have your own report and that provided by the crèche leader. The social worker has shared some information via the consultation process; however she refuses to attend the meeting unless concerns escalate but asks you to inform her of any outcomes. The social worker from the learning disability team sends a brief report. The team has known Susan Oxley's family for 15 years. Susan spent a period in care as a teenager when her mother was unable to cope with her behaviour. Her younger brother and sister were removed due to neglect. She has mild learning difficulties.

A representative from the probation services attends the meeting. Dave Smith is the subject of a two-year probation order for burglary. He has a long history of offending and has spent time in prison for assault. He has admitted that he hits Susan occasionally, usually when he is drunk. His probation officer thinks he has an alcohol problem but he denies this. The probation officer has arranged for Dave to attend anger management sessions. He also thinks the family are in debt: neither parent is working and there doesn't seem to be much money available. Dave talks fondly of Louise but has a lot of conflict with Jamie. In addition to supervising offenders, probation officers provide a service to child victims of serious sexual or violent offences and supervise 16–17 year olds on community punishment. They also staff youth offending teams and support victims of domestic abuse (DCSF 2010: 62–3). The Multi-Agency Risk Assessment Conference (MARAC) is part of a coordinated community response to domestic abuse and includes probation officers.

Voluntary organizations

The youth club leader attends the meeting as Jamie attends the weekly youth club. Jamie is always poorly dressed and has few social skills. He is very good at games, especially football. He helps to look after some of the younger members and is very good with them. He talks to one of the mentors regularly. He has told him that he hates Dave Smith and would like to live with his 'real' dad, Brian Oxley. He sees his birth dad every week. Home Start has received a referral from the health visitor, but has not managed to see Susan yet as she does not appear to be in when the worker calls. Voluntary and private sectors provide a wide range of services, including preventative interventions, support, specialist support, information and advocacy. They need to be fully aware of the safeguarding process and able to refer appropriately. Note: the NSPCC is the only organization (other than social services and the police) that is allowed to initiate proceedings to protect children, and who can receive referrals about child abuse.

Police

A report of an incident was sent to the health visitor. Police officers were called to a domestic violence incident. The perpetrator was Dave Smith, the victim was Susan Oxley and three children were present in the house. The police have a responsibility to investigate the criminal element of child abuse. Indeed Lord Laming suggested that: 'the investigation of crimes against children is as important as the investigation of any other serious crime and any suggestions that child protection policing is of lower status than any other form of policing should be eradicated' (quoted in DCSF 2010: 60). The police work in cooperation with advice and assessment (e.g. they are part of the strategy meeting) and are responsible for gathering evidence and prosecuting adults or young people who have committed a crime, such as neglect, physical abuse, sexual abuse.

The police keep records of children who have child protection plans and are often the first point of contact in domestic abuse cases. They have a responsibility to keep and share relevant information and to contribute to multi-agency meetings. The police can receive direct referrals regarding child abuse and have emergency powers (police protection order) to enter premises and remove children (72 hours).

Practice reflection points

Case study 5

- Do you feel you could chair a child action meeting such as this?

- How could you develop these skills?

- Who could support you?

While you may know more about the family than your manager or designated person with responsibility for safeguarding, you could discuss your assessment and possible actions. They could also support you by reflecting, reviewing and discussing how to proceed. If you are not experienced in chairing meetings there will be Local Safeguarding Children's Board multi-agency training available, your manager could also act as a role model or in this case someone else could act as lead professional and also chair the meeting, such as the health visitor, who may be more experienced and have more involvement with the family. The decision regarding lead professional should be made at this initial meeting, as this person will ensure that care is coordinated, thus avoiding omissions and duplication in care. There should also be goals set, with regular reviews of support given and outcome monitoring to avoid delay and drift. If there is no improvement then it may be that the concern needs to be escalated.

Practice reflection points

Case study 5

- Do you feel the social worker should have attended the meeting?

- How would you refer a child to advice and assessment?

A referral would be done by telephone followed by a written referral in the form of a CAF form. If the social worker doesn't agree with you regarding thresholds for intervention, you need to take advice from the designated person within your organization, who may then consult with the line manager of the social worker. It may be helpful to write down the key areas you want to address, what your specific concerns are and concrete examples of why you feel there is a need for further assessment or action. It may be that in this case the child action meeting would be sufficient to raise the level of concern with the family and consider means of addressing the needs of the children and carers, however if the concerns continue to escalate and/or the family does not engage with services this could justify increasing the level of need and a referral to social worker to consider a child protection plan.

Children's social care services advice and assessment

The advice and assessment team offer social work service to children in need and children at risk of significant harm or in need of protection (levels 3 and 4 of the child action model). Duty social workers usually work between 9 am and 5 pm (with out of hours on call provision) and take referrals from anyone who has a concern for a child's well-being. If an assessment is deemed necessary, social workers will undertake specialist assessments (initial and core) to assess levels of need and then assist to develop a multi-agency plan to meet any needs of children and their families. Close coordination and multi-agency working with other professionals and agencies is required to share information and assist in meeting the needs of the family.

Work often undertaken includes the following:

- Investigating all allegations of child abuse. Children at risk of protection are immediately safeguarded via safeguarding procedures, and implementing Section 47 enquiries.
- Accommodating children at risk (where an immediate safeguarding plan within the family cannot be established).

- Undertaking Initial and Core Assessments.
- Initiating child protection conferences.
- Assessing children in need, and convening child action meetings.
- Attending child in need meetings.
- Offering advice and consultation.
- Private fostering assessments.

Referral process is via a CAF to the appropriate advice and assessment team (usually based on the address where the child resides).

If there is an urgent concern, a telephone call is required to make a referral, to be followed up via a CAF by the referring agency or person. Any child presenting with an injury or alleging abuse must be referred immediately via the phone so Section 47 enquiries can commence and safeguarding of the child can be assessed. Social workers can take immediate action to protect a child: they have to apply to a magistrate for an Emergency Protection Order (lasts up to eight days).

Children's services are also responsible for caring for children who have been removed from their primary carers (they may be living with other family, with foster parents or in residential care, or they may be adopted). They also provide specialist teams, for instance a disability team, and contribute to specialist teams, such as child and adolescent mental health service and drug action teams.

Alerts and warnings for Case study 5

Considerations	Possible responses	Useful agencies and contacts to support the family or you as a professional
Initial alert – what concerns you about this scenario? What have you noticed? Why is it of concern to you? How can you respond immediately? How do you believe the child is experiencing this moment? What is he or she likely to be feeling? How do you feel at this stage?		
Applying definitions of safeguarding and child protection: • Is this child being ill-treated? • Is it easy to recognize in this instance?		

(Continued)

(Continued)

Considerations	Possible responses	*Useful agencies and contacts to support the family or you as a professional*
• What is the child's understanding of this situation likely to be? • Are there any factors within the context of the scenario that may add to your concerns? • Are there any existing strengths you can identify in terms of existing factors or possible sources of support?		
How would you feel about initiating any action? Possible actions? What can you do? How will this impact on the child and the family, including the parents or carers?		
What is already known? What else do you need to know? Where could you get the information you need?		
Risks and benefits of action: consider the needs and impact on • the children, Jamie, Kylie and Louise • the parents, Susan, Dave and Brian • the family and extended family • you as a professional • the service setting you work in		

Is teamwork easy to organize?

This scenario demonstrates the difficulties involved in coordinating safeguarding between multi-agency teams. It may be easy to share information and concerns with professionals within your own team or agency, particularly if you have regular contact with them. It is important for all professionals to contribute and to feel valued in terms of the experience and knowledge they can offer. Each professional can operate in different ways to implement an effective safeguarding response; however this requires engagement with the assessment process, providing a report, attending the meeting.

We now consider Case study 5 within the context of the five chapters in part 1 of the book.

History: what can it teach?

We know from research that domestic abuse does impact on children: the link between child physical abuse and domestic violence is high, with estimates ranging between 30 per cent to 66 per cent depending upon the study (Edleson 1999; Hester et al. 2000; Humphreys and Thiara 2002). In 90 per cent of domestic violence cases, the children are in the same room or the room next door during an attack on their mother. In the UK, one in three child protection cases show a history of domestic violence to the mother. Abrahams (1994) found that 75 per cent of mothers said their children had witnessed domestic violence, 33 per cent of children had seen their mothers beaten up and 10 per cent of children had witnessed sexual violence. The Women's Aid organization website (www.womensaid.org.uk) cites the following evidence: in 40–70 per cent of cases where women are being abused, the children are also being directly abused themselves (Stark and Flitcraft 1996).

Children can also be a factor in women staying with violent partners, in order to keep the family together; in response to perceived family, societal and cultural pressure or negative responses from agencies. There may be financial issues or fear of what may happen if they leave.

How are the child's rights being recognized?

We know that it is important to maintain a child focus: the children's needs are paramount, they are entitled to basic care, nutrition and loving relationships. In this case they are at risk of physical injury due to domestic abuse, their basic needs are not being met in terms of cleanliness or provision of food and there is often associated emotional abuse in violent abusive homes. The parents' problems can sometimes detract and distract from the children's needs, but while meeting parents' needs can impact positively on the children, they should not be the prime consideration.

Focusing in on the child: what is the baby or young child experiencing?

Seeing this scenario from the children's perspective, it is important to consider what it is really like for the children within this family. Jamie is an adolescent, who has a positive relationship with his biological father, but difficulties with his stepfather, Dave. Although this is common, it should not be normalized. Jamie also has significant involvement with his younger siblings and relates well to younger children at the youth club. While Jamie is old enough to wash and dress himself, older children sometimes need encouragement to do so. Kylie's medical needs are not being met in that she is not being taken for eye appointments and there are basic care deficits. Louise is underweight and has not completed her immunizations. Her developmental delay could be a direct result of poor bonding with Susan due to postnatal depression, and there are also basic care deficits.

All of the children are experiencing inadequate basic care. The parents should ensure that children are well presented in terms of hygiene and appropriate clothing and nutrition. The younger children need physical care, whereas with an older child such as Jamie, the parent should teach and encourage the child regarding hygiene and appearance. Children should have nutritious food bought and prepared for them to provide a diet that meets nutritional, health and energy requirements. There are indications in the scenario that this is not happening – Kylie's hunger, Louise's poor weight gain and Jamie's food stealing.

What have the carers to say about your concerns?

The parents' response in this meeting would give an indication of their concern for the children's welfare and willingness or ability to work with agencies to effect change. Do they all attend? Do they listen to the concerns of the professionals? Do they agree with the concerns about the children? Do they offer any explanations? How do they respond? Do they engage with the plan and goals set? For instance Dave's willingness to acknowledge his behaviour, discuss his anger and attend the classes arranged by the probation service could be crucial to effecting a positive outcome. Much of Susan's ability to care for the children could be restricted because of her postnatal depression.

Key messages

- Multi-agency working is not only desirable, but also clearly indicated in legislation and policy as a requirement.
- Effective communication and information-sharing between professionals working with children can aid prevention of problems, or at least facilitate early intervention.
- It is particularly important when abuse is suspected or confirmed that all professionals working with the family contribute to multi-agency assessments and investigations.
- Ongoing monitoring and support will also often be required: it is important that seamless services are provided to avoid duplication and omission. Effective communication between the various professionals will be crucial in this instance.
- Communication between agencies is often criticized in serious case reviews, therefore a culture of working together effectively needs to be developed.

10 Working with the parents and carers of an abused baby or young child

---

Chapter Overview

This chapter discusses the likely nature of working through a safeguarding investigation with the parents and carers of an abused child. A case study is used to illustrate the complexity of emotion and anxiety that may surround professional intervention. The chapter develops potential strategies for dealing with difficult dilemmas, while remaining focused on the needs of babies and young children.

Balancing relationships with parents and carers effectively

The involvement of any early years professional in the identification of potential ill-treatment or other safeguarding concerns can be extremely traumatic, particularly for the parents and carers of the baby or young child in question. This can make it difficult to maintain positive partnerships that focus clearly on the child, parents may have negative feelings towards being monitored or even accused of abuse. However, it is important for practitioners to sustain a relationship with parents and carers that will inevitably lead to more positive outcomes for the child. In this chapter we consider how practitioners may develop their ongoing relationship with the parents or carers from the initial moments of investigation through to some sort of culmination and withdrawal to more normal relations, if that is deemed appropriate.

Balancing the maintenance of a positive relationship with parents or carers while meeting the needs of the child can be a delicate exercise. If the relationship is too positive there is a danger of at best focusing on the parents' or carers' needs to the detriment of the child. At worst collusion can occur where you could be manipulated to think the best of a situation or serious indicators of abuse are covered up, such as the chocolate smeared on Baby Peter's face to cover up bruising. This perhaps fits in with a rule of optimism (Dingwall et al. 1983) where it is hard to imagine anyone wanting to deliberately harm a child. It may also occur where there is an overemphasis on process and procedure, resulting in pressures of high workloads for practitioners and little time to carry out duties effectively such as a home visit.

Equally the difficulties of categorizing levels or thresholds of abuse can also be applied to parenting skills and behaviours. Many practitioners recognize that there is no such thing as a perfect parent, but the level of the 'good enough' parent as introduced by Winnicott (1951) can be difficult to determine. A judgement is effectively being made on aspects of the parenting, with support and partnership being offered, while potentially monitoring or investigating them for abuse or neglect. A general rule of thumb would be to always treat the parent or carer with respect, informing them where possible unless to do so would compromise the safety of the child, which should of course be prioritized as the paramount concern.

Negotiation and partnership with families are key principles of the Children Act 1989 in order to balance family support with child protection. Focusing on preventative services is important while still recognizing the primary responsibility for parents and carers to care for their children. The duty of the state is also evident in terms of not only ensuring this happens but also facilitating it through appropriate service provision and support. Intervention from the state does need to be proportionate: accusations of paternalism in past cases such as Cleveland in 1987 (Butler-Sloss 1988) highlighted potential for inappropriate intrusion into family life by services. This means that practitioners can face criticism at either extreme of the tightrope for either getting too involved or not intervening appropriately. Together with the issues surrounding confidentiality and sharing concerns discussed in Part 1 you may find that Table 10.1 helps you to identify the level of involvement required and responses from parents or carers at various stages of proceedings.

Even when being mindful of the potential for collusion and overemphasis on the needs of parents and carers, partnership working can be effective in terms of balancing the needs of the child while maintaining a positive relationship with the parents or carers. Providing support to parents promoting positive parenting will potentially impact on the well-being of the child. However, if communication breaks down, there is arguably less opportunity for practitioners to be able to improve the situation and work effectively with families. When working with difficult or resistant families, it must be remembered that frustration and anger can precipitate aggressive behaviour; this can be caused by anxiety about any safeguarding investigation, fear of what may happen to them and their children, or a sense of injustice. Some of this may be directed at you as an early years professional, raising the importance of avoiding misunderstandings or omissions, such as by turning up when you say you will, avoiding unnecessary unplanned visits, including clients in assessment and decision-making where possible, and being professional and respectful towards clients.

Effective partnership should include aspects such as informing parents of procedures and processes, involvement in assessments and proceedings, attendance at meetings including child in need, core groups and conferences. These procedural elements form only a basic level of partnership, which on a broader level could also include expressing views, influencing decisions and involvement in assessment, planning, providing and evaluating service provision. Clearly this is not necessarily advisable in some cases where state intervention is required such as court proceedings, but parents or carers and children still have rights to be kept informed, involved and to complain.

Techniques to employ with resistant or difficult individuals include focusing on aims and goals, negotiating, facilitating empowerment and advocacy. Occasionally confrontation and ultimatums may be required to ensure that parents or carers

Table 10.1 Level of professional involvement and associated responses

Stage 1	Concerns are raised in relation to a baby or young child and an initial set of monitoring procedures are initiated.	At this stage the parents or carers may not be notified. Throughout this period it is important for the practitioner to keep clear and concise records.
Stage 2	Concerns are raised with the parents or carers. Are concerns resolved at this stage?	The practitioner can expect a number of potential reactions, including anger, denial, or alternatively distress and an admission of difficulty in caring for the child.
Stage 3	Concerns continue and the situation in relation to the child's well-being deteriorates. Are concerns resolved at this stage?	The practitioner should discuss this change with appropriate managers, who in turn may wish to relate this to a wider group of practitioners. Parents or carers are likely to be informed and will be aware of the gradual escalation in concern. It is unlikely that they would be informed in the case of child sexual abuse.
Stage 4	If concerns continue appropriate review meetings will be convened to consider appropriate action to safeguard and protect the child. Are concerns resolved at this stage?	Parents or carers will be invited to review meetings particularly if there is any likelihood of legal action being considered. Of course, if a Common Assessment Framework (CAF) meeting is considered appropriate then they will have to attend for the meeting to go ahead.
Stage 5	Levels of concern persist or escalate.	A conference will take place to discuss whether the child will be placed under a child protection plan (formerly on the child protection register) and to determine an appropriate set of interventions, possibly by a range of different agencies. Regular core group meetings will be set up to assess progress, made up of the family and key professionals working with them. If however the concern is that an emergency intervention needs to take place, this could result in immediate action prior to any meeting to assess the situation and to determine appropriate action such as the application of an Emergency Protection Order (EPO).
Stage 6	Concerns cannot be resolved with the parents or carers and the safety of the child is assessed as being at risk and needing to be resolved by the Family Court.	It may be necessary for social workers to submit an application for a care order to the Family Court where there has been little improvement in home circumstances and the risk to the child is considered to be unacceptable.

understand what is required. At all times you need to be mindful of ensuring your own safety, which may mean visiting with someone else, or seeing the family in a neutral environment. Never enter a situation if you feel you may be in danger. Consider that situations may change and keep an eye open for warning signs and a potential escape route. A sense of danger may be raised by warning signs such as escalation of anger, people blocking your access (particularly to exits), obvious intoxication or drug use, verbal or physical threats or intimidation. Most services and organizations recommend that you never visit alone, particularly if there are known risks or a history of any previous violent incidents. Risk assessments should be undertaken and policies such as lone visits guidance followed, this would include measures such as carrying a mobile phone and ensuring someone knows where you are.

We include the following case study as a focus for discussion and consideration noting however that the key features of it are concerned with early prevention and partnership working.

Case study 6: the Williams family

- Tracy (30 years old)
- Zoe (12 years old)
- Abby (10 years old)
- Jade (9 years old)
- Jack (7 years old)
- Adam (5 years old)
- Megan (3 years old)
- Millie (1 year old)

Tracy is nine weeks pregnant; she has been refused a requested termination of the pregnancy as it was getting too late and complicated by being twins. There is little involvement from the fathers of any of the children. Tracy prefers not to name them for records and she reports she doesn't know who the twins' father is. The family live in a three-bedroomed semi-detached council property; the dining room is utilized as a fourth bedroom for the three older girls. She has applied for rehousing due to neighbour disputes and family size; she does not like the area, which is considered a 'rough' estate. She moved here originally to be near her sister, but they don't get on now. She has rent arrears and other debts.

Zoe will not attend secondary school and is often at home helping with the younger children. Tracy has reported incidents of bullying to the school, but feels they are 'not taking her on' despite the presence in the school and estate of a community police officer. Abby and Jade attend a free council-run after school club. Megan and Millie are at home. The other children attend the same primary school. Adam has just started in reception. Jack has speech delay, behaviour problems and wets the bed at night. He has missed several speech therapy appointments and subsequently been removed from the list.

Jack and Adam are missing some immunizations, Megan and Millie have had none. Megan and Millie have both had six-month placements in family day care, with two sessions per week with a childminder. Megan was frequently sent home due to repeated episodes of head lice infestation and impetigo. Megan and Millie's development is age appropriate. Megan is particularly lively with advanced speech, including a few swear words. Millie is often strapped in the pram during visits and particularly clingy with mum. Mum often spends time with neighbours and in summer is often seen outside drinking vodka alcopops and smoking.

Tracy reports that she loves her children and only thought about termination as she was worried how she would cope; she has had episodes of postnatal depression in the past. Although the house is chaotic, the family appears loving towards each other. Tracy usually cooks a large pot of food for tea such as a stew or lasagne; the children help themselves to a bowl of food with the older children helping the younger ones.

Tracy rings up worried about an incident at the weekend where police were called to the home anonymously reporting that all the children were at home alone in the care of the eldest, Zoe. The police waited for some time and were about to remove the children, when Mum arrived home at 9 pm. She was worried what social services were going to do. On looking back through the notes, you observe that this is not the first incident when the children had been left alone. Upon ringing social services they report that they are sending Mum a warning letter.

Alerts and warnings for Case study 6

Considerations	Possible responses	Useful agencies and contacts to support the family or you as a professional
Initial alert – what concerns you about this scenario? What have you noticed? Why is it of concern to you? How can you respond immediately? How do you believe the child is experiencing this moment? What is he or she likely to be feeling? How do you feel at this stage?		
Applying definitions of safeguarding and child protection: • Is this child being ill-treated? • Is it easy to recognize in this instance?		

(Continued)

(*Continued*)

Considerations	Possible responses	Useful agencies and contacts to support the family or you as a professional
• What is the child's understanding of this situation likely to be? • Are there any factors within the context of the scenario that may add to your concerns? • Are there any existing strengths you can identify in terms of existing factors or possible sources of support?		
How would you feel about initiating any action? Possible actions? What can you do? How will this impact on the child and the family, including the parents or carers?		
What is already known? What else do you need to know? Where could you get the information you need?		
Risks and benefits of action: consider the needs and impact on • the seven children • the mother, Tracy • the extended family • you as a professional • the service setting you work in		

Initial responses

It is clear that Tracy has a lot of responsibility with seven children to care for and support, and there are some deficits in terms of the basic care she is able to provide. It is unacceptable to leave 12-year-old Zoe with responsibility for six younger siblings. However, the police did not remove the children under an Emergency Protection Order and the social worker appears happy to deal with the situation with a warning letter. Tracy was very worried about the situation and was expecting more formal and serious action on the part of social care services. It could be argued that the time is right to introduce a safer cultures approach to prevent this situation deteriorating. As Tracy is expecting two more children, she could be receptive to advice and support.

What actions might be considered by the practitioner?

As a practitioner you are aware that two agencies who could initiate more formal proceedings have chosen not to do so; however your concern for the children in this family may prompt some discussion of these decisions. You could consult with your line manager or named person with responsibility for safeguarding within your organization, particularly if you are unhappy with the decisions made by other agencies or professionals.

It is also apparent that Tracy may be more receptive to advice and support, particularly as she has had a 'near miss' in terms of having her children removed. She is also aware of the responsibilities that two more children will bring, especially as she has little support available to her from family, friends or neighbours. This situation presents an opportunity to promote factors that may improve the well-being of the children and remove factors that hinder, building on any identified strengths and addressing any assessed needs.

As the consultation process has not resulted in the social worker taking the lead in the form of a Core Assessment or Section 17 enquiry, you have the option of calling a child in need or child action meeting yourself. Key professionals working with the family can be invited to discuss how the needs of the children can be met more successfully to prevent deterioration in their well-being.

Tracy was receptive to this idea as a means of identifying what services may be helpful to support her. At the same time it is important to ensure that she understands that the well-being of the children will be monitored and further action taken if deemed necessary. This ensures that the needs of the children remain of paramount importance rather than detracting from them towards Tracy's needs alone, to the detriment of the children.

The meeting was held in the local health centre where Tracy attends her GP, midwife and health visitor appointments. Childcare was arranged for the younger children and the older children were at school. The health visitor was happy to chair the meeting and minutes were taken. The midwife and staff from the children's schools were invited. The local community police officer attended to discuss neighbourhood issues and reports were provided by the GP. The social worker did not attend but did offer some financial support for after school clubs.

While Zoe, Abby and Jade were excited about the twins, it was made clear that their education should be maintained. The teachers at the primary school and secondary school were supportive in terms of monitoring issues affecting attendance and putting supportive measures in place such as breakfast clubs, and safe zones/clubs within school. The primary school reported that some of Jack's appointments could be held in school as practitioners were able to visit the premises; an educational assessment of his needs was also discussed. While Adam had not demonstrated any overt problems, it was important to consider his development needs and well-being, particularly as starting school and the arrival of more siblings can be emotionally traumatic for children.

Strengths evident within the family included the care and affection they demonstrated towards each other. Tracy provided reasonable basic care, although additional stimulation and boundaries were required at times. Some of these issues could be addressed to some extent with supportive visiting, parenting advice and behaviour management strategies. Key practitioners could include a nursery worker, family support services, the health visitor and midwife. The respite for Tracy provided by the after school clubs was also enhanced by social services funded day care for the two younger children, although these are often limited in terms of number of sessions and duration of provision, if provided at all in some areas. It is also important to offer appropriate praise where due: Tracy was particularly good at providing a cost-effective, nutritious meal for the children for example and clearly demonstrated affection and love towards them.

As Tracy's due date for the twins approached, it became apparent that she would require a caesarean birth, therefore together with the midwife and obstetrician, she decided to have a sterilization procedure performed at the same time. A support plan was discussed for going into hospital. Rather than the children going into temporary foster care, Tracy resolved some of her disputes with her sister, who agreed to look after the children while Tracy was in hospital.

This scenario has demonstrated how a positive relationship can be maintained with parents or carers while still remaining focused on the needs of the children. Positive elements can be reinforced while addressing any impeding factors that may affect the well-being of the children to effect a safer culture and prevent the situation deteriorating into significant harm. This also echoes earlier chapters in the book that focused on prevention, for instance if these children had been taken into care, the cost to society both financially and in terms of the children's future well-being could have been far worse than the efforts to support the family to make some adjustments.

Key messages

- You may find it difficult to maintain positive partnerships with parents and carers that focus clearly on the child. Parents may have negative feelings towards being monitored or even accused of abuse.
- It is important for you to aim to work positively with parents and carers in order to promote factors that help. However, you can be in a contradictory position of monitoring and surveillance to prevent significant harm.
- You may even have to initiate assessment and investigative proceedings if you feel abuse has taken place or that there is a risk of harm.
- You need to communicate effectively with parents and carers while avoiding collusion and remaining focused on the needs of the child or children. However it is important to ensure the safety of yourself and the child or children. This may mean not visiting and/or not informing the parents or carers of the accusation or investigation if this would prejudice the case or place the child or children at further risk of harm.
- Balancing the maintenance of a positive relationship with parents or carers while meeting the needs of the child can be a delicate exercise. However, if you can do it successfully the well-being of the child or children can be promoted effectively and further harm avoided.

11 What might happen after the case has been referred: mapping the potential impact of intervention

Chapter Overview

This chapter uses a case study to reflect on the potential for the future of a baby or young child and their family following a child abuse investigation under Section 47 of the Children Act 1989. The case study highlights potential difficulties for both children and families who have been the focus of concern to become rehabilitated back into their local communities. The chapter considers positive strategies that may lead to successful outcomes for the future safeguarding of babies and young children while making clear the importance of remaining vigilant.

Introduction

Following from Chapter 10 where the process of assessment and investigation was highlighted, we now consider how to work with families after the Section 47 investigation has taken place. If the child has been abused or considered at risk of abuse, they may have been removed to local authority care, perhaps foster care or another family member depending on the severity and context of the abuse (whether parental or carer contact is going to be allowed). However, if the child remains with the parents or carers a system of ongoing support and monitoring needs to be in place, usually in the manifestation of a child protection plan (previously referred to as registration) and should be considered to be a starting point rather than a finishing point. This will usually take the form of a core group of key practitioners involved with the child and family and also include the parents or carers. The core group will need to meet at regular intervals to discuss ongoing needs and developments, action plans and evaluation of any outcomes. Any improvement in the situation for the child needs to be maintained. Key aspects of these processes will be discussed and applied to a case study.

Initial child protection conferences

The initial child protection conference usually occurs following a Section 47 enquiry to bring together the family with key professionals from all the agencies most involved with the child and family participating. It will also include a range of other agencies, which may not have direct contact with the family at this moment in time but still hold relevant information. The aim of the conference is to review and analyse the information presented and make a decision regarding the likelihood of significant harm to the child. Information reviewed will include focusing on the child's health and development status; the nature, extent and impact of any abuse or neglect; as well as the parents' or carers' capacity to meet the child's needs in terms of promoting safety, ensuring well-being, and any wider family, social and environmental factors that may be relevant.

Timing of initial child protection conferences

The timing of the conference will depend on the urgency of the case and on the time needed to obtain the relevant information about the child and family. However, all initial conferences should take place within 15 working days of the initial or latest strategy meeting. As this timescale is quite short, plans are likely to be made early on in the Section 47 enquiry in terms of setting a date. Children's social care has the responsibility to convene child protection conferences, although any professional or agency involved with the family or the Section 47 enquiry can request that one is convened, particularly if they have serious concerns regarding a child's welfare and are supported by their manager or designated safeguarding professional. The conference considers all the children of the household even if concerns are being expressed about one child only.

Attendance at child protection conferences (initial and review conferences)

The quality of information presented and shared responsibility of the professionals involved are crucial to ensure effective implementation of a child protection plan. All agencies directly involved with the child and family, or holding information relevant to the safety or welfare of the child should be invited. The following must always be invited:

- Social workers who have undertaken an assessment of the child and family
- Police officers involved in investigations
- Health visitors and/or school nurse
- GP for the child and parents
- School (where one or more children are of school age)

- Other doctors involved in recent medical assessment or treatment of the child
- Midwifery services (particularly where the conference concerns an unborn or newborn child)
- Children's guardian (if applicable, usually where there are current court proceedings).

Other professionals who may contribute include the following:

- Professionals involved with the parents or other family members (e.g. family support services, adult mental health services, probation, housing department and other housing services, Sure Start)
- NSPCC or other involved voluntary organizations
- The fostering supervising social worker or, in some instances, the foster carers (current or former)
- Local authority legal services
- Professionals with expertise in the particular type of harm suffered by the child or in the child's particular condition (e.g. disability, medical condition or long-term illness).

While it is the responsibility of the social worker to draw up the list of those to be invited, other agencies should alert the social worker to any professionals involved with the family who may have a significant contribution to make. Wherever possible, the date and timing of the conference should be set at a time convenient for those who are key to that conference.

All agencies and professionals invited are expected to attend or send a representative, to contribute information and to be part of the evaluation and decision-making process. Wherever possible, agencies should be represented by those with first-hand knowledge of the child and family, who can commit resources, if necessary, following prior discussion with managers. In deciding who should attend, each agency should be mindful of the need to limit the size of the conference, to minimize the intimidating effect of large meetings on parents and children and to ensure efficiency. An observer can attend only with the prior consent of the chairperson and with the prior consent of the family.

Professionals attending the conference should prepare their contribution in advance, preferably summarizing their involvement in a written report: this is usually in the form of a Common Assessment Framework (CAF). Any written report should be made available to those attending, including family members. Professionals who are invited but unable to attend for unavoidable reasons should always submit a written report, which sets out the context of and information about their involvement with the family and relevant information concerning each child's health and development; the capacity of the parents to safeguard the child and promote each child's health and development; any other relevant family and environmental factors.

Information should be summarized. Care should be taken to distinguish between fact, observation and opinion, to identify both strengths and concerns, and to avoid jargon or overlong detail. Opinion and interpretations are important, but should be substantiated. Opinion should be included about what needs to change, and about what further supports and services should be made available to the child and family members.

Attendance by professionals is particularly important as a quorum is required. This means that sufficient agencies should be present to enable safe decisions to be made in the individual circumstances. There should normally be representation from children's social care and at least two other agencies or professional groups who have had direct contact with the child. The chairperson is responsible for deciding, in the best interests of the child, to proceed if the conference is not quorate, taking into account: whether the most relevant professionals are available; the urgency of the need to safeguard the child; the importance of effective decision-making based on relevant information and completing reviews within prescribed timescales.

Information for the conference

The social worker should provide to the conference a written report which summarizes and analyses the information obtained in the course of the Core Assessment and the Section 47 enquiries. This report should include: the nature of concerns; a chronology of significant events and any professional contact with the family; information on the child's current and past state of health and development; the capacity of the parents and family members to ensure the child's safety from harm and to promote the child's well-being; family and environmental factors which affect the care of the child; the views, wishes and feelings of the child, parents and other family members; and analysis of the implications of the information obtained for the child's future safety, health and development and recommendations developed from this analysis. Parents and children, if appropriate, should be be provided with a copy of the report, and have the opportunity to read, question and discuss it with the social worker. This should be prior to the day of the conference. Exceptionally, if the social worker has to do this on the day of the conference, sufficient time must be allowed for this task before the conference is due to start. The social worker should help children and family members in advance to think about what they want to say in the conference and how best to get their points across. Some may find it helpful to provide their own written submission, which an advocate may help to prepare.

Decision regarding a child protection plan

The conference should consider if the child is at a continuing risk of significant harm when determining whether there is a need for a child protection plan. This means that the child can be shown to have suffered ill-treatment or impairment of health or development as a result of physical, emotional or sexual abuse or neglect, and professional judgement is that further ill-treatment or impairment are likely. Or professional judgement, substantiated by the findings of enquiries in this individual case or by research evidence, is that the child is likely to suffer ill-treatment or the impairment of health or development as a result of physical, emotional or sexual abuse or neglect. If the child is judged to be at continuing risk of significant harm, safeguarding the child will require inter-agency help and intervention delivered through a formal child protection plan. This should be considered separately in respect of each child in the family or household.

The aim of the conference is to reach a consensus of opinion between the agencies involved. The role of the chairperson is to facilitate this, ensuring that a clear focus is kept on the child and on the issues of safeguarding the child. The wishes and feelings of the child and family members are represented and taken into account, ensuring that all views are represented. If there is not clear consensus, the chairperson will seek more explicit views amd may make a decision reflecting the child's best interests and weight of opinion (particularly of those most involved with the child and family members).

Disagreements with the decision or recommendations of a conference may arise which should be recorded in the conference record. Where a participant believes that a decision or recommendation leaves a child at risk of significant harm, this should immediately be brought to the attention of a senior manager and/or the named or designated professional for their own agency. This would then be raised with the conference chair, who will review the case and liaise with other managers involved.

Category of abuse or neglect

If the decision is taken that the child is in need of a child protection plan, the chairperson will determine which category, or combination of categories, of abuse or neglect the child is at risk of suffering. A child may be subject of a child protection plan as a result of one or more categories of abuse. The categories used are as defined in the guidance *Working Together to Safeguard Children* (DCSF 2010): physical, emotional, or sexual abuse, and neglect. The full definition of each is given in Chapter 1.

The category or categories determined by the conference chairperson represents the primary presenting concern at the time the child became subject of a child protection plan, and thus indicates to anyone consulting the child's social care record the nature of current and previous concerns. This categorizing also allows for the collation and analysis of information locally and nationally. The use of more than one category is reserved for those circumstances where the evidence is sufficiently strong – not where there are merely some additional concerns or early suspicions. The category of emotional abuse should normally only be used where this is the sole or main form of abuse.

When a child protection plan is not instigated

If a child protection plan is not needed, the child may still be in need of help to promote his or her well-being, health or development, the conference should ensure that arrangements are made to consider with the family what further help and support might be offered. Subject to the family's views and consent, it may be appropriate to continue a Core Assessment of the child's needs, to help determine what support might best help promote the child's health and development; make recommendations about what support and help should be provided; ensure continued commitment to inter-agency working, particularly where the child's needs are complex. Any Core Assessment or subsequent child in need plan should be reviewed at intervals of not more than six months.

Decision to make a child protection plan

Whenever a child is made subject to a child protection plan, the conference must appoint a key worker; identify the core group of professionals and family members who will develop and implement the plan; set a date for the initial core group within ten working days and for the first review conference within three months; establish how children, parents and wider family members should be involved and the support and advice available to them; identify in outline what needs to be done to complete the Core Assessment; identify what specialist assessment is required or is under way to further assist sound judgements on how best to safeguard the child and promote his or her welfare; and set out the outline child protection plan.

The outline child protection plan

The outline plan defines the objectives of the detailed plan developed subsequently by the core group. Its focus is on what needs to change in order to safeguard the child and how the child is to be safeguarded meanwhile. It must therefore identify the risks of significant harm; establish short-term and long-term aims and objectives that clearly link to reducing the risk of harm and promoting the child's welfare; be clear about who will have responsibility for what actions, including actions by family members, and within what specified timescales; outline ways of monitoring and evaluating progress against the plan; and consider the need for a contingency plan if agreed actions are not completed or circumstances change quickly.

Pre-birth conferences

Where a Core Assessment under a Section 47 enquiry gives rise to concern that an unborn child may be at future risk of significant harm, there may be a need to convene an initial child protection conference prior to the birth. Such a conference has the same status and proceeds in the same way as other initial child protection conferences, with the exception that it will not normally be convened before the twentieth week of pregnancy, but should wherever possible be held at least six weeks before the expected birth and where the baby or young child is to be subject of a child protection plan, this becomes effective at the birth of the child.

Core groups

Core groups are set up to implement the child protection plan, enabling the key professionals working with a family to engage with the family. It is usually established at the case conference and made up of those professionals working most closely with the family, the parents and children and foster carers if applicable or appropriate. The child's experience, voice and needs must be represented in the child protection plan. The core group meets at set intervals to monitor progress and plan supportive measures, and success is often dependent upon the degree of engagement and participation of the family together with a commitment from all the professionals within the core group. The aim is to ensure that progress is made with the plan developed at the case conference, registration or a child protection plan should not be seen as an end point.

Although the core group is led by a key worker from social care, core group members are jointly responsible for the development and implementation of the child protection plan, including refining it as needed and monitoring it against the specific objectives. This means that you as an early years professional would have to be mindful of the work of other agencies, ensuring that services are coordinated and seamless, avoiding repetition and omissions. The date of the first meeting is usually set at the case conference and takes place within ten working days, there is an expectation that the group will meet at least every six weeks to ensure effective working, review outcomes against the goals of the child protection plan and make adjustments as required. The idea is that there should be some improvements made. This could be monitoring of the child within the family setting or if the child is in foster care it could concern the parents making changes to facilitate returning the child to the family.

It should be recorded at each meeting who attended, the date of the meeting, details of the child and the family, a summary of how the key tasks are progressing, decisions made and actions agreed to progress the specified objectives, and the date of the next meeting.

The focus of the ongoing core group assessment is the safety and well-being of the child, supporting the parents to develop awareness and skills to promote the child's health and development and relevant therapy for the child or carers. This could include counselling following abuse, parent education or anger management, for example. However the professionals working with the family need to be mindful of ongoing signs of abuse, particularly if the decision at the case conference was to keep the child in the family setting. Any new concern would need to be dealt with through the core group, or if more serious, such as an injury or other signs of abuse, then the police may need to be contacted or a new Section 47 enquiry instigated.

Case conference reviews

The purpose of the review child protection conference is to review the safety, health and development of each child against the intended outcomes set out in the child protection plan; ensure that the child continues to be adequately safeguarded; and consider whether the child protection plan should continue in place, should be changed or is no longer needed. Every review child protection conference should thus consider explicitly whether the child continues to be at risk of significant harm.

The first review child protection conference must be held within three months of the initial child protection conference. Subsequent review conferences must be held at intervals of no more than six months for as long as the child remains the subject of a child protection plan.

Any agency may request an early review conference where there is concern that the child protection plan no longer safeguards the child. The decision about whether this should be agreed rests with the chairperson, in consultation with the key worker and his or her line manager. The key worker should consult the chairperson as to whether an earlier review conference is needed in any of the following circumstances:

- Where child protection concerns relating to a new incident or allegation of abuse have been substantiated.
- Where departure from conference recommendations by any agency or parent has a significant effect on the safety of the child.
- Where consideration is to be given to the return home of a child who is subject to a child protection plan and is also currently looked after by the local authority or placed with relatives for his or her safety, and the planned rehabilitation had not been anticipated at the previous conference.
- Where a pre-birth initial conference is needed because a further child is to be born into the household and pre-birth assessment indicates that a conference is necessary to consider the safety of the baby.
- Where a person assessed as presenting a risk to children is to join or commences regular contact with the household.
- Where the core group believes that the child protection plan is no longer needed.

In most circumstances the decision to discontinue the child protection plan must be made at a review child protection conference. A child should no longer be the subject of a child protection plan if the risk of harm has been reduced by action taken through the child protection plan; the child and family's circumstances have changed; reassessment of the child and family indicates that a child protection plan is no longer necessary; or the child is now looked after by the local authority.

The child protection plan may be discontinued without a review conference where the child and family have moved permanently to another local authority area. In such cases the child protection plan may be discontinued once the receiving authority has convened a child protection conference (within 15 working days). Other circumstances include if the child reaches 18 years of age, has died or has permanently left the UK.

It is important to note that any child who ceases to be the subject of a child protection plan may still require additional support and services. Discontinuation should never lead to the automatic withdrawal of help. The key worker should discuss with the parents and the child what services might be wanted and needed, based upon the reassessment of the child and family. Where the identified needs remain complex and require a coordinated inter-agency approach, the conference should draw up the child in need plan and agree the timescales for its review.

A case study now explores a situation following instigation of a child protection plan.

Case study 7: Barbara and Imogen

Barbara is a 43-year-old single parent living in a high-rise block of flats in a deprived urban area. As a young mother she had a large family of five children, all of whom had been taken into local authority care because of her poor parenting caused by alcohol and drug misuse. The details of her relationship with the children was characterized by neglect and physical abuse. The last of her children had come into local authority care when Barbara was 30 years old. Now at 43 years old Barbara discovered that she was pregnant again. The midwife responsible for her care contacted the social services department to report this information. The latest situation regarding her alcohol and drug misuse was that it was controlled and in fact she claimed not to be using for some considerable time, in excess of five years.

Initial responses

Following the initial contact from the midwife, the previous history was reviewed by the social worker in the form of a case review. This can involve contacting key practitioners involved in the case and reviewing records (particularly in view of the time passed as professionals are likely to have moved on). A Core Assessment and Section 47 enquiry was undertaken by the social worker to assess the nature and extent of any risk to this unborn baby. A case conference was called resulting in the unborn baby being placed under a child protection plan, which included monitoring and assessment for potential risk. This involved ongoing support and planning for the birth by the multidisciplinary team, with a view to assessing whether Barbara was fit to keep this baby.

Barbara was noted to be attending regular antenatal appointments with the midwife. Part of the midwife's role includes monitoring the well-being of the mother-to-be and unborn baby and offering advice regarding nutritional and dietary requirements. The general practitioner and obstetrician expressed no concerns regarding Barbara's pregnancy and general health status. There was no current involvement of drug team services in view of Barbara's lack of recent drug misuse.

When the baby girl, Imogen, was born there were some concerns regarding low birth weight, decreased muscle tone and that her head was small. These are potential signs of fetal alcohol syndrome or neonatal abstinence syndrome, meaning that Barbara could have potentially been covering up ongoing drug misuse during her pregnancy, presumably as she was aware this may damage her chances of keeping the baby. However, these signs can also be attributed to other factors.

There may be an assumption at this stage that the baby should be removed into care, but there are strengths that can be identified even where the parent may be misusing alcohol or drugs. In cases such as this it is important to consider factors such as sources of support available to Barbara and her willingness to engage with services, particularly regarding her past alcohol and drug use and the impact on her potential to parent Imogen effectively. Imogen's safety needs to be of paramount concern to the practitioners involved in this case.

Barbara was allowed to take Imogen home and allocated to a social worker. Imogen and her mum attend the mother and baby group at her local children's centre. During the social worker visits Barbara was extremely cooperative and ready to act on advice regarding her parenting skills and Imogen flourished. There was one situation in which Barbara had difficulties, following Imogen being hospitalized for a chest infection, which resulted in her getting very drunk and assaulting a member of ward staff. Police were called and Barbara was arrested. Reassessment heightened the potential risks to Imogen resulting in a change from a supervision order to care order.

Please apply the alerts and warnings to this more complex scenario and consider what additional services Barbara and Imogen may need. Also consider the support and skills you may need to work with this family together with other practitioners and agencies. There will be provision within your Local Safeguarding Children's Board multi-agency training to develop skills in working with more complex situations with more resistant families.

Alerts and warnings for Case study 7

Considerations	Possible responses	Useful agencies and contacts to support the family or you as a professional
Initial alert – what concerns you about this scenario? What have you noticed? Why is it of concern to you? How can you respond immediately? How do you believe the child is experiencing this moment? What is he or she likely to be feeling? How do you feel at this stage?		
Applying definitions of safeguarding and child protection: • Is this child being ill-treated? • Is it easy to recognize in this instance? • What is the child's understanding of this situation likely to be? • Are there any factors within the context of the scenario that may add to your concerns? • Are there any existing strengths you can identify in terms of existing factors or possible sources of support?		
How would you feel about initiating any action? Possible actions? What can you do? How will this impact on the child and the family, including the parents or carers?		
What is already known? What else do you need to know? Where could you get the information you need?		
Risks and benefits of action: consider the needs and impact on • the baby, Imogen • the mother, Barbara • the extended family • you as a professional • the service setting you work in		

Monitoring and subsequent interventions

Once Barbara has been arrested for this incident of aggressive behaviour, potential risks to Imogen need to be reviewed. This would be in the form of a strategy meeting or case conference. A number of considerations arise from this scenario, not only in terms of Barbara's behaviour, but also the events leading to it. Imogen's illness resulting in poor health and well-being could be purely coincidental, but it could be questioned whether the basic care she is receiving is adequate for her health needs. Barbara may be feeling guilty that Imogen has become ill. She may feel that she is not being fully included in the care of Imogen in hospital: are her frustrations justified? All of these aspects need to be assessed.

While the relationship between Barbara and professional agencies has been good most of the time, this does not mean that there is a good connection or fit with that aspect of the professional role that pertains to authority. For example, while Barbara appears to listen to professional advice and strategies as a response to perceived parenting issues, she has found it difficult to put the advice into practice. She does not appear to have organizational skills capable of improving or overcoming her lack of social support and feelings of isolation.

Because Imogen is very young, there is little external contact through pre-school services, such as a crèche, children's centre, contact with other parents or support groups, Home Start, local mums' support, family centre, family support or Sure Start. It is therefore advisable to refer to a local service directory for information regarding what is available in the area. This would include identifying places and opportunities where Barbara would have the opportunity to meet other parents in similar situations (perhaps providing role modelling of good parenting strategies and techniques). Barbara should also be given access to professional support and opportunistic advice together with targeted support such as parenting course or one-to-one. Conversations in a support group, whether formal, informal and/or targeted at a specific element of parenting or childcare, could work in a number of ways: peer support, reduce feelings of guilt or inadequacy knowing that others are in a similar position. Individual targeted support would require careful handling to retain a positive relationship with Barbara, to ensure she understands the benefit of any intervention and feels that it addresses her needs while keeping Imogen's needs and safety as the paramount consideration. However, the work undertaken to support Barbara can impact on Imogen directly if parenting skills improve, if Barbara feels more fulfilled and confident in her ability.

While the situation undoubtedly requires monitoring and ongoing assessment of strengths, needs and concerns, this will not be achieved effectively if Barbara becomes resistant to working with agencies. The review conference, strategy meeting and/or subsequent core group meetings would need to identify what each agency knows about the recent hospital admission and incident, and the events and context leading up to it. A key worker is usually identified to work more closely with the family: this would ideally be someone who Barbara can communicate with effectively.

Applying a safer cultures approach

What are the values of Barbara towards Imogen? This relatively straightforward question is actually complicated. Barbara begins her caring of Imogen in a very positive and committed way and retains this after Imogen is born, seeing herself within this context as a last chance to do a good job as a parent. However, conversely Barbara can behave in a manner that puts into jeopardy the well-being of Imogen through her occasional inability to control her own aggression and her possible reliance on alcohol and perhaps even drugs. The question arises then as to what safeguards can be put into place within the immediate environment that will sustain the Barbara–Imogen relationship. Barbara's mother Mary has been off the scene for several years. When Mary was told of Imogen's birth, she began in a rather sceptical manner to question Barbara's suitability to care for her properly. This view is one which is questioned by the social worker, who asks whether it is possible for her daughter and granddaughter to have a positive and loving relationship. After consideration Mary believes it can and that if Barbara will let her, she could herself offer some support; this could perceptibly change the situation towards a safer culture. There are some key questions that this raises, including the nature of the support and the durability of it if Mary disagrees with Barbara's style of childcare. Another question is whether Barbara would be willing to accept any support from her mother since she may have had a fairly negative experience as a child herself. It is also unclear whether they have been in touch over the years and what exactly the nature of the contact has been.

To gain further insight and to progress the safer culture by including Mary, the appropriate social care worker may set up a meeting with Mary to ask about Barbara's childhood and how she, Mary, coped as a mother with Barbara. We can speculate that there might have been a number of difficulties in Mary bringing up Barbara, which in turn may have affected the way that Barbara developed as a young person. The chief concern is to establish areas of connection between the two women, particularly in relation to childcare practices, and to support and encourage areas of agreement where they match previously agreed objectives determined with the early years professional and other concerned colleagues.

Further considerations in developing and sustaining a safer culture for Imogen

1. Can the practitioner map the range of family, friends and practitioners who come into contact with Imogen and are able to offer some form of positive childcare input?
2. Are there particular times when Barbara might be more vulnerable and therefore lacking in her consideration towards Imogen?
3. How can these times be clarified and resolved?

4. What can Barbara add that can help to understand her situation better and improve how she responds to Imogen?
5. Are there particular moments where Barbara clearly shares the same concerns for Imogen as the early years professional? And by the same token can the practitioner identify moments when she is clearly at odds with the professional perspective?
6. Are there safer cultures that exist for Imogen outside the home and in the community such as at a crèche or settings such as a Sure Start centre?
7. It is important to recognize that this will always be a work in progress which requires ongoing monitoring and review.

Key messages

- Initial child protection conferences are designed to review and analyse the information presented and make a decision regarding the likelihood of significant harm to the child.
- It is crucial that all agencies are represented at the conference and that each practitioner involved with the family sends a written report.
- As a practitioner you are likely to work with a family after a child protection conference has taken place, particularly if the child or children remain with the family.
- Therefore a system of ongoing support and monitoring needs to be in place, usually in the manifestation of a child protection plan, with a core group of key practitioners involved with the family.
- If the decision is taken that the child is in need of a child protection plan, the chairperson will determine which category, or combination of categories, of abuse or neglect the child is at risk of suffering. A child may be the subject of a child protection plan as a result of one or more categories of abuse.
- The category or categories determined by the conference chairperson represents the primary presenting concern at the time the child became subject of a child protection plan, and thus indicates to anyone consulting the child's social care record the nature of current and previous concerns.
- If a child protection plan is not needed, the child may still be in need of help to promote his or her well-being, health or development. The conference should ensure that arrangements are made to consider with the family what further help and support might be offered.
- The first review child protection conference must be held within three months of the initial child protection conference. Subsequent review conferences must be held at intervals of no more than six months for

as long as the child remains the subject of a child protection plan. Any agency may request an early review conference where there is concern that the child protection plan no longer safeguards the child.
• Applying a safer cultures approach can not only aid assessment of potential risks, but can also consider how to introduce positive factors to reduce the potential for harm to occur.

12 Conclusions: reflections on considerations for developing future practice and detailed requirements of effective intervention

Chapter Overview

Key messages arising from Parts 1 and 2 are explored bearing in mind the importance they have for readers as well as other practitioners within early years practice. This chapter supports a more personal set of reflections for developing appropriate practices for safeguarding babies and young children who may be suffering from abuse. Key practical, ethical and anti-discriminatory positions are highlighted for you to consider in your daily practice. Detailed points and requirements when managing a safeguarding case are set against a background of all the case studies. This includes making explicit the need for verbatim and contemporaneous recording, confidentiality and its complex meanings particularly in multidisciplinary teamwork contexts as well as many other important messages arising from the analysis of the case studies. This chapter draws together the central messages for practice and the advice for future developments in safeguarding babies and young children.

The following discussion offers a summary of the previous chapters for consideration by practitioners, early years managers and students who are engaged in appraising aspects of safeguarding and child protection or are involved in community-based placements.

At its heart the book offers the opportunity for you to develop your understanding through an interactive learning process that takes as a starting point the embedded nature of safeguarding and child protection as an ideal that all practitioners strive to achieve. In those cases that have been offered as examples in Part 1 of the book we acknowledge that although mistakes were made and that this has on very rare occasions led to the death of a child that has come to the attention of the public through the media and impacted on social policy – the practitioners attempting to support those children at the time were often undermined by a lack of resources, lack of access to supervision from a manager and perhaps most notably often the lack of time to do the job in a thorough and effective way. There is therefore something implicit in interventionist practice that needs to be made more explicit so that we as practitioners may learn and subsequently develop and refine our practice.

Brookfield points out that:

> Conceiving learning as always being embedded in society and always reflective of particular group mores, means it is irrevocably contextual... One cannot speak of adult learning in a generic, abstract way or as a decontextualized model of stages or phases. Learning is relational, always framed by the interaction 'of purely individual and subjective elements with which the individual is in an active relationship' (Gramsci 1971:391). The focus and processes of learning spring from the social contexts of individuals' lives, and these change according to the political conditions under which they live.
>
> (Brookfield 2005: 105)

Each situation therefore, whether it is one that is encountered professionally or privately (although these terms may not be particularly helpful as a means of separating experience) presents each of us with a set of questions about our practice, its effectiveness and rationale. The implications for each of us and our ability to continuously adapt dynamically may be achieved through the learning opportunities available through reflective discussions which keeps practice alive and practitioners alert to the effects of practice rather than taking it for granted and watching it fall short. The strategies highlighted in this chapter are offered as a means by which you may consider addressing practice through a critical yet reflective discourse and can be used by early years managers.

Early years managers

The summary set out below may be employed as part of an agenda for discussion about most aspects of safeguarding and child protection concerns and considerations. The work based or inter-professional team involvement in discussion is useful in opening up practice as a dynamic discourse able to overcome personal and professional barriers.

Wenger (1998: 152) argues that 'practice defines a community [of practitioners] through three dimensions: mutual engagement, a joint enterprise and a shared repertoire'. Wenger (1998: 152) adds that a mutuality of engagement can lead to a shared understanding of the ways that 'people treat each other', which is likely in turn to support the idea of practitioners' accountability and how each of them operates differently in pursuing a common set of objectives. Wenger argues that

> as an identity this translates into a perspective. It does not mean that all members of a community look at the world in the same way. Nonetheless, an identity in this sense manifests as a tendency to come up with certain interpretations, to engage in certain actions, to make certain choices, to value experiences – all by virtue of participating in certain enterprises.
>
> (Wenger 1998: 153)

The sharing of each practitioner's practice in safeguarding and protecting babies and children supports the development of a shared discourse which may offer the opportunity to engage creatively in problem solving possibly in ways similar to those employed in this part of the book.

Students

As well as being important for practitioners in engaging and sharing practice, it is equally important for students to have the opportunity to rehearse real-life situations that can prepare them for the workplace or higher level courses.

Team meetings

The meeting of a team of early years professionals focused around concerns relating to a child might consider as part of its agenda the following points for inclusion. The purpose is to articulate how active considerations for the child's well-being have been attended to by practitioners in their routine practice.

The Etter Wheeler principle

One of the first lessons for practice arising at different parts throughout the book and repeated as a core idea is the principle of maintaining a strong focus on the child, particularly at those times when other aspects of workload may be deflecting your attention. This principle was in evidence in the way that Etter Angell Wheeler remained focused in supporting Mary Ellen Wilson (see Chapter 1 and the case of Mary Ellen Wilson), which refers to the child and her well-being as the point of professional focus.

The Etter Wheeler principle could be summarized as follows:

- Act as a concerned individual.
- Remain focused to verify, as far as is feasible, that the child is experiencing a positive sense of well-being and appears cared for.
- Where this principle is relaxed or compromised, a child's needs are less likely to be met.

This principle requires practitioners to always keep returning to the way that the child seems to be and whether he or she seems to be enjoying improving care and consideration provided by immediate parents and carers. It was interesting to note that even in the case of Mary Ellen Wilson, which was over a hundred years ago when there were very few practitioners to support the child and her family, and no specific childcare legislation, the part played by Etter Wheeler was pivotal in the relentlessness that she pursued her objective of ensuring that Mary Ellen was safe. There is the important lesson to be learnt of persisting stubbornly in supporting a child and in certain circumstances if this is not done may lead to problems that to some degree were in evidence in the Victoria Climbié and Maria Colwell cases. In these cases and for different reasons, the child was not given the preferred status of practitioner focus, in a sustainable or enduring form, required to ensure improvements in child safety and well-being. In the Victoria Climbié case there was clearly another factor at play, that is time – and the long hours that the doctors and other professionals were working then. Overworking impacted on the ability of practitioners to reflect and discuss the situation carefully with each other. This breakdown in communication led to decisions being made to a default position dependent on internal hierarchy and status which in turn was over-reliant on the version of events offered by Victoria's great-aunt and carer.

Practice reflection points

- It is important to discuss the ways that you interact with parents and carers, especially in cases where there are safeguarding concerns.
- Do you include the child's perspective? How do you communicate with children? What skills do you have or need to develop?
- Are you tenacious enough in ensuring children are protected? Is there more that you could do? Begin to reflect on what this might be.
- How do you communicate with practitioners from other disciplines? Do you feel empowered to challenge the opinions of experienced practitioners? If you wished to do this, how might you go about it that could be perceived as a legitimate thoughtful concern and not simply an attempt to be difficult?
- If a senior colleague made a decision that you believed could put a child at risk, how might you address this concern?

The principle of the child as having rights and a voice (see Chapter 2)

This principle recognizes children as possessing rights that should be taken into consideration at all times, even when they appear to be too young or immature to directly contribute to decision-making. Further rights confirm the central principles that children should be treated with respect and free of abuse. The real challenge for you is to develop this principle from a symbolic understanding to one that is central to your practice. This means that you need to remind yourself of the fact that children have rights and that you are there to recognize them.

In addressing this point it is useful to reflect what can be done to ensure that a rights agenda remains a prominent concern for practice. Workplace discussions need to reflect 'rights' as a part of any agenda where practice is being considered so that they are then able to be integrated into a developing professional discourse.

Ross (1996: 95) argues that 'total listening [to children] uses all one's senses and includes seeing, smelling, feeling as well as hearing'. Gersch (1996) identifies 'six main issues worth highlighting', as follows:

(a)   Adults' attitudes
(b)   The capacity and maturity of children
(c)   Parent–child disputes
(d)   'Who pays the piper...'
(e)   Changing one's mind; negotiating, counselling and exploring, and
(f)   What the child needs as opposed to says s/he wants.

(Gersch 1996: 39)

Of course the above issues are likely to be met at some point and each represents a possible difficulty to open practitioner–child communication. The attitude of adults and the significance they attach to the child's view may vary substantially according to context. Alderson (2000b) reminds us that:

> Public and academic discussions about children are dominated by notions of 'development' and of 'early experiences as the path to the whole person'. People still repeat theories of the developing mind as if these are factual, and as if children's minds develop like their bodies through one universal pattern of ascending growth marked out by 'milestones' from zero to adult maturity.

(Alderson 2000b: 52)

This can obviously affect the way that we listen to children as well as our attitude to what we hear and a degree of significance we give to their views. In the case of babies, communication is unlikely to be very verbal or at least in an articulate way but through their body language and their general disposition to those around them, they may be extremely expressive conveying their sense of pleasure or alternatively their sense of unhappiness or distress.

Additionally if children's rights can be included in workplace documents, including those that relate to assessment, they are likely to become embedded into thinking and discussion about practice. The voice of the child was discussed in Chapters 2, 3 and 4. It is important to ensure wherever possible that it is included in practitioner discussions. In Chapter 5 we emphasized the significance of the professional community and the importance of maintaining clear opportunities for communication across professional boundaries.

- You need to be able to articulate sensitively, but honestly, any concerns felt about a particular child to the parents or carer and your colleagues. The issues here are concerned with personal feelings, values and beliefs; it is difficult to discuss childcare where there are considered shortcomings, and for carers not to feel offended for at least being considered a poor parent and not want to have further contact, which could be extremely problematic, particularly for the baby or young child concerned.

- You should be able to explore and assert your position with colleagues, both from within the familiar workplace and also with those from outside agencies who may have a different set of values and perspectives.
- It is important to be aware of current guidance and policy and to some extent the underpinning legislation that informs it. This is particularly important in the case of a situation where a professional action is being contemplated such as recording or visiting the home of a parent or carer. It is important to have a sense of security that the action that is about to be performed is appropriate, professional and linked to legal understandings.
- Most of all, it is essential for you to understand yourself as a vital resource for babies and young children and for their parents and carers. Failure to do so may result in the safeguarding agenda not being taken seriously, which might result in the continuation of a safeguarding situation that otherwise might have been supported or resolved earlier.
- You should be persistent and focus on the needs of the child in each case, including the child's perspectives and experiences, giving the opportunity for the child to tell their side of the story. In our view the relationship with the parents or carers, while important, should always wherever possible allow the child to give voice to matters that clearly are important to them and their future well-being.
- Reflection on practice is essential, because it will help you to review your actions or perhaps your lack of them as being part of a considered professional examination, leading to continuous learning opportunities and improvements.
- Children's rights can be maintained only by vigilant practitioners who are prepared to continuously preface children's rights within any discussion on safeguarding.
- You should as a high priority recognize the importance of babies and young children being consulted and included and where feasible supported to participate in communicating about their thoughts and feelings.
- Children clearly have the right to a happy and contented childhood, free from abuse or ill-treatment.
- You should be aware of communication as an essential skill, and its importance in maintaining a more inclusive participatory relationship with babies and young children, parents and carers and other practitioners.
- You need to be clear about the ways in which you can behave in a discriminatory and even oppressive manner if you are not prepared to be reflective or reflexive in their practice.
- Babies and young children have identities, which should be acknowledged and respected.
- You should reflect on the diverse ways in which you interact with different aspects of social divisions.

> ## Practice reflection points
>
> - How can the child be supported in taking a fuller part in the safeguarding process? Are there particular skills and abilities that you possess that makes you a good communicator with children?
> - What skills do you feel you need to develop further to support direct work with children?
> - How might you include parents and carers more in the process of relating to their children?

Safer cultures

Safer cultures refers to the practice of developing a strong proactive philosophy based on agreeing a set of practitioner and parent or carer values to support agreed parenting–child practice. Safer cultures is linked to a systems theory approach that emphasizes the person and their environment.

Payne (2005) shows the main issues and concepts of practice as follows:

- Systems theory focuses on the resources and connections available to families or groups and their effective functioning rather than inputs such as health work or counselling; thus the family itself can hinder or improve functioning, health or well-being.
- Life stressors apply energy in the form of stresses to a system; this may be a person or more commonly a family or community.
- Fit or adaptation between individuals and their social environments. Working to initiate, maintain and improve social networks and mutual support.

(Payne 2005: 143)

The important feature of safer cultures is that it views the family members or carers as part of a wider interacting set of relationships that will not only operate in a deficit mode, even when there are issues, but will also work in positive ways as well, even if those moments are less in evidence than the practitioner might wish. The key idea is concerned with how the parent or carer or significant other such as grandparent is supported in relating positively towards their child or grandchild. Where there are issues they may arise in the ways that the 'fit' between parents or carers and the child is disconnected or inconsistent. There also may be a poor 'fit' with potentially supportive systems, such as the day nursery, children's centre or school. This theory encourages the early years professional to examine the relationship that each individual in the adjoining systems has with the family and vice versa and how well those relationships might be supported to make a better and sustainable fit.

Ongoing discussion between the practitioner and the parents or carers and other individuals outside the family system may also be consulted to support change. A plan of action should be drawn up that highlights what is agreed, which parts of the connecting systems are problematic and the nature of the issue. Agreements should pay attention to parent or carer engagement with the process by focusing on evidence such as specific behaviour that needs to be demonstrated.

Where there is progress, it is important for this to be commented on and further encouragement given as deemed appropriate. This ethos should facilitate the promotion of a positive feeling of being part of a joint community culture that has the best interests and the well-being of the baby and young child at the forefront of any considerations.

A safer cultures approach is likely to include:

- A proactive ethos regarding safer cultures should be at the forefront of practitioner considerations.
- This ethos should facilitate the promotion of a positive community ethos that has the best interests and the well-being of the baby and young child at the forefront of any considerations.
- There should be a sharing of understanding of any issues relating to safer cultures with carers and/or colleagues.
- A common position regarding establishing ground rules for a safer culture needs to be developed within any context felt to be problematic for the baby or young child.
- Procedures need not be implemented directly unless the situation is concerning enough to do so. However partnership and cooperation should be agreed that is linked to an agreed set of values articulated possibly in an action plan and reviewed as an ongoing conversation.
- The processes and procedures that are relevant to safeguarding should be visible and clear and understood by all parties involved as being there and available if and when required.
- Recommended agreed areas of work should be negotiated with all parties involved particularly including the carers and child/ren and practitioners from different disciplines.

Practice reflection points

- In what situations could you imagine introducing the safer cultures strategy?
- How will you set up agreements with parents and carers that will be achievable and improve the relationship they have with their children.

- How will you agree time and availability for progress to be reviewed?
- When might it be appropriate for you to move from a safer cultures approach to one that is more concerned with the protection of the child?

Acting ethically in safeguarding contexts

Ethical behaviour is an important aspect of practice in safeguarding and child protection situations. Earlier the importance of transparent relationships and direct communication with parents and carers regarding concerns and actions was highlighted. This is extremely important in developing relationships that are based on trust as they set the standard for what is expected from both parents and carers and practitioners.

An ethical approach provides the focus for early years professionals and a reminder of the importance of their need to be aware of the influence of power dynamics. There are clearly strong hierarchical structures of power in place not simply in terms of practitioners being perceived as more powerful by parents and carers which can result in apparent compliance, it can also result in resistance towards the early years professional from the parent or carer. Dynamics and hierarchies of power may also have an impact on the relationships between practitioners, particularly from different disciplines where a 'pecking order' may operate, usually in favour of the more 'senior' professions such as law and medicine (see Powell 2005a).

The needs and concerns for the child must remain of paramount concern, bearing in mind that they are the most vulnerable and least likely to have power in their relationships with adults. As part of the dynamic of transparent communication between practitioners and parents or carers, it is important that the process of forewarning is held to (McLaren 2007). This means that if any information that concerns the child's well-being is introduced, the parent or carer knows that you will have to act on it by reporting it to a line manager. If it is information that suggests that a crime has been committed, the police would have to be informed. A problem sometimes encountered concerns what to do if you have passed on information concerning abuse of a child and you then discover that it is not being acted upon internally but instead is shelved. In the circumstances and depending on the urgency of the situation, you might consider making direct contact with another agency so that they can act instead.

It is ethically acceptable to note key aspects of concern about a child as and when they arise. Equally you should note if your information is shared at a meeting with practitioners and if any action results as well as its effectiveness. Of course case reviews and conferences will usually be confidential, at least during the meeting. Information will be most likely shared with those members at the meeting and not with others outside the group. Teachers often express concern that they might have been excluded from receiving information about a safeguarding issue, that they should know about because of the contact they have with the child but often confidential information in either verbal or written form will be strictly limited on a 'need to know' basis. This situation is arguably arrived at for pragmatic reasons and particularly at the stage of a Section 47 investigation, to limit the possibility of sensitive information 'leaking' because the number of practitioners in the know was not recorded and had stretched beyond the initial review or conference group. Information about a conference should not be discussed unless there is a formal need to do so and never in public places where there is the chance of being overheard. The question of who should 'need to know' is often not clearly articulated and it might be that someone who has a strong connection to the child or family has not been considered. While this might be due to an oversight, it is also possible that there are situations when a practitioner is excluded for personal reasons which are not shared with the remainder of the group. It is therefore a useful practice to discuss the required membership of a group and its likely effectiveness in safeguarding terms by considering the key contacts with the child particularly those who have a regular contact such as nursery workers, early years, reception and infant teachers who have the child in their room every day and therefore are most likely to know her or him well.

Practice reflection points

- How will you ensure that you remain ethical in your practice?
- How will you maintain an ethical dynamic with a busy workload?
- Are there skills that you believe that you and/or others in the team have that could be described as ethical? What are those skills? How might they be successfully disseminated?
- Reflect on your recent practice and identify times when you believe that a stronger ethical approach might have led to a better outcome. How might the situation that you have identified be incorporated into a team discussion?

The development of community involvement

The sense that there is a community as a coherent group 'out there' is problematic, particularly in light of recent funding cuts to local authorities. This has impacted on projects that were starting to deliver a proactive service to the 'hardest to reach populations' described as follows in the National Evaluation Summary (Barlow et al. 2007):

> A focus on the relationship between parent and child suffused all the activities offered to families in some SSLPs [Sure Start Local Programmes] beginning during pregnancy and continuing through toddlerhood and beyond. One local manager described the approach: *'Everything we do is ultimately aimed at influencing the way in which parents parent, every single thing from the minute they [parents] walk through the door hopefully, in the way that we are, the way we talk with parents, and the way that we talk with their children...'* The philosophy and culture of these SSLPs was distinctive, and evident in the emphasis on a relationship between parent and child beginning before birth.
>
> (Barlow et al. 2007: 4)

Early years professionals need to be aware of the context of the families they work with; this may include geographical or cultural factors relevant to the lives of the babies and young children. Professionals themselves belong to a variety of communities influencing their values and judgements, including their upbringing, their own cultural, family and living circumstances and the professional and organizational influences on their working practices (Barlow et al. 2007).

Following the 2010 general election and the emergence of the UK coalition government, there has been a shift for community provision of childcare services delivered by Sure Start from the statutory to the private, voluntary and independent sectors. This may make a difference to the services that will be provided and whether family support or outreach work will be encouraged in the ways it had prior to the general election. If the development of support of vulnerable families is not as forthcoming, there may well be an increase in concern for babies and young children and their well-being. Particularly in the light of evidence from the NSPCC:

> The number of serious child abuse cases referred to police or social services by the NSPCC reached an all-time high last year, the children's charity says. NSPCC counsellors referred 16,385 serious cases to police or social services in 2010/11, which is 37 per cent higher than the previous year.
>
> (BBC News 2011a)

Early years professionals and their managers will be aware of the geography and demographics of the community they work in, the sense of ethnic diversity and class, and whether there is high or low employment level. In areas where there are high levels of deprivation and poverty, there may well be an increase in concerns relating to safeguarding with potentially fewer experienced practitioners available to support vulnerable families in dealing with these issues. This suggests that the likelihood of child abuse increasing may well be linked to a reduction in available staff to carry out prevention work in the community.

There are serious questions that you as a practitioner or manager may be able to raise about ways that the prevention of child abuse could be considered in your agency. Equally if you are a student on placement, you will be able to study the agency where you are currently training and critically analyse the ways in which it seems to be represented to a wider community. The diversity of experiences and perspectives of practitioners can influence relationships with families and other professionals and agencies.

Most practitioners working in early years aim to maximize efforts to work closely with practitioners involved with families and to avoid making assumptions, not only about behaviour of families, but also regarding the knowledge and actions of other professionals and agencies in contact with families in the community. This is a complex area.

Effort is required to communicate effectively, build positive working relationships and share responsibility for assessment and support of families. There are many barriers to interprofessional cooperation including the practitioner position in a professional model of hierarchy and the potential for expert views to sometimes appear to close down communication from the wider professional group. The value attributed to different views may also be related to professional hierarchy with those at the top of the hierarchy such as paediatricians likely to be considered by others at case review or conference as being of more value than a practitioner with a lower status such as a nursery worker but who has a greater knowledge of the family and the child (Powell 2007).

Positive working relationships can be facilitated by developing shared understanding of roles and perspective through joint training and meetings. Co-location and integrated teams are sometimes recommended to achieve this, but it is not always necessary to be in the same building to work together well. Indeed the opposite can be true, as professionals can equally communicate and work together effectively while retaining separate roles and responsibilities.

The benefits to the family of good interprofessional work cannot be overemphasized. It can provide seamless provision of services, avoiding overlap while ensuring that services are actually being provided (misunderstandings can occur when everyone thinks someone else is involved – so they don't need to be). For the parents and carers, the benefit is avoiding repetition of their story to a number of different professionals, and avoiding contradictions and conflicting advice.

Effective communication between all professionals involved with a family can result in appropriate support being provided at the right time, with a focus on prevention rather than dealing with the results of abuse. Delay and drift can also be avoided in dealing with issues as they arise.

While following procedures and process is important, this must not be at the expense of direct engagement and interaction with families, professional judgement and quality assessment of need, or indeed timely and appropriate action.

Practice reflection points

- How might you facilitate better interprofessional relationships? If you are a manager, are there policy developments that could facilitate improved communication? If you are a practitioner or a student, are there skills that you believe you may have which support the process of inter-agency relationships? What are the skills?

- Are there skills and practices that on reflection you believe could be refined and improved? What are they and how will you go about developing them?

Conclusion: questions for your practice

- How can a historical perspective be considered in terms of your personal practice or into the way that the team thinks about practice?
- How can the rights of the child be integrated into your practice and that of the team?
- How can you ensure that a child's voice will be included in practice contexts? How can this be supported throughout the team?
- How can you ensure that you are maintaining a focus on the child while at the same time not alienating the parents? If you are a manager, are there practical ways that this question can be addressed?
- How can ethics be incorporated into your personal and the team's everyday practice?
- If you don't get the response to your concerns that you feel is necessary, what can you do?
- How do you believe your focus on the child will be maintained despite potential distractions?
- What is it you expect to happen at the point where you share your concerns for the first time? Are your expectations reasonable?
- What can you do if you are working with families who are resistant to your intervention and concerns? Is a team response possible? Can others in the team support aspects of work that may help overcome family resistance?
- What can you do if you are working with practitioners who seem resistant to working in an acceptable interdisciplinary way?
- What is expected of you by others – including the child, his or her parents or carers and the community of practitioners that you are part of?
- What is confidentiality? How do you understand it in terms of your role relating to safeguarding situations in particular?
- Will you be able to incorporate strategies of 'forewarning' into everyday practices that emphasize telling the parent or carer that confidentiality means that you may have to pass on concerns? Is it possible as a team manager to develop a policy relating to this? Can documents include a statement relating to forewarning?
- How will you keep records? Do you think you should tell parents or carers that you are doing so? Is it appropriate for this to be developed into a team approach?

- If you don't agree with the system or procedures, what will you do? How would you assert your view? Is there a policy of whistle blowing? Would you use it if necessary?
- There are occasions when policy can be viewed as an obstacle – what is your strategy for overcoming situations when this appears to be the case?

Key messages

- Awareness of power in dynamic interprofessional relationships and practitioner relationships with parents and carers.
- Confidentiality and developing an understanding of the importance of issues relating to the confidential relationship.
- Process and procedures – not only their significance but also their ability to undermine action.
- Systems theory and how it links to the concept of safer cultures.
- Children's rights – recognizing 'voice and agency' – while retaining a clear understanding that the needs of the child is paramount (Children Act 1989).
- The ability to develop meaningful interactions with parents or carers and at the same time recognizing the need to avoid collusion with them because the child is the central focus of consideration.
- The key concept for practice is to always act on behalf of the child.
- Remember children have rights and may need you to be their advocate to recognize them.
- It is probably important to relate to a general rule of optimism while at the same time ensuring that your practice is strongly embedded to reality.
- Make sure that you are as active and proactive as possible when intervening, and at the same time fully record any actions or discussions that you have been involved in. You may also need to explain your rationale or reason for this.
- Remember to act ethically at all times in line with the principles outlined in Chapter 4.
- Remember to remind the parent or carer that child protection issues override confidentiality concerns.
- The central practice for you is therefore one that carefully includes a strong child focus and incorporates the notion of the child as an active participant in child protection.

References

Abrahams, C. (1994) *The Hidden Victims: Children and Domestic Violence*. London: NCH Action for Children.

Action for Children (ACH) (2008) *Supporting Families: Children on the Edge of Care*. Action for Children Briefing. Available at www.actionforchildren.org.uk/media/95626/action_for_children_supporting_families_on_the_edge_of_care.pdf (accessed 14 July 2011).

Adair, J. (1987) *Effective Teambuilding*. London: Pan.

Alderson, P. (2000a) 'UN Convention on the Rights of the Child: Some common criticisms and suggested responses.' *Child Abuse Review* 9(6): 439–443.

Alderson, P. (2000b) *Young Children's Rights: Exploring Beliefs, Principles and Practice*. London: Jessica Kingsley.

Allison, G. (1971) *Essence of Decision: Explaining the Cuban Missile Crisis*. Boston, MA: Little, Brown.

Banks, S. (2006) *Ethics and Values in Social Work*, 3rd edn. Basingstoke: Palgrave Macmillan.

Banks, S. and Gallagher, A. (2009) *Ethics in Professional Life: Virtues for Health and Social Care*. Basingstoke: Palgrave Macmillan.

Barlow, J., Kirkpatrick, S. and Wood, M., Ball, D. and Stewart-Brown, S. (2007) *Family and Parenting Support in Sure Start Local Programmes: National Evaluation Summary*. London: DfES. Available at www.ness.bbk.ac.uk/implementation/documents/34.pdf (accessed 26 July 2011).

BBC News (2011a) NSPCC says child abuse referrals at all-time high 21 April 2011. Available at www.bbc.co.uk/news/uk-13147650 (accessed 9 May 2011).

BBC News (2011b) Child protection system shake-up urged, Richardson, H., 10 May 2011. Available at www.bbc.co.uk/news/education-13335150 (accessed 10 May 2011).

Beauchamp, T.L. and Childress, J.F. (2001) *Principles of Biomedical Ethics*, 5th edn. Oxford: Oxford University Press.

Behlmer, G. (1982) *Child Abuse and Moral Reform in England 1870–1908*. Stanford, CA: Stanford University Press.

Bichard, M. (2004) *The Bichard Inquiry Report*. London: The Stationery Office.

Bion, W.R. (1961) *Experience in Groups*. London: Tavistock.

Blythe, E. and Milner, J. (1990) 'The process of inter-agency work.' In Violence Against Children Study Group, *Taking Child Abuse Seriously: Contemporary Issues in Child Protection Theory and Practice*. London: Unwin Hyman.

Bolam v Friern Hospital Management Committee [1957] 2 All ER 118 [1957] 1 WLR 582.

Bolitho v City and Hackney HA [1997] *Lloyds Law Reports Medical*. Part 1, pp. 26–37.

Bolton, G. (2005) *Reflective Practice: Writing and Professional Development*, 2nd edn. London: Sage.

Bolton, G. (2010) *Reflective Practice: Writing and Professional Development*, 3rd edn. London: Sage.

Bolton Safeguarding Board (2007) *Framework for Action*. Bolton: Bolton Safeguarding Children Board.

Bowlby, J. (1951) *Maternal Care and Maternal Health: A Report Prepared on Behalf of the World Health Organization as a Contribution to the United Nations Programme for the Welfare of Homeless Children*. Geneva: World Health Organization.

Brandon, M., Owers, M. and Black, J. (1999) *Learning How to Make Children Safer: An Analysis for the Welsh Office of Serious Child Abuse Cases in Wales*. Norwich: University of East Anglia and Welsh Office.

Brandon, M., Bailey, S., Belderson, P., Gardner, R., Sidebottom, P., Dodsworth, J., Warren, C. and Black, J. (2009) *Understanding Serious Case Reviews and their Impact: A Biennial Analysis of Serious Case Reviews 2005–7*. London: Department for Children, Schools and Families.

British Association of Social Workers (BASW) (2011) *Code of Ethics*. Birmingham: BASW. Available at www.basw.co.uk/about/code-of-ethics/ (accessed 25 July 2011).

Bronfenbrenner, U. (1979) *The Ecology of Human Development*. Cambridge, MA: Harvard University Press.

Brookfield, S.D. (2005) *The Power of Critical Theory for Adult Learning and Teaching*. Maidenhead: Open University Press.

Browne, K.D. and Saqi, S. (1987) 'Parent–child interaction in abusing families: Its possible causes and consequences.' In P. Maher (ed.) *Child Abuse: The Educational Perspective*. Oxford: Blackwell Scientific.

Buckley, B. (2003) *Children's Communication Skills: From Birth to Five Years*. London: Routledge.

Butler-Sloss, E. (1988) *Report of the Inquiry into Child Abuse in Cleveland 1987*. London: The Stationery Office.

CAFCASS (2009) *The 'Baby Peter Effect' and the Increase in s31 Care Order Applications*. Available at www.cafcass.gov.uk/PDF/Baby%20Peter%20exec%20summary%20final.pdf (accessed 16 January 2011).

Children Act (2004) Children Act. Available at www.opsi.gov.uk/acts/acts2004/ukpga_20040031_en_3 (accessed 14 August 2008).

Children's Rights Alliance (2010) Children's Rights Alliance website. Available at www.crae.org.uk (accessed 27 April 2011).

Cicchetti, D. and Rizley, R. (1981) 'Developmental perspectives on the intergenerational transmission, and sequelae of child maltreatment.' In R. Rizley and D. Cicchetti (eds) *Developmental Perspectives on Child Maltreatment*. San Francisco, CA: Jossey-Bass.

Clémant, M.E. and Tourginy, M. (1997) 'A review of the literature on the prevention of child abuse and neglect: Characteristics and effectiveness of home visiting programs.' *International Journal of Child and Family Welfare* 1: 6–20.

Clyde, J.J. (1992) *The Report of the Inquiry into the Removal of Children from Orkney in February 1991*. Edinburgh: HMSO.

Cohen, A.P. (1985) *The Symbolic Construction of Community*. London: Tavistock.

Cohen, A.P. (1989) *The Symbolic Construction of Community*, reprint. London: Routledge.

Commission for Social Care Inspection (2005) *Safeguarding Children: The Second Joint Chief Inspectors' Report on Arrangements to Safeguard Children*. Newcastle: Commission for Social Care Inspection. Available at www.safeguarding children.org.uk (accessed 16 January 2010).

Corby, B. (2006) *Child Abuse: Towards a Knowledge Base*. Maidenhead: Open University Press.

Cunningham, H. (1995) *Children and Childhood in Western Society Since 1500*. London: Longman.

Department for Children, Schools and Families (DCSF) (2008) *Information Sharing: Guidance for Practitioners and Managers*. London: DCSF and Department for Communities and Local Government.

Department for Children, Schools and Families (DCSF) (2010) *Working Together to Safeguard Children 2010: A Guide to Inter-Agency Working to Safeguard and Promote the Welfare of Children*. London: HM Government.

Department for Education and Skills (DfES) (2003a) *The Birth to Three Matters Framework*. London: HMSO.

Department for Education and Skills (DfES) (2003b) *Every Child Matters*. London: HMSO. Available at http://webarchive.nationalarchives.gov.uk/ 20080915105927/everychildmatters.gov.uk/children/

Department for Education and Skills (DfES) (2004a) *Every Child Matters: Change for Children*. London: HMSO.

Department for Education and Skills (DfES) (2004b) *Every Child Matters: Next Steps*. London: HMSO. Available at www.everychildmatters.gov.uk (accessed 12 August 2008).

Department for Education and Skills (DfES) (2004c) *Working Together: A Sure Start Guide to the Childcare and Early Education Field*. Available at www.education.gov.uk/publications/eOrderingDownload/SSWT0304PDF.pdf (accessed 12 August 2008).

Department for Education and Skills (DfES) (2005) *Safeguarding Children in Education*. London: HMSO.

Department for Education and Skills (DfES) (2006a) *Information Sharing: Practitioner's Guide*. London: DfES.

Department for Education and Skills (DfES) (2006b) *What To Do If You're Worried a Child is Being Abused – Summary*. London: HM Government.

Department for Education and Skills (DfES) (2007) *Early Years Foundation Stage*. London: DfES.

Department of Health (DH) (1991) *Child Abuse: A Study of Inquiry Reports 1980–1989*. London: HMSO.

Department of Health (DH) (1995) *Child Protection: Messages from Research*. London: HMSO.

Department of Health (DH) (1999) *Working Together to Safeguard Children*. London: DH.

Department of Health (DH) (2000) *Framework for the Assessment of Children in Need and their Families*. London: The Stationery Office.

Department of Health (DH) (2003) *What To Do If You're Worried a Child is Being Abused*. London: DH.

Department of Health (DH) (2004) *National Service Framework for Children, Young People and Maternity Services*. London: DH.

Department of Health (DH) (2006) *Working Together to Safeguard Children: A Guide to Inter-Agency Working to Safeguard and Promote Welfare of Children*. London: DH.

Department of Health (DH) (2010) *Liberating the NHS*. London: DH.

Department of Health (DH) and Home Office (1991) *Working Together Under the Children Act 1989: A Guide to Arrangements for Inter-Agency Co-operation for the Protection of Children from Abuse*. London: HMSO

Department of Health and Social Security (DHSS) (1974) *Report of the Committee of Inquiry into the Care and Supervision Provided in Relation to Maria Colwell*. London: HMSO.

Department of Health and Social Security (DHSS) (1980) *Child Abuse: Central Register Systems*, Circular LASSL (80)4. London: HMSO.

Department of Health and Social Security (DHSS) (1988) *Working Together: A Guide to Inter-Agency Co-operation for the Protection of Children from Abuse*. London: HMSO.

DHSS (1975) *The Report of the Committee of Inquiry into the Provision and Co-ordination of Services to the Family of John George Auckland*. London: HMSO.

Dimond, B. (2003) 'Child protection and the midwife.' *British Journal of Midwifery* 11(12): 737–740.

Dingwall, R., Eekelaar, J. and Murray, T. (1983) *The Protection of Children: State Intervention and Family Life*. Oxford: Blackwell.

Douglas, M. (1992) *Risk and Blame Essays on Cultural Theory*. London: Routledge.

Dunford, J. (2010) *Review of the Office of the Children's Commissioner (England)*. London: Department of Education.

Edleson, J. (1999) 'Children witnessing of adult domestic violence.' *Journal of Interpersonal Violence* 14(4): 839–870.

Frazer, E. (2000) *The Problem of Communitarian Politics: Unity and Conflict*. Oxford: Oxford University Press.

Freeman, M.D.A. (1983) *The Rights and Wrongs of Children*. London: Francis Pinter.

Freeman, M.D.A. (1987) 'Taking children's rights seriously.' *Children and Society* 1(4): 299–319.

Furedi, F. (2009) *Paranoid Parenting: Why Ignoring the Experts May Be Good for your Child*. London: Continuum.

Gateshead Children and Young People's Partnership (CYP) (2009) *Signs of Wellbeing Tool*. Available at www.gatesheadcyptrust.co.uk/processes/caf/index.htm (accessed 25 July 2011).

General Teaching Council for England (GTC) (2009) *Code of Conduct and Practice for Registered Teachers*. London: GTC. Available at www.gtce.org.uk/publications/code_of_conduct_2009/ (accessed 25 July 2011).

Germain, C. and Glitterman, A. (1996) *The Life Model of Social Work Practice: Advances in Theory and Practice*. New York: Columbia University Press.

Gersch, I.F. (1996) 'Listening to children in educational contexts.' In R. Varma, G. Upton and V. Varma (eds) *The Voice of the Child: A Handbook for Professionals*. London: Falmer.

Gibbs, G. (1988) *Learning by Doing: A Guide to Teaching and Learning Methods*. Oxford: Oxford Further Education Unit.

Giddens, A. (1991) *Modernity and Self-Identity*. Cambridge: Polity.

Gillick v West Norfolk and Wisbech AHA (1986) AC 112 [1985] 3 ALL ER 402 (1985) 2 BMLR 11 (HL).

Hall, D. and Elliman, D. (eds) (2003) *Health for All Children*, 4th edn. Oxford: Oxford Medical Publication.

Hall, P. (1982) 'Approaching the problem.' In A. McGrew and M. Wilson (eds) *Decision Making: Approaches and Analysis*. Manchester: Manchester University Press.

Hardiker, P., Exton, K. and Barker, M. (1991) 'The social policy contexts of prevention in child care.' *British Journal of Social Work* 21: 341–359.

Haringey LSCB (2008) *Baby Peter Serious Case Review Executive Summary*. London: Haringey Local Safeguarding Children Board.

Hart, J.T. (1971) 'The inverse care law.' *The Lancet* 1(7696): 405–412.

Hawkes, N. (2005) ' Hospital may ban treatment for smokers and drinkers.' *The Times* 9 December. Available at www.timesonline.co.uk/tol/news/uk/article755775.ece (accessed 14 July 2011).

Healy, K. (2005) *Social Work Theories in Context: Creating Frameworks for Practice*. London: Macmillan.

Hester, M., Pearson, C. and Harwin, N. (2000) *Making an Impact: Children and Domestic Violence – A Reader*. London: Jessica Kingsley.

Hoff, B. (1982) *The Tao of Pooh*. London: Methuen.

Holland, S. (2004) *Child and Family Assessment in Social Work Practice*. London: Sage.

Home Office, Ministry of Health and Ministry of Education (1951) *Joint Circular Home Office 157/50, Ministry of Health 78/50, and Ministry of Education 225/50*. Quoted in Home Office (1951) *Sixth Report of the Children's Department*. London: Home Office.

Human Rights Act (1998) Human Rights Act. Available at www.legislation.gov.uk/ukpga/1998/42/contents (accessed 17 January 2011).

Humphreys, C. and Thiara, T. (2002) *Routes to Safety: Protection Issues Facing Abused Women and Children and the Role of Outreach Services*. Bristol: Women's Aid Federation England.

Ingleby, O. (1960) *Report of the Committee on Children and Young Persons*, Cmnd 1191. London: HMSO.

Jack, G. (2006) 'The area and community components of children's well-being.' *Children and Society* 20: 334–347.

Johns, C. (1994) 'Guided reflection.' In A. Palmer, S. Burns and C. Bulman (eds) *Reflective Practice in Nursing*. Oxford: Blackwell Science.

Jones, S.R. and Jenkins, R. (2004) *The Law and the Midwife*, 2nd edn. Oxford: Blackwell.

Kemp, S., Whittaker, J. and Tracy, E. (1997) *Person–Environment Practice*. New York: Aldine de Gruyter.

Kempe, R., Silverman, F., Steele, B., Droegemueller, W. and Silver, H. (1962) 'The battered child syndrome.' *Journal of the American Medical Association* 181: 17–24.

Laming, H. (2003) *The Victoria Climbié Inquiry: Report of an Inquiry by Lord Laming*. London: HMSO. Available at www.victoria-climbie-inquiry.org.uk/

Laming, H. (2009) *The Protection of Children in England: A Progress Report*. London: HMSO.

London Borough of Brent (1985) *Jasmine Beckford Inquiry Report: A Child in Trust*. London: Brent Borough Council.

London Borough of Greenwich (1987) *Report of the Commission of Inquiry into the Circumstances Surrounding the Death of Kimberley Carlile: A Child in Mind. Protection of Children in a Responsible Society*. London: London Borough of Greenwich.

London Borough of Lambeth (1987) *Whose Child? The Report of the Panel Appointed to Inquire into the Death of Tyra Henry*. London: London Borough of Lambeth.

Macdonald, G. and Winkley, A. (1999) *What Works in Child Protection*. Ilford: Barnados.

McLaren, H. (2007) 'Exploring the ethics of forewarning: social workers, confidentiality and potential child abuse disclosures.' *Ethics and Social Welfare* 1: 22–40.

Macmillan, H.L., Macmillan, J.H., Offord, D.R., Griffith, L. and Macmillan, A. (1994) 'Primary prevention of child physical abuse and neglect: A critical review. Part I.' *Journal of Child Psychology and Psychiatry* 35: 835–856.

Marcellus, L. (2005) 'The ethics of relation: Public health nurses and child protection clients.' *Journal of Advanced Nursing* 51(4): 414–420.

Mason, J.K., McCall Smith, R.A. and Laurie, G.T. (2002) *Law and Medical Ethics*, 6th edn. London: Lexis Nexis Butterworths.

Meadows, R. (1977) 'Munchausen syndrome by proxy: The hinterland of child abuse.' *The Lancet* 57: 92–98.

Morrison, T. (1998) 'Partnership, collaboration and change under the Children Act.' In M. Adcock and R. White (eds) *Significant Harm: It's Management and Outcome*. Croydon: Significant Publications.

Muir, J. (1911) *My First Summer in the Sierra*. Boston, MA: Houghton Mifflin.

Munro, E. (1999) 'Common errors of reasoning in child protection work.' *Child Abuse and Neglect* 23: 745–758.

Munro, E. (2007) 'Confidentiality in a preventative child welfare system.' *Ethics and Social Welfare* 1: 41–56.

Munro, E. (2008) *Effective Child Protection*, 2nd edn. London: Sage.

Munro, E. (2010) *The Munro Review of Child Protection: Part One, A System's Analysis*. Available at www.education.gov.uk/munroreview/downloads/TheMunroReviewofChildProtection-Part%20one.pdf (accessed 2 May 2011).

Munro, E. (2011) *The Munro Review of Child Protection: Interim Report – The Child's Journey*. Available at www.education.gov.uk/munroreview/downloads/Munrointerimreport.pdf (accessed 2 May 2011).

Myers, J.E.B. (2004) *A History of Child Protection in America*. Philadelphia, PA: Xlibris.

Nursing and Midwifery Council (NMC) (2008) *The Code: Standards of Conduct, Performance and Ethics for Nurses and Midwives*. London: NMC. Available at www.nmc-uk.org/Nurses-and-midwives/The-code/The-code-in-full (accessed 25 July 2011).

Oates, R.K. and Bross, D.C. (1995) What have we learned about treating child physical abuse? A literature review of the last decade. *Child Abuse and Neglect Review* 19: 463–473.

Oberle, K. and Tenove, S. (2000) Ethical issues in public health nursing. *Nursing Ethics* 7: 426–438.

O'Hanlon, B. (1995) 'Breaking the bad trance.' London Conference.

Olds, D.L. and Henderson, C.R. (1986) 'Preventing child abuse and neglect: A randomised trial of nurse home visitation.' *Pediatrics* 78: 65–78.

Olds, D.L. and Kitzman, H. (1993) 'Review of research on home-visiting for pregnant women and parents of young children.' *The Future of Children* 3: 53–91.

Olds, D.L., Eckenrode, J., Henderson, C.R., Kitzman, J.H., Powers, J., Cole, R., Kimberley, S., Morris, P., Pettitt, L. and Luckey, D. (1997) 'Long-term effects of home visitation on maternal life course and child abuse.' *Journal of the American Medical Association* 278(8): 637–643.

P v East Berkshire Community Health Trust (2003) EWCA Civ 1151.

Parton, N. (2006) *Safeguarding Childhood: Early Intervention and Surveillance in a Late Modern Society*. Basingstoke: Palgrave Macmillan.

Parton, N. and O'Byrne, P. (2000) *Constructive Social Work: Towards a New Practice*. Basingstoke: Palgrave Macmillan.

Payne, G. (ed.) (2000) *Social Divisions*. Basingstoke: Palgrave Macmillan.

Payne, M. (1997) *Modern Social Work Theory*, 2nd edn. Chicago, IL: Lyceum.

Payne, M. (2005) *Modern Social Work Theory*, 3rd edn. Basingstoke: Palgrave Macmillan.

Peckover, S. (2002) 'Supporting and policing mothers: An analysis of the disciplinary practices of health visiting.' *Journal of Advanced Nursing* 38: 369–377.

Powell, J. (2005a) 'Child protection.' In L. Jones, R. Holmes and J. Powell (eds) *Early Childhood Studies: A Multiprofessional Perspective*. Maidenhead: Open University Press.

Powell, J. (2005b) 'Safety matters.' In L. Abbott and A. Langston (eds) *Birth to Three Matters: Supporting the Framework of the Effective Practice*. Maidenhead: Open University Press.

Powell, J. (2007) 'Multi-agency development and issues of communication.' In A. Nurse (ed.) *The New Early Years Professional: Dilemmas and Debates*. Abingdon: Routledge Fulton Press.

Powell, R. (2001) *Child Law: A Guide for Courts and Practitioners*. Winchester: Waterside Press.

R v Harrow London Borough Council, ex p D [1990] Fam 133, [1990] 3 All ER 12, CA.

R v Norfolk County Social Services Department, ex p M [1989] 2 All ER 359.

Reder, P. and Duncan, S. (1999) *Lost Innocents: A Follow-up Study of Fatal Child Abuse*. London: Routledge.

Reder, P. and Duncan, S. (2003) ' Understanding communication in child protection networks.' *Child Abuse Review* 12: 82–100.

Reder, P., Duncan, S. and Gray, M. (1993) *Beyond Blame: Child Abuse Tragedies Revisited*. London: Routledge.

Robinson, R.M., Anning, A., Cottrell, D., Frost, N. and Green, J.M. (2004) *New Forms of Professional Knowledge in Multi-Agency Delivery of Services for Children (The MATCh Project): Summary End of Award Report to the Economic and Social Research Council*. Leeds: University of Leeds.

Ross, E.M. (1996) 'Learning to listen to children.' In R. Varma, G. Upton and V. Varma (eds) *The Voice of the Child: A Handbook for Professionals*. London: Falmer.

Sameroff, A.J. and Chandler, M.J. (1975) 'Reproductive risk and the continuum of caretaker casualty.' In F.D. Horowitz (ed.) *Review of Child Development Research*, Volume 4. Chicago, IL: University of Chicago Press.

Seebohm, F. (1968) *Report of the Committee on Local Authority and Allied Personal Social Services* (Seebohm report). London: HMSO.

Sinclair, R. and Bullock, R. (2002) *Learning from Past Experience: A Review of Serious Case Reviews*. London: Department of Health.

Sinclair, R., Hearn, B., and Pugh, G. (1997) *Preventive Work with Families: The Role of Mainstream Services*. London: National Children's Bureau.

Singer, P. (1993) *Practical Ethics*. New York: Cambridge University Press.

Smale, G., Tuson, G., Behal, N. and Marsh, P. (1993) *Empowerment, Assessment, Care Management and the Skilled Worker*. London: National Institute of Social Work.

Stark, E. and Flitcraft, A. (1996) *Women at Risk: Domestic Violence and Women's Health*. Thousand Oaks, CA: Sage.

Stevenson, O. (1963) 'Co-ordination reviewed.' *Case Conference* 9(8): 208–212. Reprinted in E. Younghusband (ed.) (1967) *Social Work and Social Values*. London: Allen & Unwin.

Stevenson, O. (1998) *Neglected Children: Issues and Dilemmas*. Oxford: Blackwell Science.

Sullivan v Moody (2001) 207 CLR 562.

Thompson, N. (2003) *Promoting Equality: Challenging Discrimination and Oppression*, 2nd edn. Basingstoke: Palgrave Macmillan.

Turnell, A. and Edwards, S. (1999) *Signs of Safety: A Solution and Safety Oriented Approach to Child Protection Casework*. New York: Norton. (Also see www.signsofsafety.net/)

UNCRC (1989) *United Nations Convention on the Rights of the Child*. Unicef. Available at www.unicef.org/crc/fulltext.htm (accessed 16 January 2011).

W v Egdell (1990) 1 All ER 835 (1989) 4 BMLR 96 (CA).

Wakefield, J.C. (1996a) 'Does social work need the eco-systems perspective? Part 1: Is the perspective clinically useful?' *Social Service Review* 70: 1–32.

Wakefield, J.C. (1996b) 'Does social work need the eco-systems perspective? Part 2: Does the perspective save social work from incoherence?' *Social Service Review* 70: 183–213.

Ward, L. (2005) 'Serious failings persist in care of vulnerable children: Five years after Climbié case concerns are highlighted.' *Guardian* 14 July. Available at www.guardian.co.uk/society/2005/jul/14/childrensservices.politics?INTCMP= SRCH (accessed 14 July 2011).

Wenger, E. (1998) 'Communities of practice: Learning as a social system.' *Systems Thinker* 5. Available at www.ewenger.com/pub/pub_systems_thinker_wrd.doc (accessed 29 September 2010).

Wenger, E. (1999) *Communities of Practice: Learning, Meaning and Identity*. Cambridge: Cambridge University Press.

Winnicott, D. (1951) 'Transitional objects and transitional phenomena.' In D. Winnicott (1958) *Collected Papers*. London: Tavistock.

Winter, R., Buck, A. and Sobiechowska, P. (1999) *Professional Experience and the Investigative Imagination: The Art of Reflective Writing*. London: Routledge.

Index

Abrahams, C. 150
abuse
    definitions of 106–9
    levels of, difficulties in categorization of
        152–3
    neglect or, categories of 165, 174
    problems of child abuse, longstanding
        nature of 50
    recognition of child abuse 55–6
    referrals for, increasing numbers of 186
    signs on the child 21–22
Act Utilitarianism 77, 78
action, framework for 103
Action for Children (ACH, 2008) 116
Adair, J. 70, 88
adaptation to situations 71, 83, 177, 182
Adoption Act (1976) 36
Adoption and Children Act (2002) 26, 36
adults acting for children, role of 42–3
agencies
    checks and information gathering by
        129–30
    contextual situations, regular review by
        62
    responses of, information sharing and
        94–6
    responsibilities and roles of 97
    roles of, early years professionals and
        96–7
Alderson, P. 40, 41, 180
alerts and warnings
    raising concerns and identification of
        abuse 105–6
Allan, Graham 110
Allison, G. 126
anxiety in contemporary society, extent of
    33
Area Child Protection Committees (ACPC)
    14, 88
assessment
    ongoing core group assessment, focus of
        167–8
assessment and referral 5, 125–37
    agency checks and information gathering
        129–30

assessment
    decision-making process and 126,
        137
    definition of 125–7
    focus of 125–6
    risk within processes of 126–7
case study 132–7
    actions, consideration of 136–7
    benefits of action 133
    carers views on concerns 135–6
    child, focus on 135
    child protection plan 137
    child's rights, recognition of 134
    community involvement 135
    ethical practice 134–5
    experiences of child 135
    family history, lessons from 133–4
    information requirements and sources
        133
    initial alert 133
    initiation of action, feelings about 133
    interventions, coordination and
        implementation of 136–7
    prior knowledge 133
    risks of action 133
    safeguarding and child protection,
        application of definitions 133
core assessment 131
emotions, thoughts and actions,
    distinction between 126
initial assessment
    carrying out of 129, 137
    outcome of 130–31
key messages 137
notification of police 130
overview 125
purpose of initial assessment (section 17,
    Children Act, 1989) 128
risk as concept in child protection 127
risk assessment, implementation of
    127–8, 137
section 47 enquiries 131–2, 137
seeing the child 129
timescale of initial assessment 128
assumptions, avoidance of 98

Auckland, Susan 14
Aynsley-Green, Professor Al 34–5

baby and young child as focus of
    safeguarding 3, 48–64
  agency context, regular review of 62
  child beating in public
    example of 53–5
    foreseeable outcomes of intervention
      53
    issues illustrated 54–5
    key reasons for intervention 54
    lessons from example 53–4
    reflection on 53–4
  child protection, development of
    framework for 48–9
  children are our future 48
  children at risk, concept of 49
  communication, importance of clarity in
    63
  concerns about possible abuse,
    prioritization of 63
  creativity and inclusiveness 62
  cross-agency involvement 62
  discussions with other practitioners 63–4
  encouragement of positive behaviour 62
  Every Child Matters (DfES, 2004) 48–9, 50
  everyday practices 52–5
  focus, strength and clarity of 52
  home context 61
  key messages 63–4
  local community context 62
  objectivity 64
  opinions of others, dealing with 64
  overview 48
  problems of child abuse, longstanding
    nature of 50
  professional expectations 51
  promotion of safer cultures 61–3
  recognition of child abuse 55–6
  record-keeping 64
  relationship with close carers 61–2
  safeguarding agenda, challenge of 50–51
  safer cultures 57–9
  safer cultures approach, development of
    64
  safer cultures approach, principles for 61
  systems approach 59–60
  values of support, clarity and focus in 63
  worst case scenario 51
Baby P *see* Connelly, Peter
balancing relationships 152–5, 160
Banks, S. 66, 67–8, 71–2

Banks, S. and Gallacher, A. 72
Barlow, J., Kirkpatrick, S. et al. 185–6
BBC News 1, 186
Beauchamp, T.L. and Childress, J.F. 77
Beckford, Jasmine 15, 50
Behlmer, G. 10
beneficence 77
Bichard Report (2004) 60
Bion, W.R. 87
Blythe, E. and Millner, J. 87
Bolam v Friern Hospital Management
    Committee (2010) 78–9
Bolitho v City and Hackney HA (1997) 78–9
Bolton, G. 44, 46
Bolton Safeguarding Board 103
Bowlby, J. 11
Brandon, M., Bailey, S. et al. 94
Brandon, M., Owers, M. and Black, J. 86
Brent, London Borough of 15
British Association of Social Workers
    (BASW) 65–6
Bronfenbrenner, U. 57–9, 108
Brookfield, S.D. 177
Browne, K.D. and Saqi, S. 108
Buckley, B. 41
Butler-Sloss, E. 15, 16, 55, 153

Caldicott Guardian 96
Carlile, Kimberley 15
case studies
  assessment and referral 132–7
    actions, consideration of 136–7
    benefits of action 133
    carers views on concerns 135–6
    child, focus on 135
    child protection plan 137
    child's rights, recognition of 134
    community involvement 135
    ethical practice 134–5
    experiences of child 135
    family history, lessons from 133–4
    information requirements and sources
      133
    initial alert 133
    initiation of action, feelings about 133
    interventions, coordination and
      implementation of 136–7
    prior knowledge 133
    risks of action 133
    safeguarding and child protection,
      application of definitions 133
  child beating in public
    example of 53–5

foreseeable outcomes of intervention 53

issues illustrated 54–5

key reasons for intervention 54

lessons from example 53–4

reflection on 53–4

ethical practice 80–82

assessment of strengths and needs of children 82

ethical considerations arising 81

focus on improvement of lives of children 81

positive well-being, development of 81

role of early years professionals, importance of 81, 82

significant adults, attachment with 82

support for or hindrance to well-being 81–2

vulnerability of babies and young children, factors influencing 82

intervention, potential impacts of 169–74

alerts and warnings 171

benefits of action 171

child protection plan, instigation of 169–74

development and sustenance of safer culture 173–4

information requirements and sources 171

initial alert 171

initial responses 169–70

initiation of action, feelings about 171

monitoring and subsequent interventions 172

prior knowledge 171

risks of action 171

safeguarding and child protection, application of definitions 171

safer cultures approach, application of 173, 175

support group conversations 172

parents and carers of abused baby or young child, working with 155–9

actions, consideration of 158–9

alerts and warnings 156–7

benefits of action 157

identification of appropriate support services 158–9

information requirements and sources 157

initial alert 156

initial responses 157–8

initiation of action, feelings about 157

positive relationship, maintenance of 159

prior knowledge 157

risks of action 157

safeguarding and child protection, application of definitions 156–7

strengths within family 159

raising concerns and identification of abuse

alerts and warnings 111–12

benefits of action 112

courses of action, consideration of 113

early intervention, dichotomy in 110

further action, consideration of 114

information requirements and sources 112

initial alert 111, 112–13

initiation of action, feelings about 112

levels of prevention 109–10

prevention, child protection within context of 109–14

primary prevention 110, 115

prior knowledge 112

quaternary prevention 110, 115

risks of action 112

safeguarding and child protection, application of definitions 111–12

secondary prevention 110, 115

tertiary prevention 110, 115

support for "at risk" babies and young children

accident prevention advice 123

alerts and warnings 119–20

balance, objectivity and 122

benefits of action 120

child protection in context of secondary prevention 117–23

childcare options, exploration of 123

concern, alarm bells and feelings of 121–2

courses of action, consideration of 120–21, 122–3

information requirements and sources 120

initial alert 119

initiation of action, feelings about 120

interventions, examples of 117, 118–19

parental skills improvement, impact on well-being of children 123

prior knowledge 120

risks of action 120

safeguarding and child protection, application of definitions 119–20

case studies (*Continued*)
  safeguarding intervention, initiation of
    122–3
  support for mother, impact on
    well-being of children 123
teamwork and safeguarding 140–51
  alerts and warnings 148–9
  benefits of action 149
  carers views on concerns 151
  child, focus on 150–51
  child action meeting 143–8
  child action meeting, attendees at
    144–5
  health visitor 141–3
  health visitor, attendance at child
    action meeting 143, 144
  historical perspective, lessons from 150
  information and actions from each
    agency, picture built up from 143
  information requirements and sources
    149
  initial alert 148
  initiation of action, feelings about 149
  management, consultation with 146–7
  Multi-Agency Risk Assessment
    Conference (MARAC) 145
  police, contribution of 143, 146
  practice reflection points 141, 142, 143,
    146, 147
  prior knowledge 149
  probation service representative,
    attendance at child action meeting
    143, 145
  provision of services, self-reflection on
    personal and agency capacities 140
  risks of action 149
  safeguarding and child protection,
    application of definitions 148–9
  school representative, attendance at
    child action meeting 143, 144–5
  social care services advice and
    assessment 143, 147–8
  team leadership at child action meeting
    145
  teamwork, organization of 149–50
  voluntary organizations, contribution
    of 143, 145
categories of child abuse 24–5
causation factors
  raising concerns and identification of
    abuse 115
  support for "at risk" babies and young
    children 124

centrality of child to concerns 31, 32
  see also needs of children
Centre for Maternal and Child Enquiries
  (CMACE) 93
Chapman, Jessica 60
child beating in public
  example of 53–5
  foreseeable outcomes of intervention
    53
  issues illustrated 54–5
  key reasons for intervention 54
  lessons from example 53–4
  reflection on 53–4
child-centredness, common failing of lack
  of 77
child development, notions of 180
child protection
  designated leaders on issues of 104–5
  development of framework for 48–9
  early prevention practice 115
  rights of children and 37–8
  safeguarding, welfare and 27
child protection conferences
  aims of 165
  attendance at 162–4, 174
  case conference reviews 168–9, 174–5
  early review conference, circumstances
    requiring 168
  information for 164
  initial conferences 162, 174
  pre-birth conferences 166–7
  preparation in advance for 163
  quorum in, need for 164
  timing of initial conference 162
child protection plans
  assessment, referral and 137
  decision concerning 164–5, 174
  discontinuance of 168–9
  instigation of 169–74
  making decisions about 166
  non-instigation of 166, 174
  outline for 166
  review and reassessment of action plans
    105
Childcare Act (1989) 105
children
  families and
    provision of support for 116–17
    relationship with 18–19, 31
  identities of children
    acknowledgement of 47
    recognition of 181
  listening to children, influences on 180

needs and concerns of, primary
importance of 184
our future in 48
as rights-holders 41–2
rights of, maintenance of 181
at risk, concept of 49
treatment as adults, right to 42
voices of, consultation and 181
see also needs of children
Children, Schools and Families,
Department for (DCSF) 23, 60, 138,
144, 145, 146
*Information Sharing: Guidance for
Practitioners and Managers* (2008) 96
safeguarding, determination of 60
Working Together to Safeguard Children
(2010) 19, 23–4, 25, 26, 27, 73, 97,
112, 138–9, 165
Children Act (1889) 10
Children Act (1894) 11
Children Act (1904) 11
Children Act (1908) 11
Children Act (1948) 11
Children Act (1975) 14
Children Act (1989) 15, 16, 26, 27, 28, 73,
86, 106–7, 138, 153, 161
child-centred approach of 36
children in need, family support for 28
Core Assessment 128, 130, 131, 148, 158,
164, 166–7, 169–70
cultural sensitivity, recognition of 37
initial assessment (section 17) 19–20, 27,
102, 114, 128–31, 135, 136, 137, 158
investigative duties of local authorities 20
needs of children, categorisation of levels
of 102–3
significant harm (section 47) 5, 20, 24,
97, 128, 130, 131–2, 147, 148, 161,
162, 164, 166–7, 168, 169–70, 185
welfare checklist 20
Children Act (2004) 18, 27, 34, 35, 38, 40,
54, 69, 73, 95, 110, 138
Children and Families Court Advisory and
Support Service (CAFCASS) 21–2
Children and Young Persons Act (1932) 11
Children and Young Persons Act (1933) 11,
14, 136
Children and Young Persons Act (1963) 11
Children and Young Persons Act (1969) 11
Children's Commissioner, role of 34–5
Children's Guardian 38–9, 43
Children's Rights Alliance 35
Cicchetti, D. and Rizley, R. 108

Clément, M.E. and Tourginy, M. 118
Cleveland affair (1987) 15, 16, 153
Climbié, Victoria 11, 13, 14, 17–18, 55–6,
57, 81, 85, 86, 88–9, 92, 121, 134, 179
Clyde, J.J. 16
Cohen, A.P. 84
Colwell, Maria 13–16, 18, 31, 50, 179
Commission for Social Care Inspection 79
Common Assessment Framework (CAF) 1,
67, 74, 103, 114, 154, 163
assessment and referral 126, 128, 135, 137
community involvement and 88, 89, 92
teamwork, safeguarding and 144, 147,
148
Common Law Duty of Confidence 95
communication
across professional boundaries 180–81
between agencies 151
clarity in, importance of 63
direct communication, importance of 83
effective communication, importance of
98
effectiveness in, importance of 187
as essential skill 181
information sharing and 151
openness and effectiveness in,
importance of 115
with parents and carers 30
importance of 160
practitioner-child communication,
contextual factors 180
skill of 47
communities of practice 84–5
community involvement, development of
4, 84–98
agency responses, information sharing
and 94–6
agency roles
early years professionals and 96–7
responsibilities and 97
assumptions, avoidance of 98
benefits to families of 98
communities of practice 84–5
community, definition of 84
Connexions, roles and responsibilities of
97
direct engagement, value of 98
effective communication, importance of
98
faith organizations, roles and
responsibilities of 97
family contexts, awareness of 98
future practice, development of 185–7

community involvement, development of (*Continued*)
  future prospects 90–94
  government policy 90–94
  health, roles and responsibilities for 97
  housing services, roles and responsibilities of 97
  information sharing and agency responses 94–6
  inter-agency relationships 87–8
  key messages 98
  library and youth services, roles and responsibilities 97
  organizational culture, communication and 85–7
  overview 84
  police, roles and responsibilities of 97
  policy initiatives 89–90
  positive working relationships, facilitation of 98
  probation services, roles and responsibilities of 97
  professional communities 98
  safeguarding, community involvement in 88–9
  schools, roles and responsibilities of 97
  social care advice and assessment, roles and responsibilities in 97
  sports and leisure services, roles and responsibilities 97
  voluntary and private sectors, roles and responsibilities 97
  youth offending teams, roles and responsibilities of 97
community provision, shift towards 186
concerns about abuse
  knowing when to act on 29–30
  prioritization of 63
  shelving of 184
confidentiality 185
  ethical practice of 69–71
Connelly, Peter (Baby P) 21–2, 31, 48, 57, 81, 92, 121–2, 123, 152
Connelly, Tracey 123
Connexions 145
  roles and responsibilities of 97
Connolly, Mary and Francis 12
Contact Point 69, 95
contextual factors, awareness of 186
Corby, B. 10
core assessment 131
core groups 167–8
creativity, inclusiveness and 62

Crime and Disorder Act (1998) 20
cross-agency working 62, 95, 110, 116, 123, 124, 166, 169
  discussions with other practitioners 63–4
  early intervention, importance of inter-agency working and 124
  inter-agency information sharing 14, 17, 30, 35, 52, 116
  inter-agency relationships 85, 87–8
  interprofessional cooperation, importance of 35
  interprofessional effectiveness, benefits of 187
  multi-agency contributions, need for 151
  professional boundaries, working across 30
  working with other practitioners and agencies 138–40
Cunningham, H. 10

dangers, awareness of 155
Data Protection Act (1998) 69, 86, 96
definitions
  of abuse 24, 106–9, 115
  assessment 125–7
  community 84
  defining abuse, difficulties in 115
  meanings of ethics in safeguarding contexts 66
  safeguarding 22–4
demographics of communities, awareness of 186
deontology 77, 78
designated leaders on child protection 104–5
Dimond, B. 36
Dingwall, R., Eekelaar, J. and Murray, T. 15, 17, 79, 94, 121, 134, 152
direct engagement, value of 98
discriminatory behaviour, avoidance of 47, 181
diversity of social interactions 47
Douglas, M. 127
Dunford Review (2010) 35

early intervention, importance of inter-agency working and 124
early prevention practice 115
early years professionals
  managers 177–8
  reflection and reflexivity for 43–4
  skills of safeguarding and child protection for 45

The Ecology of Human Development
(Bronfenbrenner, U.) 58, 59
Edleson, J. 150
Education Act (2002) 18–19
Education and Skills, Department for (DfES)
77, 90, 138
Birth to Three Matters Framework (2003)
40–41
Early Years Foundation State (2007) 40–41
Every Child Matters: Change for Children
(2004) 18, 26, 48–9, 50
Every Child Matters: Next Steps (2004) 86
Every Child Matters (2003) 18, 23, 33, 73,
88, 96, 101
Information Sharing: Practitioners Guide
(2006) 96
Safeguarding Children in Education (2005)
19
What To Do If You're Worried a Child is
Being Abused (2003) 24, 52, 73, 104,
112
Emergency Protection Order 105, 135, 136
emotional abuse 24, 25
emotions, thoughts and actions, distinction
between 126
ethical practice 3–4, 65–83
Act Utilitarianism 77
beneficence 77
case study 80–82
assessment of strengths and needs of
children 82
ethical considerations arising 81
focus on improvement of lives of
children 81
positive well-being, development of 81
role of early years professionals,
importance of 81, 82
significant adults, attachment with
82
support for or hindrance to well-being
81–2
vulnerability of babies and young
children, factors influencing 82
child, maintenance of ethical focus on
74
child-centredness, common failing of
lack of 77
confidentiality 69–71
deontology 77, 78
direct communication, importance of
83
ethical action in safeguardiong contexts
184–5
ethical decision-making 66–7
ethical principles 77
ethical responses, philosophies
underpinning 77
ethics and safeguarding, aspects in
practice 65–6
flexibility in relation to context 83
individual rights, welfare and 68
integration of ethical approach into
everyday thinking 65–6
justice 77
key messages 82–3
meanings of ethics in safeguarding
contexts 66
needs of child, pre-eminence of 83
negligence 78–9
non-maleficence 77
oppression, discrimination and 68–9
overview 65
policy and practice, tensions between
71–3
policy and process, dealing with 83
power and ethics 75–6
power dynamics, awareness of influence
of 83
professional roles, boundaries and
relationships 68–9
public welfare 68
reflexiveness in, development of 75
risk management 79–80
safeguarding context, ethical dilemmas in
76–8
setting scene for 69
social work and ethical issues 67–9
transparent relationships, importance of
83
vigilance 73–4
watchfulness
development through ethical lens 73–4
framework for 73
Etter Wheeler principle 178–9
European Court of Human Rights (ECHR)
36, 39
Every Child Matters see Education and Skills,
Department for
everyday practices 52–5
everyday thinking, integration of ethical
approach into 65–6

fact, observation and opinion, distinction
between 163–4
faith organizations, roles and
responsibilities of 97

family contexts
    awareness of 98
    collusion with parents, dangers of 153
    flexibility in relation to 83
    home context. baby and young child as
        focus of safeguarding in 61
    identification of families at risk 116–17
    negotiation with families 153
    parents, rights against 42
    partnership with families 153
    risks in communicating concerns with
        parents 115
    working with children and families 18–19
focus, strength and clarity of 52
    see also needs of children
Framework for Action (Bolton Safeguarding
    Board, 2007) 103
Frazer, E. 84
Freedom of Information Act (2000) 96
Freeman, M.D.A. 41–2
frustration, aggressive behaviour and 153
Furedi, F. 49, 60
future practice, development of 5–6, 176–89
    adaptation to situations 177
    child abuse referrals, increasing numbers
        of 186
    child development, notions of 180
    child needs, focus on 181
    childrens' needs and concerns, primary
        importance of 184
    children's rights, maintenance of 181
    childrens voices, consultation and 181
    communication
        across professional boundaries 180–81
        as essential skill 181
        importance of effectiveness in 187
    community involvement, development
        of 90–94, 185–7
    community provision, shift towards 186
    concerns about abuse, shelving of 184
    confidentiality 185
    contextual factors, awareness of 186
    demographics of communities, awareness
        of 186
    discriminatory behaviour, avoidance of
        181
    early years managers 177–8
    ethical action in safeguarding contexts
        184–5
    Etter Wheeler principle 178–9
    geography of communities, awareness of
        186
    guidance and policy, awareness of 181

    identities of children, recognition of 181
    interactions, diversity of means for 181
    interactive learning, process of 176
    interprofessional effectiveness, benefits of
        187
    interventionist practice 176–7
    key messages 189
    learning, embedded in society 177
    listening to children, influences on 180
    needs and concerns for child, primary
        importance of 184
    needs of child, focus on 181
    oppressive behaviour, avoidance of 181
    overview 176
    persistence, importance of 181
    positive working relationships,
        facilitation of 187
    practice, questions about your practice
        and performance 188–9
    practitioner-child communication,
        contextual factors 180
    practitioner discussions, voice of child in
        180–81
    prevention, bringing experience to bear
        on 186–7
    provision of services, yourself as vital
        resource for 181
    record-keeping, noting concerns 184–5
    reflection on practice, importance of 181
    relationships with family members or
        carers, importance of 182–3
    rights of children 179–81
    safer cultures 182–3
        approach of, elements of 183
    sensitive articulation, need for 180–81
    students 178
    support for change 183
    systems theory, safer cultures and 182
    team meetings 178
    total listening, practice of 180
    voices for children 179–81

Gateshead Children and Young People's
    Partnership 92–3
general rights 36
General Teaching Council (GTC) *Code of
    Conduct and Practice for Registered
    Teachers* (2009) 66
geography of communities, awareness of
    186
Germain, C. and Glitterman, A. 59
Gersch, I.F. 180
Gibbs, G. 105–6

Giddens, A. 46, 75
Gillick v West Norfolk and Wisbech Area
    Health Authority (1986) 42–3, 96
government policy 90–94
Greenwich, London Borough of 15
guidance
    characterisation of 102–5
    identification of abuse, guidance on 21–2,
        26–7
    policy and, awareness of 31, 181

Hall, D. and Elliman, D. 78
Hall, P. 126
happiness and contentment, rights to 47
Hardiker, P., Exton, K. and Barker, M. 109
Haringay Council 21
Hart, J.T. 79
Hawkes, N. 78
Health and Social Security, Department of
        (DHSS) 13–14
    Working Together (1988) 15
Health Department (DH) 14, 70, 107, 108,
        138
    child abuse, definitions of 24
    Child Protection: Messages from Research
        (1995) 16
    *Framework for the Assessment of Children in
        Need and Their Families* (2000) 17,
        126
    Liberating the NHS (2010) 78
    *National Service Framework for Children,
        Young People and Maternity Services*
        (2004) 19
    *Working Together to Safeguard Children: A
        Guide to Inter-agency Working to
        Safeguard and Promote Welfare of
        Children* (2006) 18, 23
    Working Together to Safeguard Children
        (1999) 16
    *Working Together under the Children Act
        1989* (with Home Office, 1991) 16
health services, roles and responsibilities of
        97
Healy, K. 59
Help4Me 82, 123, 135, 140
Henry, Tyra 15
Hester, M., Pearson, C. and Harwin, N.
        150
Hoff, B. 87
Holland, S. 126
Home Office 16
housing services, roles and responsibilities
        of 97

Human Rights Act (1998) 19, 36, 69, 78, 86,
        95
    fundamental rights 39
Humphreys, C. and Thiara, T. 150
Huntley, Ian 60

'Incidence and Concerns' books 104
inclusiveness, creativity and 62
individual rights, welfare and 68
Infant Life Protection Act (1897) 11
information sharing
    agency responses and 94–6
    communication and 151
    inter-agency information sharing 14, 17,
        30, 35, 52, 116
Information Sharing Index 18
Ingleby, O. 11
initial assessment
    carrying out of 129, 137
    outcome of 130–31
    purpose of (section 17, Children Act,
        1989) 128
integration of ethical approach into
        everyday thinking 65–6
inter-agency
    information sharing 14, 17, 30, 35, 52,
        116
    relationships 87–8
    working together 62, 95, 110, 116, 123,
        124, 166, 169
interactions, diversity of means for 181
interactive learning, process of 176
interprofessional cooperation, importance
        of 35
intervention, potential impacts of 5,
        161–75
    abuse or neglect, category of 165, 174
    aim child protection conferences 165
    attendance at child protection
        conferences 162–4, 174
    case conference reviews 168–9, 174–5
    case study 169–74
        alerts and warnings 171
        benefits of action 171
        child protection plan, instigation of
            169–74
        development and sustenance of safer
            culture 173–4
        information requirements and sources
            171
        initial alert 171
        initial responses 169–70
        initiation of action, feelings about 171

intervention, potential impacts of
(*Continued*)
monitoring and subsequent
interventions 172
prior knowledge 171
risks of action 171
safeguarding and child protection,
application of definitions 171
safer cultures approach, application of
173, 175
support group conversations 172
child protection plans
decision concerning 164–5, 174
decision to make 166
discontinuance of 168–9
non-instigation of 166, 174
outline for 166
core groups 167–8
early moments, importance of 29–30
early review conference, circumstances
requiring 168
examples of interventions in support for
"at risk" babies and young children
117, 118–19
fact, observation and opinion, distinction
between 163–4
information for child protection
conferences 164
initial child protection conferences 162,
174
interventionist practice 176–7
key messages 174–5
monitoring and support, need for
ongoing 174
ongoing core group assessment, focus of
167–8
overview 161
pre-birth conferences 166–7
preparation in advance for child
protection conferences 163
quorum child protection conferences,
need for 164
timing of initial child protection
conferences 162

Jack, G. 88
Job Centre Plus 90
Johns, C. 106, 107
Jones, S.R. and Jenkins, R. 70
justice 77

Kant, Immanuel 78
Kemp, S., Whittaker, J. and Tracy, E. 59

Kempe, R., Silverman, F. et al. 11
Keppel, William 14
key messages
assessment and referral 137
baby and young child as focus of
safeguarding 63–4
community involvement, development
of 98
ethical practice 82–3
future practice, development of 189
intervention, potential impacts of
174–5
parents and carers of abused baby or
young child, working with
159–60
raising concerns and identification of
abuse 114–15
rights of children 47
safeguarding from abuse, issues in
31–2
support for "at risk" babies and young
children 124
teamwork and safeguarding 151
Kouao, Marie-Thérèse 17

Lambeth, London Borough of 15
Laming, H.
*Protection of Children in England: Progress
Report* (2009) 48, 71, 79, 92
Victoria Climbié Inquiry Report (2003) 11,
14, 17–18, 24, 30, 51, 52, 55, 77, 85,
86, 94, 138
learning
embedded in society 177
interactive learning, process of 176
library and youth services, roles and
responsibilities of 97
listening to children, influences on 180
Liverpool for the Prevention of Cruelty to
Children 12

Macdonald, G. and Winkley, A. 108, 117
McLaren, H. 70, 184
Macmillan, H.L., Macmillan, J.H. et al. 117,
118
Manning, Carl John 17
Marcellus, L. 80
Maria Colwell (March 1965-January 1973)
13–16
Mary Ellen Wilson (1864-1956) 12–13
Mason, J.K., McCall Smith, R.A. and Laurie,
G.T. 79
Meadows, R. 14

monitoring and support, need for ongoing intervention and 174
teamwork and safeguarding 151
Morrison, T. 87
Muir, J. 78
multi-agency contributions, need for 151
Multi-Agency Risk Assessment Conference (MARAC) 145
Munchausen's by proxy 14
Munro, Professor Eileen 1, 51, 69, 87, 109, 113, 126–7
Munro Review (2010) 71, 72–3, 79, 91–2, 93, 94, 95, 109, 110, 127, 138
Myers, J.E.B. 9–10, 12

National Childcare Strategy 89–90
National Evaluation Summary 185–6
National Institute for Clinical Excellence (NICE) 78
National Society for the Prevention of Cruelty to Children (NSPCC) 10, 12, 97, 105, 136, 145, 163, 186
needs of children
    assessment of strengths and 82
    categorisation of levels in Children Act (1989) 102–3
    child-centredness, common failing of lack of 77
    children and families, provision of support for 116–17
    focus on 181
    maintenance of ethical focus on 74
    pre-eminence of 83
    primary importance of concerns about 184
neglect 24, 25
negligence 78–9
New York Society for the Prevention of Cruelty to Children (NYSPCC) 12
non-maleficence 77
Nursing and Midwifery Council (NMC) 66, 95

Oates, R.K. and Bross, D.C. 117
Oberle, K. and Tenove, S. 80
objectivity 64
    balance and 122
Ofsted 104–5
O'Hanlon, B. 126
Olds, D.L. and Henderson, C.R. 109
Olds, D.L. and Kitzman, H. 118
Olds, D.L., Eckenrode, J. et al. 117, 118–19

opinions of others, dealing with 64
oppression
    discrimination and 68–9
    oppressive behaviour, avoidance of 47, 181
organizational culture, communication and 85–7
Orkney ritualistic abuse affair 16
overviews
    assessment and referral 125
    baby and young child as focus of safeguarding 48
    community involvement, development of 84
    ethical practice 65
    future practice, development of 176
    intervention, potential impacts of 161
    parents and carers of abused baby or young child, working with 152
    raising concerns and identification of abuse 101
    rights of children 33
    safeguarding from abuse, issues in 9
    support for "at risk" babies and young children 116
    teamwork and safeguarding 138

P v East Berkshire Community Health Trust (2003) 79
parents and carers of abused baby or young child, working with 5, 152–60
    abuse levels, difficulties in categorization of 152–3
    balancing relationships 152–5, 160
    case study 155–9
        actions, consideration of 158–9
        alerts and warnings 156–7
        benefits of action 157
        identification of appropriate support services 158–9
        information requirements and sources 157
        initial alert 156
        initial responses 157–8
        initiation of action, feelings about 157
        positive relationship, maintenance of 159
        prior knowledge 157
        risks of action 157
        safeguarding and child protection, application of definitions 156–7
        strengths within family 159
    collusion with parents, dangers of 153

parents and carers of abused baby or young child, working with (*Continued*)
communication with parents and carers, importance of 160
dangers, awareness of 155
frustration, aggressive behaviour and 153
key messages 159–60
negotiation with families 153
overview 152
partnership with families 153
personal safety 155
positive relationships, maintenance of 152
professional involvement, levels of 154
resistance, techniques for overcoming 153–5
responses associated with levels of involvement 154
Parton, N. 28, 49
Parton, N. and O'Byrne, P. 126
Payne, G. 46–7
Payne, M. 59, 182
Peckover, S. 80
persistence, importance of 181
personal feelings 28–9, 32
personal safety 155
Peter (Baby P) Connelly (March 2006-August 2007) 21–22
physical abuse 24, 25
police
notification of 130
roles and responsibilities of 97
policy
policy initiatives 89–90
and practice, tensions between 71–3
and process, dealing with 83
translation into practice of 40–41
Powell, J. 13, 18, 24, 86, 184, 187
Powell, R. 42–3
power
dynamics of, awareness of influence of 83
ethics and 75–6
practice reflection points
concerns of possible child abuse, responses to 56
development of focus to safeguard children 50
intervention or not, child beating in public example 53
multidiciplinary team 30
organization or team, thinking about aspects of 85

practitioners, managers and students, considerations for reflection for 179, 182, 183–4, 185, 187–8
questions about your practice and performance 188–9
representatives of children's rights 35
safer cultures framework of practice, establishment of 63
values and beliefs, consideration of personal attitudes 28–9
practitioner-child communication, contextual factors 180
pre-birth conferences 166–7
prevention
accident prevention advice 123
bringing experience to bear on 186–7
child protection in context of secondary prevention 117–23
early prevention practice 115
levels of 109–10
primary prevention 109, 110, 115
protection and 28
quaternary prevention 17, 110, 115
secondary prevention 109, 110, 115, 116, 117–18, 123
tertiary prevention 109, 110, 115, 117, 118
principles and practice 2–6
assessment and referral 5, 125–37
baby and young child as focus of safeguarding 3, 48–64
case studies 2, 3, 4, 80–82, 111–14, 119–23, 132–7, 140–46, 155–9, 169–74
community involvement, development of 4, 84–98
effective intervention, requirements for 5–6, 176–89
ethical practice 3–4, 65–83
focus on core concerns 2–3
future practice, development of 5–6, 176–89
intervention, potential impacts of 5, 161–75
parents and carers of abused baby or young child, working with 5, 152–60
practical considerations 3, 4
problem resolution approach 3
raising concerns and identification of abuse 4, 101–15
rights of children 3, 33–47
safeguarding from abuse, issues in 3, 9–32

support for "at risk" babies and young
children 5, 116–24
teamwork and safeguarding 5, 138–51
probation services, roles and responsibilities
of 97
professional communities 98
professional expectations 51
professional involvement, levels of 154
professional roles, boundaries and
relationships 68–9
protection, rights to 41
provision of services
self-reflection on personal and agency
capacities 140
yourself as vital resource for 181
public welfare 68
Punishment of Incest Act (1908) 11

R v Harrow London Borough Council
(1990) 79
R v Norfolk County Social Services (1989)
79
raising concerns and identification of abuse
4, 101–15
abuse, definitions of 106–9
action, framework for 103
alerts and warnings 105–6
case study
alerts and warnings 111–12
benefits of action 112
courses of action, consideration of 113
early intervention, dichotomy in 110
further action, consideration of 114
information requirements and sources
112
initial alert 111, 112–13
initiation of action, feelings about 112
levels of prevention 109–10
prevention, child protection within
context of 109–14
primary prevention 110, 115
prior knowledge 112
quaternary prevention 110, 115
risks of action 112
safeguarding and child protection,
application of definitions 111–12
secondary prevention 110, 115
tertiary prevention 110, 115
causative factors 115
communication, importance of openness
and effectiveness in 115
defining abuse, difficulties in 115

designated leaders on child protection
issues 104–5
early prevention practice 115
Every Child Matters (2003), outcomes from
101
guidance, characterisation of 102–5
'Incidence and Concerns' books 104
key messages 114–15
overview 101
practical concerns 102
record-keeping 104
reflective practice, Gibbs' model for 105–6
review and reassessment of action plans
105
risks in communicating concerns with
parents 115
record-keeping
baby and young child as focus of
safeguarding 64
noting concerns and 184–5
raising concerns and identification of
abuse 104
Reder, P. and Duncan, S. 85–7
Reder, P., Duncan, S. and Gray, M. 13, 18,
44
reflection
essential nature of 32
need for 44–5
on practice, importance of 181
see also practice reflection points
reflective practice, Gibbs' model for 105–6
reflexivity
in ethical practice, development of 75
need for 45–6
relationships
balance in, importance of 152–5, 160
with children and families 18–19, 31
with close carers 61–2
with colleagues 31
collusion with parents, dangers of 153
encouragement of positive behaviour 62
with family members or carers,
importance of 182–3
interactions, diversity of means for 181
partnership with families 153
positive relationships, maintenance of
152
positive working relationships,
facilitation of 98, 187
professional roles, boundaries and 68–9
transparent relationships, importance of
83

resistance, techniques for overcoming
153–5
rights of children 3, 33–47
adults acting for children, role of 42–3
anxiety and surveillance, contemporary
society and 33
child protection 37–8
children as rights-holders 41–2
Children's Commissioner, role of 34–5
communication, skill of 47
discriminatory behaviour, avoidance of
47
diversity of social interactions 47
early years professionals
reflection and reflexivity for 43–4
skills of safeguarding and child
protection for 45
Every Child Matters (DfES, 2003) 33–4
feelings and thoughts of babies and
young children, consideration for
47
further rights for consideration 46–7
future practice, development of 179–81
general rights 36
happiness and contentment, rights to 47
Human Rights Act (1998), fundamental
rights 39
identities of children, acknowledgement
of 47
interprofessional cooperation,
importance of 35
key messages 47
oppressive behaviour, avoidance of 47
overview 33
parents, rights against 42
policy, translation into practice of
40–41
protection, rights to 41
reflection, need for 44–5
reflexivity, need for 45–6
safeguarding context, application of
children's rights to 35–6
treatment as adult, right to 42
UNCRC central tenets 37
UNCRC specific rights 37–8
vigilance, need for 47
voice of the child 38–9
welfare, rights to 41
risks
in communicating concerns with parents
115
management of, ethical practice and
79–80

risk as concept in child protection 127
risk assessment, implementation of
127–8, 137
Robinson, R.M., Anning, A. et al. 87
Ross, E.M. 180

Safeguarding Children Boards 88, 104, 146
safeguarding from abuse, issues in 3, 9–32
categories of child abuse 24–5
centrality of child to concerns 31, 32
child protection, safeguarding and
welfare 27
children and families, relationship with
18–19, 31
communication with parents and carers
30
community involvement, development
of 88–9
concerns, knowing when to act on 29–30
defining safeguarding 22–4
emotional abuse 24, 25
guidance and policy, awareness of 31
historical perspective 9
identification of abuse, guidance on 21–2,
26–7
intervention, early moments 29–30
key messages 31–2
legal framework 19–20
Maria Colwell (March 1965-January
1973) 13–16
Mary Ellen Wilson (1864-1956) 12–13
neglect 24, 25
overview 9
personal feelings 28–9, 32
Peter (Baby P) Conneily (March
2006-August 2007) 21–22
physical abuse 24, 25
prevention and protection 28
professional boundaries, working across
30
reflection, essential nature of 32
relationship with colleagues 31
safeguarding agenda, challenge of 50–51
safeguarding context
application of children's rights to 35–6
child protection, shifts in social policy
12–18, 31
ethical dilemmas in 76–8
sensitivity and honesty, importance of 31
sexual abuse 24, 25
significant cases informing current
practice 12–18
significant harm, identification of 26

signs on the child 21–22
state involvement, growth of 9–11
values and beliefs, consideration of
    personal attitudes 28–9
Victoria Climbié (November
    1991-February 2000) 17–18
working with children and families
    18–19
safer cultures
    baby and young child as focus of
        safeguarding 57–9
    development of approach 64
    elements of approach 183
    future practice, development of 182–3
    principles for 61
    promotion of 61–3
Sameroff, A.J. and Chandler, M.J. 108
schools, roles and responsibilities of 97
section 47 enquiries 131–2, 137
Seebohm Report (1968) 11
sensitivity
    honesty and, importance of 31
    sensitive articulation, need for 180–81
sexual abuse 24, 25
significant cases informing current practice
    12–18
significant harm, identification of 26
Signs of Well-Being (Gateshead Children
    and Young People's Partnership)
    92–3, 128
Sinclair, R. and Bullock, R. 17, 86
Sinclair, R., Hearn, B. and Pugh, G. 127
Singer, P. 72
Smale, G., Tuson, G. et al. 126
social care advice and assessment, roles and
    responsibilities in 97
social interactions, diversity of 47
social work and ethical issues 67–9
sports and leisure services, roles and
    responsibilities 97
Stark, E. and Flitcraft, A. 150
state involvement, growth of 9–11
Stevenson, O. 11, 87
stigmatization 117, 124
students, future practice for 178
Sullivan v Moody (2001) 80
support for "at risk" babies and young
    children 5, 116–24
    case study
        accident prevention advice 123
        alerts and warnings 119–20
        balance, objectivity and 122
        benefits of action 120

child protection in context of
    secondary prevention 117–23
childcare options, exploration of 123
concern, alarm bells and feelings of
    121–2
courses of action, consideration of
    120–21, 122–3
information requirements and sources
    120
initial alert 119
initiation of action, feelings about 120
interventions, examples of 117, 118–19
parental skills improvement, impact on
    well-being of children 123
prior knowledge 120
risks of action 120
safeguarding and child protection,
    application of definitions 119–20
safeguarding intervention, initiation of
    122–3
support for mother, impact on
    well-being of children 123
causation factors 124
children and families, provision of
    support for 116–17
early intervention, importance of
    inter-agency working and 124
identification of families at risk 116–17
inter-agency working 116, 124
interventions, examples of 117, 118–19
key messages 124
overview 116
quaternary prevention 117
stigmatization 117, 124
tertiary prevention 117
Sure Start 22, 34, 43–4, 80, 89, 90, 96, 110,
    163
Sure Start Local Programmes (SSLPs)
    186
surveillance, contemporary society and
    extent of 33
systems theory
    baby and young child as focus of
        safeguarding 59–60
    safer cultures and 182

teamwork and safeguarding 5, 138–51
    case study 140–51
        alerts and warnings 148–9
        benefits of action 149
        carers views on concerns 151
        child, focus on 150–51
        child action meeting 143–8

teamwork and safeguarding (*Continued*)
    child action meeting, attendees at
        144–5
    health visitor 141–3
    health visitor, attendance at child
        action meeting 143, 144
    historical perspective, lessons from 150
    information and actions from each
        agency, picture built up from 143
    information requirements and sources
        149
    initial alert 148
    initiation of action, feelings about
        149
    management, consultation with 146–7
    Multi-Agency Risk Assessment
        Conference (MARAC) 145
    police, contribution of 143, 146
    practice reflection points 141, 142, 143,
        146, 147
    prior knowledge 149
    probation service representative,
        attendance at child action meeting
        143, 145
    provision of services, self-reflection on
        personal and agency capacities 140
    risks of action 149
    safeguarding and child protection,
        application of definitions 148–9
    school representative, attendance at
        child action meeting 143, 144–5
    social care services advice and
        assessment 143, 147–8
    team leadership at child action meeting
        145
    teamwork, organization of 149–50
    voluntary organizations, contribution
        of 143, 145
communication and information sharing
    151
communication between agencies 151
key messages 151
monitoring and support, need for
    ongoing 151
multi-agency contributions, need for 151
multi-agency working, requirement for
    151
overview 138
team meetings 178
working with other practitioners and
    agencies 138–40

Thompson, N. 68–9
total listening, practice of 180
transparent relationships, importance of 83
Tunbridge Wells Group 11
Turnell, A. and Edwards, S. 92

United Nations Convention on the Rights
    of the Child (UNCRC, 1989) 34,
    35–6, 39, 40, 42, 43, 46–7
central tenets 37
specific rights 37–8

values and beliefs, consideration of
    personal attitudes 28–9
values of support, clarity and focus in 63
Victoria Climbié (November 1991-February
    2000) 17–18
vigilance 5, 21–2, 48, 49, 80, 101, 161, 181
    ethical practice 73–4
    need for 47
    safer cultures and 57
    see also watchfulness
voice of the child
    consultation and 181
    future practice, development of 179–81
    practitioner discussions, voice of child in
        180–81
    rights of children 38–9
voluntary and private sectors, roles and
    responsibilities 97

W v Egdell (1990) 80
Wakefield, J.C. 59
Walker, Ainlee 50
Ward, L. 79
watchfulness
    development through ethical lens 73–4
    framework for 73
welfare, rights to 41
Wells, Holly 60
Wenger, E. 72, 84, 85, 177
Wheeler, Etta Angell 12, 17–18, 178–9
Wilson, Mary Ellen 12–13, 14, 17, 178–9
Winnnicott, D. 152–3
Women's Aid 150
Working Families Tax Credit 91
worst case scenario 51
Wright, Lauren 50

youth offending teams, roles and
    responsibilities of 97

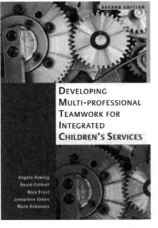

DEVELOPING MULTIPROFESSIONAL TEAMWORK FOR INTEGRATED CHILDREN'S SERVICES 2/E

Angela Anning, David Cottrell, Nick Frost, Jo Green & Mark Robinson

9780335238118 (Paperback)
2010

eBook also available

The first book to combine theoretical perspectives, research evidence from the 'real world' of children's services, and reflections on policy and practice in inter-agency services in England. This fully updated new edition retains its popular approach, while reflecting the numerous changes to policy, practice, and research. The book:

- Exemplifies what multi-professional work looks like in practice
- Examines real dilemmas faced by professionals trying to make it work, and shows how these dilemmas can be resolved
- Considers lessons to be learnt, implications for practice and recommendations for making multi-professional practice effective

www.openup.co.uk

OPEN UNIVERSITY PRESS
McGraw - Hill Education

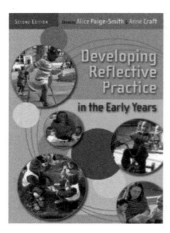

DEVELOPING REFLECTIVE PRACTICE IN THE EARLY YEARS 2/E

Alice Paige-Smith & Anna Craft

9780335242351 (Paperback)
2011

eBook also available

This book supports early years' practitioners in articulating and understanding their own practice in greater depth, exploring ways in which they can be encouraged to engage in reflecting on their practice.

The authors introduce ideas around creativity, inclusion, children's well being, partnership with parents and multidisciplinary team working, which will enable you to develop and explore the role of the early years' practitioner in further detail.

Key features of the book include:

- Updated and revised throughout to reflect latest policy changes and documents
- The role of the early years professional Reference to Children's Plan and Common Core of Skills and Knowledge for Children's Work Force
- New reflective questions and extended case studies
- Reference to safeguarding and child protection through joint-working

www.openup.co.uk

OPEN UNIVERSITY PRESS
McGraw - Hill Education